AGGRESSIVE
INVESTING
PROVEN
STRATEGIES
FOR
BOLD
INVESTORS

RICHARD CROFT

PRENTICE HALL CANADA

Canadian Cataloguing in Publication Data

Croft, Richard, 1952–
Aggressive investing : proven strategies for bold investors

Includes index.
ISBN 0-13-929268-3

1. Securities. 2. Investments. I. Title.

HG4521.C85 1998   332.67'8   C98-932070-7

Prentice-Hall, Inc., Upper Saddle River, New Jersey
Prentice-Hall International (UK) Limited, London
Prentice-Hall of Australia, Pty. Limited, Sydney
Prentice-Hall Hispanoamericana, S.A., Mexico City
Prentice-Hall of India Private Limited, New Delhi
Prentice-Hall of Japan, Inc., Tokyo
Simon & Schuster Southeast Asia Private Limited, Singapore
Editora Prentice-Hall do Brasil, Ltda., Rio de Janeiro

ISBN 0-13-929268-3

Director, Trade Group: Robert Harris
Editor: Bruce McDougall
Copy Editor: Jim Leahy
Assistant Editor: Joan Whitman
Production Editor: Lu Cormier/Andrew Winton
Production Coordinator: Shannon Potts
Art Director: Mary Opper
Cover Design: Alex Alter
Page Layout: B.J. Weckerle

1 2 3 4 5   02 01 00 99 98

Printed and bound in Canada.

Visit the Prentice Hall Canada Web site! Send us your comments, browse our catalogues, and more.
www.phcanada.com

CONTENTS

ACKNOWLEDGMENTS

A special thanks to my editors, Bruce McDougall and James Leahy, for their support and patience.

To Robert Harris and the staff at Prentice Hall, who saw a need for a book geared to the aggressive investor in all of us.

To my family, who put up with me through the worst of times, which I define as writing a new book over the summer holidays.

To aggressive investors everywhere. Those who provide liquidity to the financial markets, and who are willing to take on the risks others would prefer to avoid.

Richard N. Croft

To my mother, Minnie, who taught me to be judiciously aggressive!
To my wife, Barbara, who taught me to be practical.
To my children, Christopher, Loa and Machaela, who taught me to be patient.
These are the attributes of the Aggressive Investor.

PART I
WHY BE
AN AGGRESSIVE
INVESTOR?

1
INTRODUCTION

Traders, turn the key, rev your engines and open your pocketbook. You are about to embark on a special road to investment performance. It's reserved for only a part of your investment portfolio. It's not for your retirement money, your home savings program, your children's college education or your estate plan. On this road, you'll take the speculative part of your portfolio through some aggressive investment strategies. You should probably put no more than 20% of your investment assets into this program. And then use only excess cash flow—if there is such a thing—which you can afford to lose.

Most of us have an affinity for aggressive situations. They give us something to talk about at cocktail parties. You can lose money in speculative situations, but you can also make money. Sometimes a lot of money. In fact, the potential is limitless!

Electronics for Imaging—symbol EFII—trades on the The National Association of Security Dealers Automated Quotation (NASDAQ).[1] It was trading at $16 (all prices in US$) per share on January 12, 1998. This company designs products that allow for high-quality printing in short production runs. According to Morningstar Research,[2] "the company's Fiery Color Servers are workstations that connect color copiers with computer networks. Clients include corporations, advertising agencies, graphic design studios, and print-for-pay businesses." EFII controls about 80% of this market, and one of the largest customers is Canon.

EFII dominates the market in a high-growth business. Not surprisingly, the stock market rewarded EFII stockholders big time. Its stock value rose from $3 per share in 1994 to over $50 per share in December 1997. That's a 1,700% increase over four years, or if you like, 102% compounded annually. Give or take a few percentage points. The chart in Figure 1.1 speaks a thousand words, in telling the story of EFII.

Hmmm ... is that what we mean when we talk about aggressive trading? Seems simple enough. Look for companies that dominate their particular industry, that grow earnings faster than expected, and whose stock price reflects that earnings growth. Then buy and hold.

Not surprisingly, that's the approach used by most wealth-building books. They simply attempt to fine-tune a system. And the systems generally follow one of two basic philosophies: buy value and buy for the long term, or buy growth and trade for profit.

FIGURE 1.1

ELECTRONICS FOR IMAGING—FIVE-YEAR CHART

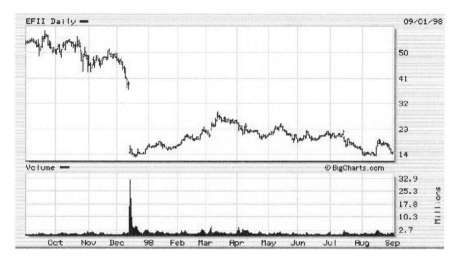

Source: www.bigcharts.com

The buy-value approach relies heavily on fundamental analysis. You pore over financial statements and, in the process, calculate a number of financial ratios—always seeking companies whose intrinsic value is worth more than the market is willing to pay.

Value investors believe that the market will eventually recognize this untapped potential and, at some point, bid up the share price—"eventually" being the key word in a value investor's vocabulary. The fact that it usually takes a lot of time for the market to recognize what the value investor sees explains the second basic tenet in this position. When you buy value, you buy for the long term.

The buy-growth strategy seeks to find companies with positive price momentum and whose share price is rising, usually because of a favorable trend in the earnings—quarterly earnings numbers that continue to beat the estimates of analysts. EFII is a classic example of just such a company.

Usually growth/momentum investors will follow chart patterns, believing that historical price and volume patterns speak volumes about the stock and tell investors all they need to know about the future.

I am not here to downplay either of these approaches. In fact, for a large part of your portfolio, they have merit. For the aggressive part of your portfolio, information gleaned from these approaches will provide support for each aggressive position. But the fact is, most aggressive trading is short-term. Positions are never held long enough to reap the benefits of the buy-value or buy-growth analysis.

DECEMBER 12, 1997

The chart of EFII tells a long-term success story. But what intrigues me about Figure 1.1 is the performance of the stock on December 12, 1997. That's the point on the left side of the chart where volume (seen along the bottom of the chart) spikes up, and the stock price spikes down. On December 12, 1997, the price of EFII fell to $14.875—24.125 points lower than the previous day's close of $39.

On December 12, EFII was front-page news. The company that had regularly beaten earnings estimates had just warned analysts and investors that their fourth-quarter profits would be substantially less than expected. The best fourth-quarter guess had earnings coming in at 60 cents per share. At the close of trading on December 11, the company announced that profits would be around 6 cents per share.

On December 12, 1997, EFII became an aggressive trading candidate. I'm not suggesting that we only seek out fallen angels. However, on December 12, 1997, we knew with a degree of certainty that most of the news likely to affect EFII was a matter of public record.

Now let's go beyond the news—put yourself in management's position. You have news that will negatively affect the price of your company's stock. Wouldn't you expect management to make certain all of the bad news comes out at the same time? Why keep skeletons in the closet? It can't get much worse.

The company cited the principal reasons for the lower-than-expected earnings to be delays in purchases associated with product transitions, aggressive reductions of inventory by its customers and weakness in the Asian economies. Read into that a new line of Canon products requiring a new upgraded controller from EFII.

In other words, there was no fundamental long-term change in the business of EFII. The company still dominated its field and continued to provide the best controllers for its customer base. The company was not losing market share to upstart competitors, and its main line of business was still growing at double-digit rates. We need to know that. Before embarking on any aggressive trade, we need to understand the long-term fundamentals of the company.

The next question is, why wait until January 12, 1998, one month after the stock's collapse, to initiate a trade? Think of the timing as a safety check. Time to make certain that all of the critical information was out in the open. Give the stock some time to settle into a reasonable trading range.

AND NOW THE TRADE

The stock has settled into a trading range. That tells us that most of the investors who were going to sell already have—either during the day the stock collapsed, in which case they would have sold in a panic, or during the ensuing 20 trading days when the stock failed to break out of its trading range. Either way, most of the sellers were already on to other things.

We also know from the trading range that investors remain fearful. Not enough to drive the price down further, but enough to keep the stock from rallying to new levels. That's an important point, because it will affect the potential return from an aggressive trade.

What we know, then, is that EFII is stuck in a narrow range. We know that investors remain fearful about the future prospects for the company. And we believe that most of the critical information is already part of the public record.

To implement an aggressive trade, the position must hold out the promise of a profit even if the stock remains within its current trading range. Between December 12, 1997, and January 12, 1998, EFII traded between $14 and $17.50.

The aggressive trade must also take advantage of the fear in other investors. In other words, we need to capitalize financially on that anxiety. The aggressive trade must take place in a defined time frame, usually no longer than four months. And finally, before entering any aggressive trade, we must define the downside risk. EFII met all of the criteria on January 12, 1998.

ANATOMY OF AN AGGRESSIVE TRADE

To implement an aggressive trade:
• *The position must hold out the promise of a profit even if the stock remains within its current trading range.*
• *The aggressive trade must also take advantage of the fear in other investors. In other words, we need to capitalize financially on that anxiety.*
• *The aggressive trade must take place in a defined time frame, usually no longer than four months.*
• *Before entering any aggressive trade, we must define the downside risk.*

For the aggressive trade, we buy the stock at $16 per share. We immediately agree to sell the shares for $17.50 by April 1998. That's three months from the date of purchase, well within our defined time frame. The price we are agreeing to sell at is $17.50, the high end of the trading range over the previous 20 trading days.

Because we are agreeing to sell the stock at $17.50 between now and April, we will receive a fee, which in this case is $2.50 per share. The fee quantifies financially the amount of risk other investors perceive in EFII. By collecting the fee, we capitalize on that anxiety, meeting yet another criterion for our aggressive trade. We keep the fee no matter what happens to EFII.

5

The fee is paid by another investor—obviously, someone who thinks the stock will rise to $20 or $25 by April. They may be right, but I'm not willing to make that kind of bet when the returns from this strategy are so high.

Finally, the fee helps us define the downside. Remember, we are buying the stock at $16 per share, and on the same day, collecting a $2.50 fee for agreeing to sell it at $17.50. If we subtract the fee from the purchase price, our actual out-of-pocket cost is $13.50 per share ($16 purchase price less $2.50 per share fee = $13.50 per share).

Looking at the trade from this perspective helps us define our downside risk. What we are saying is that EFII can fall to $13.50 between now and April, and we still break even. Again keeping within our trading parameters, $13.50 is below the trading range for the stock over the past 20 trading days.

Now for the potential. Remember, after the anxiety fee is collected, the net out-of-pocket cost for this investment is $13.50 per share. If the stock rises above $17.50 by April 1998, we will receive $17.50 per share, for a total profit of $4 per share. That's a $4 per share profit on a $13.50 investment. That's a 29.6% return over three months.

If that's not enough, then consider adding some leverage to the position. Rather than paying for EFII with your own money, borrow 50% of the cost of the stock from your broker. In this case you can borrow half of your out-of-pocket costs, or $6.75 per share. In this case, if we sell the stock at $17.50 in April, the profit is $4 per share on the total out-of-pocket cost of $6.75 per share. That produces a return in excess of 59% over three months—less borrowing costs of course. For the record, borrowing costs will eat up about 2% of your total return. So you make 57% instead of 59%.

That's what I mean when I talk about aggressive investing.

IS THIS SPECULATION OR GAMBLING?

You can be excused for thinking that the aggressive trader is nothing more than a streetwise gambler. Aside from the tax advantages of being able to write off losing positions, what's the difference?

There may be some truth to this observation, at least with respect to the personality traits of the aggressive investor. However, I'm not convinced that gambling and speculative investing deserve a place at the same table.

Gambling is, by definition, a zero-sum game. For one to win, another must lose. You could argue, given that odds are tilted in favor of the house, that gambling is a negative-sum game. For one to win, two must lose. But I'm splitting hairs.

Speculation is not a zero-sum game. For one person to profit does not imply that another MUST lose. EFII provides a compelling case study. If we sold the shares at $17.50, we earned our maximum profit, the bulk of which came from the anxiety fee we collected.

If this were gambling, our success would imply that the individual who paid the fee must have lost. But in April 1998, the shares of EFII were trading at $24 per share. We would have sold at $17.50, maximizing our profit. But the individual who bought the stock from us at $17.50 would also have earned a decent profit.

Think about it. The investor who paid the fee—call him Harry—agreed to buy the stock from us at $17.50 per share. What Harry did was buy an option on our stock. Come April, Harry's option would be worth more than the $2.50 per share he initially paid. Harry's option would be worth the difference between the price of EFII in April (i.e., $24 per share) and the price at which Harry could exercise his option and buy the stock ($17.50). That's $6.50 per share for those of you keeping track of such things. That means Harry earned 180% on his initial $2.50 per share investment over the same time frame as we earned between 25% and 57%.

This is not meant to promote one approach over the other, but merely to point out that both sides of this trade earned a profit. Not what you would expect from a zero-sum game. With speculative investing one's profit does not always mean another's loss.

Throughout this book, we will look at a number of aggressive investing strategies. I'll discuss how to line up a position and then how to assess which approach makes the most sense under a specific circumstance.

And even then, recognize that the strategies discussed in this book are not panaceas. They will help tilt the odds in your favor, but they will not eliminate the possibility of a loss. With more than 25 years of investing behind me, 23 years investing options, I can tell you there will be highs and lows. Sometimes too many lows.

But if you can see capital losses as real-world education aimed at helping you develop discipline and cash management skills, then the financial pain becomes your price of admission.

WHY ME?

It's a fair question. What gives me the right to write about aggressive trading strategies? While I like to think I've paid my dues, you be the judge. I have more than 25 years in the investment business—beginning in 1975 as a stockbroker—and throughout almost my entire career I traded options in one form or another. In this business, that constitutes veteran status.

I have written about financial issues since 1984—more than 1,800 published columns at last count, most of them related to options and futures. I've taught the Canadian Options Course to more than 500 prospective registrants from 1987 to 1991, and authored part of the Canadian Options Course strategy section.

In February 1993, I became licensed as an Investment Counselor/Portfolio Manager in the Province of Ontario and I manage approximately $40 million in personal client portfolios. Not institutional money, but personal portfolios. Average portfolio size about $500,000.

I like to think of my investment philosophy as a "passive-plus" strategy. My "core portfolio" includes a set of securities that provide diversification across asset class and geographic region. After establishing a diversified mix, I invest in securities that I believe will outperform the general trend in the market—specific stocks in sectors of the market I like long-term.

Generally, my clients fit into one of six investor categories, from *safety* to *aggressive growth*. Each client will have different weightings in their portfolio; a safety investor will hold a much larger percentage of bonds, an aggressive growth investor a much larger percentage of stocks. But all my clients will hold similar assets as their core holdings.

I don't believe in keeping cash as an investment, despite the oft-quoted traditional views about the role cash plays in a balanced portfolio. You've heard the commentary, "We're value-based money managers who want to maintain a conservative stance. We want to hold cash so that we can buy good-quality stocks when prices are more attractive."

The question in my mind is, how much is enough? To my way of thinking, more than a 10% cash cushion smacks of market timing. And that assumes the manager is able to time exactly when to buy and sell. Easier said than done!

When the markets are falling in a panic-driven correction—which seems to be the only type of correction we see these days—these so-called value managers should be jumping all over themselves to make new investments. Yet when the dust settles, you don't often see much change in the level of cash in the portfolio.

The bottom line is that, over long periods, cash will usually be the worst-performing asset in your portfolio. More to the point, why does a client have to pay a money manager to hold cash? Holding cash is not rocket science. I think the money you entrust to the manager is money that you want invested to earn the highest possible return within your personal risk profile. Cash you can manage yourself.

That brings me to the "plus" in the passive-plus strategy. I do not try to time the market. Attempting to sell stocks and raise cash before a correction or to buy stocks with excess cash before an upturn just doesn't work for me over the long haul.

Mind you, I still have to manage the portfolios—to smooth out the fluctuations that accompany every business cycle. To manage that risk and hopefully enhance returns, I use options—conservative strategies for the most part that never exceed the risk parameters of the client.

I also manage about $3 million in an aptly named "performance portfolio," again on behalf of my clients, with each contributing a small part of their core portfolio to be invested using more aggressive strategies. Some pan out, some don't. The goal overall is to earn a much higher return than they would get with a traditionally managed portfolio.

With the performance portfolio, I put myself in the same position as my client. I don't charge a management fee, but rather take a percentage of any return above a minimum return threshold. Every investment made on behalf of clients is also implemented at the same time and at the same price in my own corporate trading account. I feel exactly what my clients feel.

Each performance portfolio runs for one year. During that year, the performance portfolio must earn at least the one-year GIC rate plus 600 basis points[3] (which I refer to as the *minimum return threshold*) before I am eligible for a bonus. My bonus is then calculated as 25% of any return above the minimum return threshold, and is paid out only once, at the end of the year.

To put some numbers on this: Let's assume a client has $50,000 invested in the performance portfolio. And let's assume the minimum return threshold for the year is 10%. If at the end of the year, the client's portfolio is worth $65,000, the total return is 30%. The first $5,000 represents the minimum return threshold and is not subject to any bonus. The next $10,000, however, is subject to the 25% bonus. Given those numbers, I would earn a $2,500 bonus on the portfolio, and the client would net, after expenses, $12,500 or 25%.

I have been operating performance portfolios since January 1997. My 1997 gross return, taking into account all portfolios, was 44.84%. For the first eight months of 1998, gross returns (including the August 31 correction) were in excess of 30%.

Those are the kinds of returns I would expect to see from this type of program, and those are the kinds of returns that best-case scenarios can produce for aggressive investors. But, as always, there will be highs and lows, and the goal is to manage through the low periods to profit when the financial markets are rocking.

AND NOW FOR THE RISKS

Discussions about risk are always interesting. All too often, financial commentators and advisors focus on the investment potential, without referring to risk.

One reason for that is time horizon. The longer you hold an investment, the less chance you will sell at a loss. Over long periods (greater than 20 years) stocks have yielded higher returns than bonds, and bonds have outperformed treasury bills. I expect this to continue into the future. Buying for the long term, then, is the best way to reduce risk.

For aggressive investors, however, that standard doesn't hold. The time frame for an aggressive trade is always less than a year, usually less than four months. We cannot enter any aggressive trade without a firm grasp of the risks and an understanding of how to quantify risk. We'll spend considerable time on this subject because it relates to so many aspects of each trade.

For purposes of our discussions, we define risk as the volatility of the underlying investment. We measure risk in terms of standard deviation. And when all is said and done, we are really talking about the potential trading range for a security over a specific time period.

STANDARD DEVIATION

Standard deviation is the amount a stock's price is expected to vary from its mean or average price over a given period. Standard deviation is an appropriate measure of risk for aggressive investors because we will not hold diversified portfolios, but rather specific investment positions. In addition, standard deviation is simple to calculate and relatively easy to understand.

With some minor apologies to the reader, I think it's important to walk through the calculation, introducing in the process some statistical tools to add substance to the skeleton of the discussion.

To keep things as simple as possible, we will look at Intel Corp and show the step-by-step process for calculating volatility and standard deviation, using monthly closing prices from the beginning of January 1997 to the end of December 1997 (see Table 1.1).

TABLE 1.1

INTEL CLOSING PRICES FROM JANUARY 1997 TO
DECEMBER 1997

DATE	MONTHLY CLOSE
31-Jan-97	81.125
28-Feb-97	70.938
31-Mar-97	69.563
30-Apr-97	76.563
30-May-97	75.750
30-Jun-97	70.906
31-Jul-97	91.813
31-Aug-97	92.125
30-Sep-97	92.313
31-Oct-97	77.000
28-Nov-97	77.625
31-Dec-97	70.250
Average Price	$78.831

The first step in the process is to calculate an average price for 1997. To calculate the average price we simply add all the monthly closing prices and divide by the number of observations, which in this case is 12. The average price for Intel during 1997 was $78.831. But in our sampling, the price rose as high as $92.313 at the end of September 1997 and as low as $69.563 at the end of March 1997.

1 0

CALCULATING VARIANCE AND STANDARD DEVIATION

Intuitively, variance and standard deviation define for us how far the monthly prices for Intel varied from the average price, which we know to be $78.831. Looking at the September month-end price of $92.313, we see that it varied from the average price by $13.482. Table 1.2 looks at each of the variations from the mean price.

TABLE 1.2

CALCULATING VARIANCE AND STANDARD DEVIATION

DATE	MONTHLY CLOSE	DEVIATION	DEVIATION 2
31-Jan-97	81.125	2.294	5.26
28-Feb-97	70.938	−7.893	62.303
31-Mar-97	69.563	−9.268	85.900
30-Apr-97	76.563	−2.268	5.145
30-May-97	75.750	−3.081	9.491
30-Jun-97	70.906	−7.925	62.798
31-Jul-97	91.813	12.982	168.526
31-Aug-97	92.125	13.294	176.738
30-Sep-97	92.313	13.482	181.758
31-Oct-97	77.000	−1.831	3.352
28-Nov-97	77.625	−1.206	1.454
31-Dec-97	70.250	−8.581	73.629
Average Price		$78.831	
Variance (sum of Deviations 2) / 12			69.696
Standard Deviation (Square Root of Variance)			8.348

You might think that the "average deviation" for each monthly closing price could be calculated by simply adding the 12 deviations and dividing by the number of observations. However, if we do that, the result is zero. That would imply that the stock never varied from its average price, which is clearly not the case.

When you think about it, the sum of deviations around an average would always equal zero because of the central tendency of an average. The way around this problem is to square the deviations and then add the resulting numbers. By doing that, we convert any negative deviations into a positive number. The larger the deviation from the average, the larger the squared value will be. You can see the squared deviations in the far right column of Table 1.2.

With the squared deviations we can calculate the price variance for Intel stock. The price variance is simply the sum of the squared deviations divided by the number of observations. The result is shown in Table 1.2.

1 1

Standard deviation is simply the square root of the variance.

$$\text{Standard Deviation} = \sqrt{69.696} = 8.348$$

Because we're looking at actual price changes for Intel, the standard deviation represents a dollar value: $8.348 per share. What we are saying is that over any one-month period, the price of Intel could trade above or below its average price by $8.348. The $8.348 per share value, by the way, represents one standard deviation.

Statistically, we would expect the price of Intel to trade within one standard deviation of its average price approximately 66% of the time. Remember, I'm not saying that Intel is more likely to rise than to fall (or vice versa)—only that I would expect, in two out of the three observations, Intel's stock price will remain in a range bounded by one standard deviation of its average price, the average price being defined as the average of the stock's price over the observation period. Therefore, the price of Intel would not be expected to exceed $87.179 ($78.831 average price + $8.348 standard deviation = $87.179) or to fall below $70.483 ($78.831 average – $8.348 standard deviation = $70.483).

Interestingly, in Table 1.2, the stock traded within one standard deviation of the mean 7 out of 12 monthly observations, or just over 58% of the time. This confirms two things about statistical measures: they are open to interpretation, and statistics lie.

Keeping with the same theme, we would expect that in 95% of all monthly observations, Intel's per share price would fall within two standard deviations of its average price. For Intel, two standard deviations represents a monthly price that could be as high as $95.527 ($78.831 average + $16.696 two standard deviations = $95.527) or as low as $62.135 ($78.831 average – $16.696 two standard deviations = $62.135). Note from Table 1.2 that Intel never traded above or below the monthly price parameters as defined by two standard deviations.

AND THEN THERE IS VOLATILITY

In all aggressive trades we will cite a volatility number. Volatility will be expressed as a percent and will always relate to a one-year period. The calculation is relatively straightforward.

We begin by calculating the monthly volatility, which is simply the standard deviation as calculated in Table 1.2 divided by the average share price during the observation period. To wit: $8.348 divided by $78.831 = 10.59%.

At this point we have simply calculated monthly volatility. We need to translate monthly volatility into an annual number. To do that we multiply the 10.59% volatility number by the square root of time. Since there are 12 months in a year, and since we are translating a monthly number into an annual number, we must multiply the monthly volatility by the square root of 12.

$$10.59\% \times \sqrt{12} = 28.92\%$$

The annual volatility for Intel—using the monthly observations from Table 1.2—is 28.92%. We refer to this as historical volatility because it is based on historical numbers.

We have used a liberal interpretation of the volatility calculation to keep number crunching to a minimum. The monthly data only serve to illustrate the calculation. The monthly data only serve to illustrate the calculation.

In the real world, however, volatility is calculated using daily data. And over the course of a year, there are approximately 252 trading days on which to observe data. That translates into approximately 21 trading days per month. For aggressive traders, that's important. We will use that daily number to translate annual volatility into a trading range for the period of each aggressive trade.

For example, if the historical volatility for XYZ is 30%, we know that 30% represents an annual volatility based on the previous 252 daily observations. If we are looking at an aggressive trading strategy over a one-month period, we can calculate the monthly volatility number in the same way as we translated the monthly number for Intel into an annual figure.

We simply multiply the annual volatility number by the square root of time. Only in this case time is 21 (number of trading days in a month) divided by 252 (number of observations in a year).

$$30\% \times \sqrt{\frac{21}{252}} = 8.66\%$$

The final step is to translate the monthly volatility number into a trading range. If XYZ is trading at $100 per share, we simply multiply the monthly volatility number (8.66%) by the stock price ($100 per share) to arrive at an expected trading range. In 66% of the observations (one standard deviation representing 66% of all potential monthly observations) we could reasonably expect the price of XYZ over the next month to trade within a band of $91.34 and $108.66.

With greater assurance (95% of all observations), we could expect the price of XYZ to trade between $82.68 and $117.32, representing a two-standard deviation band around the current price.

One final point to this discussion: When we calculate the volatility of stock prices, we cannot assume that a stock will rise or fall by an equal dollar amount over a prescribed period. That's because stocks can rise to infinity, but cannot fall below zero.

The way around that is to use logarithms. We calculate volatility as shown, but when we translate that into a trading range we assume a lognormal distribution of prices. Without getting into further mathematical calculations—I can see your eyes glazing at the prospect—suffice it to say that a lognormal distribution allows us to calculate a real-world trading range for any security that falls somewhere between zero and infinity.

CONCLUSION

These calculations form the basis of how we will view risk in future chapters. And, like it or not, aggressive traders need to examine the risks associated with each aggressive strategy presented in this book.

So take a breather from the computational wizardry and move into the types of products we will use in our aggressive trading strategies.

NOTES

1. The National Association of Security Dealers Automated Quotation is the quote system used for stocks that trade over the counter in the US.
2. Morningstar is the largest US data provider of mutual fund information. The company also provides research on more than 6,000 US companies. Information was provided through America Online.
3. A basis point is 1/100th of a percentage point. One hundred basis points equals 1%, 600 basis points equals 6%.

PART II

INVESTMENT
PRODUCTS
FOR THE
AGGRESSIVE
INVESTOR

2

BASIC INVESTMENT PRODUCTS FOR THE AGGRESSIVE INVESTOR

WALKING THE WALK

Walk before you run. That's good advice for the aggressive investor.

Walking the aggressive investor's walk begins with a discussion of various investment products—what they are, how they're priced, and then how they fit with the strategies discussed in Part Four.

Included in this chapter will be a discussion of common and preferred stock and hybrids, known as convertible securities. More specifically, we'll focus on convertible debentures. Nor will we forget government bonds—the billions and billions of government IOUs whose prices float in cyberspace on the computer screens of the major banks and brokerage firms; where daily transactions reach into the billions of dollars, making this the most liquid market in the world for the aggressive investor. Yes, there are aggressive strategies tied to these staid and secure government bonds. We'll show you how. As a teaser, just think leverage—lots of leverage. We'll discuss this thoroughly when we examine the pros and cons of leverage at the end of this chapter.

STOCK: THE HEART OF CAPITAL MARKETS

A company is worth what someone is willing to pay for its stock times the number of shares outstanding, minus debt. We think of stock as equity. The most common form of equity is, well, common stock.

Common stock represents ownership in the underlying company. If you buy 100 shares of General Electric, you own a piece of that company. Not a big piece, but a piece nonetheless. So owners of companies usually own common shares.

Common shares are often listed on a major stock exchange, although the over-the-counter (OTC) market represents a large slice of trading activity on any given day. Over-the-counter simply means that the stocks are traded between brokers via computer screens. These are often called unlisted stocks as opposed to exchange-listed stocks. Most OTC stocks trade through the Canadian Dealing Network in Canada and, in the U.S., through NASDAQ.

Most new investors think that unlisted stocks are issued by smaller companies that are not quite ready for the prime-time exposure a company gets when listed on a recognized stock exchange.

In fairness, most unlisted stocks are small cap. But many others are blue-chip leaders in their markets. Microsoft and Intel are classic examples of stocks that trade over-the-counter. It's cheaper to have your stock traded in the unlisted market, and, with modern technology, trading stocks over the counter is really quite efficient.

> The National Association of Security Dealers Automated Quotation (NASDAQ) system is essentially a network of computers that enables brokers to see bids and offer prices for thousands of different stocks.

The granddaddy of all stock exchanges where listed stocks trade is the New York Stock Exchange (NYSE). If you watch the financial news broadcasts when they interview someone on the exchange floor, the background looks like organized chaos. How anyone can trade billions of dollars worth of stock while wading through a mountain of order tickets and communicating by hand signal I'll never know. Fortunately, aggressive investors don't have to.

The NYSE and NASDAQ are really just central meeting places where buyers and sellers of financial securities—i.e., stocks and bonds—come together to conduct business. Prices that buyers are willing to pay and sellers are willing to take are posted for everyone to see. Financial market regulators like that because the prices are visible, which, in theory, means fairness.

THE STOCK QUOTE

It's one thing to own shares of a good company: Hold for the long term, and who cares what the price is today, tomorrow or next week? But for aggressive investors or for that part of your portfolio dedicated to aggressive investing, timing is important. So, too, is an understanding of how stock prices are quoted.

Stocks come with two prices: the price someone is willing to sell at, referred to as the offer, or asking price, and the price that someone is willing to pay, called the bid price.

1 7

Let's assume a buyer is willing to pay $50 per share for XYZ stock. The bid on XYZ would then be posted at $50 per share, assuming, of course, that was the highest current bid. A seller might be willing to offer the same stock for sale at, say, $50 1/4 per share, which would then be posted as the best available asking price. The bid/ask for XYZ would be $50 to $50 1/4.

Common stocks have rather strange increments. For decades the spread between the bid and ask price had to be at least 1/8th or 12.5 cents per share. So much for tradition. The times they are a changin'.

The Toronto Stock Exchange has initiated decimal trading—a novel approach, at least for the financial community. With modern-day computers, decimal trading makes sense and, in the long run, benefits investors. It narrows the spread and means a stock could be bid $50 and offered at $50.05.

In the U.S., many stocks are now traded in 1/64th increments—i.e., $50 bid, offered at $50 2/64. Don't ask what that translates into. Bottom line: Tighter spreads between the bid and offered price provide aggressive investors with a more competitive environment in which to trade.

THE PREFERRED SHARE

Some companies also issue preferred shares. If you're class conscious, this might sound like a better investment. At first blush, preferred does infer some sort of advantage, comparable, say, to business class versus economy.

Both classes of shares represent ownership in the company. Usually, however, preferred shares participate only in the company's dividends; common shares grow as the company grows, providing investors with potential capital gains plus dividends. That capital gain potential can present a huge opportunity. On the other hand, preferred shareholders usually receive their dividends before common shareholders. Presumably, that's why they're called preferred shareholders.

In most cases, preferred shares restrict your ability to vote at shareholder meetings. Preferred shareholders usually get to vote only if the company fails to pay the dividends that were promised in the preferred shareholder agreement.

Holders of common shares may also receive dividends, although a company is under no obligation to pay dividends to common shareholders. The decision to pay or not rests with the company's board of directors. So does the decision to increase or reduce the dividend. General Electric has been paying dividends for as long as I can remember and will likely pay dividends long after we're all gone. But many other companies don't.

Dividends are usually paid four times a year. If a company is doing particularly well, its profits are growing, and there is more cash in the till than the company needs to fund future expansion, it will often declare a dividend increase. General Electric also has a long history of raising its dividend on a regular basis.

Investors can tell a great deal about a company from its dividend yield—i.e., the annual dividend divided by the company's stock price. But you have to listen carefully, because a high dividend yield can tell you one of two things:

1. The company is mature and has little prospect for double-digit growth. Regulated electric utility companies fall into this category.
2. The company is in trouble. The high yield may be based on previous dividend payments, which many investors don't believe the company can maintain in the future.

DIVIDEND YIELD: THE MACRO VIEW

Dividend yield has also been a popular barometer of stock market activity. The Standard and Poor (S&P) 500 composite index, for example, measures the price performance of the common stock of 500 of the largest U.S. companies, representing a cross-section of U.S. industry.

Many of these companies pay dividends. Add up these dividends and divide by the current level of the Standard and Poor 500 composite index, and you get the dividend yield on the overall stock market. When the dividend yield falls below 3%, according to the macro view of dividend theory, the stock market is overvalued. As of the second quarter of 1998, the dividend yield on the S&P 500 composite index was 1.5%. However, despite the low dividend yield, the bull market that began in the late 1980s just keeps going and going and going.

Dividends give rise to other strategies as well. The Dow Dividend Theory, also referred to as the Dow Dog Theory, comes to mind. It follows the philosophy that every dog has its day.

THE DOG DAYS OF DOW

There are 30 stocks in the Dow Jones Industrial Average, including General Electric, Disney, Alcoa, Eastman Kodak, IBM. They're the crème de la crème of U.S. companies. You may argue about the computational merits of a price-weighted index, but it's difficult to imagine a bad long-term investment among these 30 blue-chip performers. Not impossible, just difficult.

Familiarity with the index has given rise to a number of investment strategies that claim to consistently beat the Dow. The most common is the Dow Dog Approach. The idea is simple: Invest equal amounts in a portfolio of beaten-down Dow stocks—yesterday's dogs. Now hold that portfolio for a year. Then re-balance it and repeat the procedure at predetermined intervals.

Building the portfolio is easy:

> • *Look up the 30 Dow stocks, find their current price and dividend yield. If you can't find the dividend yield, then go back to our handy formula: Divide the annual reported dividend by the current price of the stock. (The lower the current price of the stock—i.e., the bigger the dog—the higher the yield.)*
> • *Next, rank the stocks by their dividend yield, from highest to lowest. Buy equal dollar amounts of the 10 highest-dividend-paying stocks in the Dow and hold the shares for one year. After a year, re-evaluate the positions, and replace those stocks that no longer rank as a dog, at least based on their dividend yield.*

Following the Keep-It-Simple-Stupid principle, the strategy is just that simple. And it seems to work. This Dow Dog strategy has returned better than 17% annually for the last 26 years and beaten the Dow more times than academics would like to admit.using this strategy, $10,000 would have increased to $641,897 over that 26-year period. So much for random walk.

I can just hear the academic naysayers stepping up to the microphone. "What about transaction costs?" they ask. "What about that bid/ask spread we talked about earlier, which can hamper returns when you're buying less than 100 shares of a stock?" Remember you're buying equal dollar amounts, not equal share amounts.

In the worst case, assuming you had to replace all 10 high-yielding stocks in the second year of the strategy, you could end up with 20 transactions (selling 10 former dogs to buy 10 new dogs). You'd still do all right, but it also demonstrates the difference between a paper-based and real-world trading system. Paper-based models don't do much for aggressive investors, except, perhaps, to lighten their pocketbook.

THE LANGUAGE GAME

Investor terminology is also important for the aggressive investor, if for no other reason than being able to say you made oodles of money investing in a blue-chip growth company and having a cursory understanding of what a blue-chip growth company actually is.

Growth, value, blue chip, small cap, mid cap, large cap, small and/or large P/Es, market indices—the terms go on and on. Here are the most common terms that aggressive investors use.

Cap, as in small cap, mid cap or large cap, is short for market capitalization. A company's market capitalization is the total value of all outstanding common shares at their current price. Compared with other companies, one company may have a small, mid or large market capitalization.

To use an example, XYZ has 10 million shares outstanding. XYZ is trading at $10 per share. XYZ's market capitalization is $100 million. That's the price per share multiplied by the number of shares outstanding. In the context of Canada's equity markets, XYZ would be considered a small-cap company. When thinking small cap, think of companies valued between $50 million up to, say, $500 million. Mid-cap companies usually have a market capitalization between $500 million and $1 billion. Companies with a market capitalization above $1 billion are large-cap companies.

To the aggressive investor, size is important. Small companies are not bad. But aggressive investors have to move in and out of the market quickly. That means dealing with stocks with a tight bid/ask spread and that have listed options (discussed in the next chapter), which we can use to structure aggressive trades with clearly defined potential return and risk. For our purposes, we'll focus on large-cap stocks.

Blue chip describes some, but not all, large-cap companies. Blue-chip companies are mature companies, leaders in their industry. General Motors is a blue-chip company. So are IBM, Microsoft, Intel, and Procter and Gamble. The 30 companies in the Dow Jones Industrial Average are blue chip.

But some blue-chip companies are less blue chip than others. Philip Morris, for example, is a blue-chip company. It's highly profitable. In 1998 its common stock's dividend yield exceeded 4%, which was almost three times the dividend yield on the S&P 500 composite index. By almost any financial measure, this looks like a great investment. And it may be!

However, look at Figure 2.1. It provides a one-year snapshot of Philip Morris. Despite some daily and weekly volatility, this is effectively a blue-chip stock whose price is going nowhere.

FIGURE 2.1

PHILIP MORRIS

Source: www.bigcharts.com

The longer term problem is that 50% of Philip Morris's business involves tobacco. At the time of writing, all tobacco companies operated under a judicial sword hanging over their corporate necks: The U.S. Congress was considering a $500 billion settlement to a lawsuit that promised limited liability in future tobacco lawsuits. But Congress was balking at the numbers, preferring instead an $800 billion settlement, with no limit on future liabilities.

An investor has to wonder if Congress is offering tobacco companies a deal they can't refuse or a Congressional carrot and stick—with a larger settlement being the carrot and the waffling on limited/unlimited liability being the stick.

For our purposes, it's enough to know that, when a company faces an uncertain future, equity markets err on the side of caution, and the value of the stock suffers. Until Congress reaches a decision, most investors will move cautiously.

For the aggressive investor, this type of situation provides an interesting case study:

- *a blue-chip stock, lots of liquidity;*
- *a stock on which options trade and that pays a good dividend, at least for now; and*
- *an uncertain long-term future, but significant short-term potential.*

Just what the aggressive investor ordered for some of our strategies.

In this case, we know that the stock will remain in a going-nowhere trading range. We also know that cigarettes will not become obsolete. And we know that tobacco companies will never sign a deal that has huge upfront costs and unlimited liability. At some point, the odds suggest that Congress will offer a middle-of-the-road solution. We also know that any decision from Congress will probably take six months to a year to complete. The prevailing uncertainty during this period begets opportunity. In Chapters Six and Seven, we'll show how aggressive investors take advantage of situations like this.

THE COST OF GROWTH: THE PRICE-TO-EARNINGS MULTIPLE

Not all blue-chip large-cap companies pay hefty dividends. In fact, some pay no dividend at all, with management preferring to plow profits back into the company. Not a bad strategy, if the company is making a better-than-average return on that re-invested equity.

Companies that re-invest profits and earn above-average rates of return on their capital are considered growth companies. Profits grow faster than the market average, and the stock price of the company trades at a higher price-to-earnings (P/E) multiple than the rest of the market.

When we talk about a company's P/E, we are comparing the company's stock price relative to its earnings per share. To do that, we simply divide the current stock price by the last year's earnings per share. A company that earns $1 per share and whose stock price is $20 per share is trading at a P/E of 20.

Growth companies like Microsoft trade at higher P/E multiples than the rest of the market. Microsoft often trades at a P/E of 50. Its stock is priced at 50 times the value of last year's earnings per share. This indicates that investors believe in Microsoft's future. But buying shares at such a high P/E ratio means that they're buying the prospect that Microsoft's earnings will continue to grow at a faster rate than most other companies'.

Growth companies are particularly interesting for the aggressive investor, for a couple of reasons:

1. Day-to-day price changes in a growth company's stock are usually more dramatic than the average stock.

2. The stock of a growth company tends to move even more dramatically around the time it issues a press release about its quarterly earnings. So important is the growth rate of earnings that investors pay particular attention to these quarterly releases. When a growth company fails to meet expectations, its stock price declines sharply; when it beats expectations, look for a sharp increase in the share price.

SHORT SELLING

One of the more interesting tools in the financial markets gives investors the ability to sell something they don't own. It's easy to understand the concept of buying stock at one price and selling it at another. You pay $40 per share to buy XYZ stock, you sell it at $50 per share, and you net a $10-per-share profit.

With short selling, you reverse the process. You sell XYZ stock short at $50 per share. At some point in the future, you buy it back. If the stock declines to $40 per share, then you'd buy it back at that price—$10 a share less than what you paid for it—and net a $10-per-share profit. Short selling allows you to make money in up-and-down markets, an important issue for aggressive investors.

How do you sell something you don't own? In essence you borrow the stock from another investor and pay a borrowing fee while you're holding it. That's not as difficult as it sounds. Most investors do not handle physical share certificates. They're too much trouble to keep track of and it's a hassle to deliver the certificates back to a broker every time you want to sell them. Besides, who wants to worry about losing the certificates or, worse yet, having the certificates stolen?

Most investors' share certificates remain on deposit at a brokerage firm in the name of the company that issues them. This means that the broker can lend the stock, at a price, to investors who want to borrow the share certificates for a period so they can enter short positions.

Unlike conventional stock trading, in which you can buy a stock and never sell it, you cannot sell a stock short and never buy it back. For aggressive investors that's not a major issue, because they move in and out of the market over short periods.

When you sell stock short, you are responsible for any dividends declared and paid out. You also incur the risk, in theory, of enormous losses if the value of the stock rises quickly instead of falling. This could happen if the company reports earnings that are better than expected or if the company is taken over by another company at a substantially higher price. In this case, a short seller would have to buy the stock back at the higher price and return the newly purchased shares to the brokerage firm to close out the short position.

However, following our strategies, you will never sell short without some type of hedge. You will not enter an aggressive trade in which the risk is unlimited.

GOVERNMENT BONDS

A bond is a financial arrangement between a borrower—the issuer of the bond—and a lender, who buys the bond. The borrower and lender agree on a fixed rate of interest and a future date when the agreement comes to an end, called the *maturity date*.

A bond issuer promises to pay a fixed rate of interest for the life of the bond. This fixed rate represents the *fixed income* that a lender receives from a bond, and, as we'll see, it affects a bond's price.

The *coupon rate* is the rate of interest the bond issuer promises to pay as a percentage of the bond's face or par value. The *face* or *par value* is the amount of principal owed to the lender. Take, for example, a $10,000 Government of Canada bond with a 6% coupon rate maturing on January 15, 2008:

> • *The bond's face value, or par value, is $10,000.*
>
> • *Its coupon rate is 6%, the rate of interest the bond will pay each year.*
>
> • *It matures on January 15, 2008. If you hold the bond to maturity, on January 15, 2008, you will receive guaranteed repayment of your $10,000 principal.*

Meanwhile, over the next 10 years, you will receive semi-annual interest payments, each amounting to half the total annual interest. Based on our $10,000 face value, on January 15 and again on July 15, you will receive an interest payment of $300. That reflects half the 6% annual interest rate that the bond promises to pay until maturity.

On the maturity date, the lender will receive repayment of the principal investment plus any outstanding or accrued interest. *Accrued interest* is the amount of interest owed to the bond holder from the time of the last interest payment. Accrued interest is important, because most investors sell their bonds prior to maturity.

To sell a bond before maturity, you must sell it to another investor. Like stocks, bonds trade with a bid and asked price. You will get the best price offered by other investors, which may be more or less than the principal amount of the bond. Most bonds trade over the counter so, to get a quote, you have to call your broker.

Let's say you want to sell this Government of Canada 6% January 15, 2008, bond on February 15, 1999. You would receive whatever someone is willing to pay for that particular bond on that particular date, plus interest that has accrued since the last interest payment date, January 15, 1999.

TRADING GOVERNMENT BONDS

This Government of Canada bond may be represented by a piece of paper or, more likely, by a blip on a computer terminal that defines what we own and what we can expect to receive over its life. In our example, we'll receive 20 semi-annual interest payments and the return of our principal on January 15, 2008.

Table 2.1 shows the total return if we were to buy this bond on January 15, 1998, and hold it to maturity on January 15, 2008.

TABLE 2.1

THE BOND'S TOTAL CASH FLOW

Particulars: Government of Canada 6% January 15, 2008
Start Date: 15-Jan-98
Face Value: $10,000.00

DATE	INTEREST PAYMENT	PRINCIPAL REPAYMENT
15-Jul-98	300.00	
15-Jan-99	300.00	
15-Jul-99	300.00	
15-Jan-00	300.00	
15-Jul-00	300.00	
15-Jan-01	300.00	
15-Jul-01	300.00	
15-Jan-02	300.00	
15-Jul-02	300.00	
15-Jan-03	300.00	
15-Jul-03	300.00	
15-Jan-04	300.00	
15-Jul-04	300.00	
15-Jan-05	300.00	
15-Jul-05	300.00	
15-Jan-06	300.00	

continued

2 5

TABLE 2.1 (continued)

DATE	INTEREST PAYMENT	PRINCIPAL REPAYMENT
15-Jul-06	300.00	
15-Jan-07	300.00	
15-Jul-07	300.00	
15-Jan-08	300.00	10,000.00
Totals	$6,000.00	$10,000.00

Total Interest + Income = $16,000

TABLE 2.2

THE BOND'S RETURN + RE-INVESTED INCOME

Particulars: Government of Canada 6% January 15, 2008
Start Date: 15-Jan-98
Face Value: $10,000.00

DATE	INTEREST PAYMENT	PRINCIPAL REPAYMENT	MONEY FOR REINVESTMENT	TOTAL RETURN OF REINVESTMENT
15-Jul-98	300.00		300.00	226.05
15-Jan-99	300.00		300.00	210.73
15-Jul-99	300.00		300.00	195.85
15-Jan-00	300.00		300.00	181.41
15-Jul-00	300.00		300.00	167.39
15-Jan-01	300.00		300.00	153.78
15-Jul-01	300.00		300.00	140.56
15-Jan-02	300.00		300.00	127.73
15-Jul-02	300.00		300.00	115.27
15-Jan-03	300.00		300.00	103.17
15-Jul-03	300.00		300.00	91.43
15-Jan-04	300.00		300.00	80.03
15-Jul-04	300.00		300.00	68.96
15-Jan-05	300.00		300.00	58.22
15-Jul-05	300.00		300.00	47.78
15-Jan-06	300.00		300.00	37.65
15-Jul-06	300.00		300.00	27.82
15-Jan-07	300.00		300.00	18.27
15-Jul-07	300.00		300.00	9.00
15-Jan-08	300.00	10,000.00	300.00	—
Totals	$6,000.00	$10,000.00		$2,061.11

Total Interest + Income + Re-invested Income = $18,061.11

The initial investment of $10,000 returns $16,000 over the life of the bond. Now you're thinking, "This is not what an aggressive investor looks for." And you're right. But you need to understand how a bond is valued to understand how changes in interest rates affect the bond's price and how you can utilize leverage to make the most of those changes.

Table 2.1 establishes the cash flow and principal repayment of the bond. It does not show what happens to the semi-annual interest payments and how that might affect the bond's price. If each of the interest payments were re-invested at the same 6% rate of interest, the total return of our bond would look like Table 2.2.

The combination of the semi-annual interest payments ($6,000) and the interest earned by re-investing those payments ($2,061.11), accounts for about 45% of the bond's total return (see Table 2.3).

TABLE 2.3

COMPONENTS OF A BOND'S TOTAL RETURN

Return of principal	10,000.00
Semi-annual interest payments	6,000.00
Interest earned re-investing semi-annual pmts	2,061.11
Total return	$18,061.11

If we were looking at a 30-year bond, the semi-annual interest payments and the re-investment of those payments would represent an even greater percentage of the bond's total return. That's important, because these two components of a bond's total return play a critical role in how the price of a bond will fluctuate over short periods.

THE YIELD TO MATURITY

What we know so far is that a bond guarantees a fixed stream of income. Since the income stream is fixed, the price of the bond must fluctuate so that it fits within the current interest-rate environment. To put it another way, if the going rate paid on 10-year bonds was 8%, why would investors pay the par or face value for a bond that promises only 6%? The answer is simple: They won't.

Since the income stream is fixed, the price of the 6% bond must change if a seller wants to attract investors seeking an 8% return. It's this fluctuation in a bond's price that makes it appealing to aggressive investors. The question is, how much can we expect the price to fluctuate given a change in interest rates?

To compute a bond's price change given a change in interest rates, we need to introduce another calculation: *the yield to maturity*. The yield to maturity accounts for all of the facets in the bond's total return, including the semi-annual interest payments and the repayment of principal.

The yield to maturity assigns a *present value* to all future cash flows including the principal repayment. It allows us to compare bonds with different maturities and different coupon rates using a single measure.

THE CONCEPT OF PRESENT VALUE

Present value is the current or beginning value of a quantity that is subject to compound interest. If you receive $100 today, it is worth $100. You know that, because you can spend it immediately, and it will purchase $100 worth of goods and services.

But what would $100 be worth today if you didn't receive it until two years from now? Certainly not $100. If you had the money today, you could re-invest it at today's rate. So it has a future value higher than its value today.

To calculate the present value of a $100 payment that's due two years from now, we need to determine several things, including the interest rate, the frequency of compounding and the future value. We know the future value—the payment you can expect in two years—is $100. We know the interest rate is 6%. The frequency of compounding may be 2 or 4, depending on whether the payments are annual or semi-annual. Now we can discount the amount of the ultimate payment—$100—to determine its present value using the following formula:

$$PV = \frac{FV}{(1 + R)^t}$$

Where
PV = Present value
FV = Future value
R = Interest (discount) rate
t = Number of periods before the money is received

The FV in the formula represents the amount due at some point in the future. In our example, that's $100. The number of periods (t) refers to the frequency of compounding. Again, using our $100 payment due two years from now, the number of periods could be 2 or 4, depending on whether the money is compounding annually or semi-annually. Let's assume the interest or discount rate is 6%, compounded semi-annually. The discount rate is set at 3%, which is the interest earned every six months, on four occasions.

$$PV = \frac{FV}{(1 + R)^4} = \frac{100}{(1 + .03)^4} = 88.85$$

Assuming the 6% discount rate that is compounding semi-annually, a $100 future value payment would be worth $88.85 today. Stated another way, if someone were to pay you $88.85 today and that money were invested at a 6% annual interest rate, compounding semi-annually, it would grow to $100 in two years.

At first blush, it would appear that a discussion around the concept of present value using semi-annual compounding as the basis for the discount complicates things. But as we have seen in our previous examples, that's the way it is in the bond market. So why delay the inevitable?

PRICING A BOND

A bond is worth the sum of its component parts. Table 2.1 defined the total cash flow for our Government of Canada bond. It is simply 20 semi-annual interest payments, plus the principal repayment due in January 2008.

When trying to calculate what a bond is worth, we need to look at all the cash flows due in the bond. But we're receiving cash flows at different stages, and the principal repayment will not occur for another 10 years. Since the value of a dollar in hand today is greater than the value of a dollar that we don't receive until some point in the future, we can use the present-value formula to ascertain the value today of each of the elements in the bond's cash flow. The key issue is the rate we'll use to discount the cash flow in the present-value formula.

For some numbers, let's assume it is January 15, 1999. Further, we'll assume that the current rate of interest is 10%. We want to know how much it would cost to buy $10,000 face value of the Government of Canada 6% January 15, 2008, bond.

We know that this bond will pay semi-annual interest payments of $300. We also know that we can re-invest those interest payments at 10% based on current rates. The 10% rate then becomes the discount rate to be used in the present-value formula.

The bond is worth the present value of each of the interest payments, plus the present value of the principal payment, all discounted at 10% (see Table 2.4).

Table 2.4 tells us that a bond's price is merely the sum of its parts. To determine the real value of this $10,000 face-value bond, we simply add up the present values in the third column:

Present value of principal repayment	4,155.21
Present value of semi-annual interest payments	3,506.88
Total value of bond	$7,662.09

Bond prices are based on a percentage of face value, with face value equaling 100%. Based on these calculations, we could buy a $10,000 face-value bond for $7,662.09 or about 76.62% of face value.

The discount rate we use to calculate the present value of each semi-annual interest payment and for the repayment of the principal 10 years from now is the basis on which yield to maturity is calculated. In Table 2.4, the yield to maturity for

TABLE 2.4

CALCULATING A BOND'S PRICE

Particulars: Government of Canada 6% January 15, 2008
Start Date: 15-Jan-99
Discount Rate: 10%*

DATE	INTEREST AND PRINCIPAL PAYMENTS	PRESENT VALUE INTEREST PAYMENTS	PRESENT VALUE PRINCIPAL PAYMENT
15-Jul-99	300.00	285.71	
15-Jan-00	300.00	272.11	
15-Jul-00	300.00	259.15	
15-Jan-01	300.00	246.81	
15-Jul-01	300.00	235.06	
15-Jan-02	300.00	223.86	
15-Jul-02	300.00	213.20	
15-Jan-03	300.00	203.05	
15-Jul-03	300.00	193.38	
15-Jan-04	300.00	184.17	
15-Jul-04	300.00	175.40	
15-Jan-05	300.00	167.05	
15-Jul-05	300.00	159.10	
15-Jan-06	300.00	151.52	
15-Jul-06	300.00	144.31	
15-Jan-07	300.00	137.43	
15-Jul-07	300.00	130.89	
15-Jan-08	300.00	124.66	
15-Jan-08		3,506.88	4,155.21

Total Cost to Buy Bond $3,506.88 + $4,155.21 = $7,662.09

* Assumes the interest payments were re-invested at 10%

our bond, assuming we pay 76.62% of par to buy it, is exactly 10%, which equals the current rate of interest for bonds with similar maturities.

A couple of points to consider:

The yield to maturity is more of a theoretical concept than an actual value. We discounted all the future payments at 10%. That assumes we could re-invest each of those payments at that rate, which is unlikely in the real world. Nevertheless, that's how bond traders price bonds.

Understanding yield to maturity and the concept of discounting future payments, we can also understand how changes in interest rates affect the value of a bond.

Now let's look at that same bond and assume we bought it at 76.62% of face value. Further, let's assume that interest rates dropped to 8%. Discounting all future interest payments at an 8% rate rather than 10%, what will the bond trade at? (See Table 2.5.)

TABLE 2.5

CALCULATING A BOND'S PRICE

Particulars:	Government of Canada 6% January 15, 2008
Start Date:	15-Jan-99
Discount Rate:	8%*

DATE	INTEREST AND PRINCIPAL PAYMENTS	PRESENT VALUE INTEREST PAYMENTS	PRESENT VALUE PRINCIPAL PAYMENT
15-Jul-99	300.00	288.46	
15-Jan-00	300.00	277.37	
15-Jul-00	300.00	266.70	
15-Jan-01	300.00	256.44	
15-Jul-01	300.00	246.58	
15-Jan-02	300.00	237.09	
15-Jul-02	300.00	227.98	
15-Jan-03	300.00	219.21	
15-Jul-03	300.00	210.78	
15-Jan-04	300.00	202.67	
15-Jul-04	300.00	194.87	
15-Jan-05	300.00	187.38	
15-Jul-05	300.00	180.17	
15-Jan-06	300.00	173.24	
15-Jul-06	300.00	166.58	
15-Jan-07	300.00	160.17	
15-Jul-07	300.00	154.01	
15-Jan-08	300.00	148.09	
15-Jan-08		3,797.79	4,936.28

Total Cost to Buy Bond $3,797.79 + $4,936.28 = $8,734.07

* Assumes the interest payments were re-invested at 8%

The value of our bond went from 76.62% of face value to 87.34% of face value. That's a 13.9% capital gain on this bond, before accounting for accrued interest. Again, this may not correspond to your idea of aggressive trading. But keep reading, because we've only scratched the surface.

The yield to maturity is the principal measure used by professional bond traders when comparing fixed-income assets with similar risk factors and maturities. Keeping in mind the distinction between theoretical and real-world principles, we calculate the yield to maturity assuming we can re-invest our semi-annual interest payments at a specific rate.

So far, we've talked about government bonds, which carry almost no risk of default. Without that risk, the only factor that will affect a bond's price will be interest rates. As interest rates go, so go bond prices.

Bond prices and interest rates are inversely related, much like the ends of a teeter-totter. When one goes up, the other goes down. The longer the bond's term to maturity, the more dramatic the move upward or downward.

TERM TO MATURITY

When investors talk about long- and short-term bonds, they're referring to the term to maturity, the amount of time that must pass before your principal is returned to you. In the previous example, the Government of Canada 6% January 15, 2008, bond was a 10-year bond; at least, it was a 10-year bond on January 15, 1998. Given the same starting point (June 15, 1998), a bond maturing on January 15, 2028, has a term to maturity of 30 years.

Remember, the longer the term to maturity, the greater the impact of fluctuations in semi-annual interest payments on the bond's total return. As you can see at the bottom of Table 2.5, the present value of the semi-annual interest payments on a 10-year bond was worth almost as much as the present value of the principal repayment.

If we stretch out the interest payments over 30 years and assume the same 10% discount rate that we used in Table 2.4, the semi-annual income stream would dwarf the present value of the principal repayment and assume even greater importance in the total return of the bond (see the bottom of Table 2.6).

Now let's see what happens to our 30-year bond if rates decline. We'll assume that interest rates drop from 10% to 8% as we did in Table 2.4 and 2.5.

The value of the 30-year bond went from 61.24% to 77.37% of face value, an increase of 24.51%, almost twice as large as the 10-year bond's, given the same change in interest rates. Again, I have not accounted for any accrued interest on this position.

TABLE 2.6

CHANGE THE DISCOUNT RATE, CHANGE THE BOND'S PRICE

Particulars: Government of Canada 6% January 15, 2028
Start Date: 15-Jan-98
Discount Rate: 10%

DATE	PAYMENTS	PRESENT VALUE
15-Jul-98	300.00	285.71
15-Jan-99	300.00	272.11
15-Jul-99	300.00	259.15
15-Jan-00	300.00	246.81
15-Jul-00	300.00	235.06
15-Jan-01	300.00	223.86
15-Jul-01	300.00	213.20
15-Jan-02	300.00	203.05
15-Jul-02	300.00	193.38
15-Jan-03	300.00	184.17
15-Jul-03	300.00	175.40
15-Jan-04	300.00	167.05
15-Jul-04	300.00	159.10
15-Jan-05	300.00	151.52
15-Jul-05	300.00	144.31
15-Jan-06	300.00	137.43
15-Jul-06	300.00	130.89
15-Jan-07	300.00	124.66
15-Jul-07	300.00	118.72
15-Jan-08	300.00	113.07
15-Jul-08	300.00	107.68
15-Jan-09	300.00	102.55
15-Jul-09	300.00	97.67
15-Jan-10	300.00	93.02
15-Jul-10	300.00	88.59
15-Jan-11	300.00	84.37
15-Jul-11	300.00	80.35
15-Jan-12	300.00	76.53
15-Jul-12	300.00	72.88

continued

TABLE 2.6 (continued)

DATE	PAYMENTS	PRESENT VALUE	
15-Jan-13	300.00	69.41	
15-Jul-13	300.00	66.11	
15-Jan-14	300.00	62.96	
15-Jul-14	300.00	59.96	
15-Jan-15	300.00	57.11	
15-Jul-15	300.00	54.39	
15-Jan-16	300.00	51.80	
15-Jul-16	300.00	49.33	
15-Jan-17	300.00	46.98	
15-Jul-17	300.00	44.74	
15-Jan-18	300.00	42.61	
15-Jul-18	300.00	40.58	
15-Jan-19	300.00	38.65	
15-Jul-19	300.00	36.81	
15-Jan-20	300.00	35.06	
15-Jul-20	300.00	33.39	
15-Jan-21	300.00	31.80	
15-Jul-21	300.00	30.28	
15-Jan-22	300.00	28.84	
15-Jul-22	300.00	27.47	
15-Jan-23	300.00	26.16	
15-Jul-23	300.00	24.92	
15-Jan-24	300.00	23.73	
15-Jul-24	300.00	22.60	
15-Jan-25	300.00	21.52	
15-Jul-25	300.00	20.50	
15-Jan-26	300.00	19.52	
15-Jul-26	300.00	18.59	
15-Jan-27	300.00	17.71	
15-Jul-27	300.00	16.86	
15-Jan-28	300.00	16.06	
15-Jan-28		5,678.79	535.36

Total Cost to Buy Bond $5,678.79 + $535.36 = $6,124.14 (61.24% of face value)

TABLE 2.7

$10,000 GOVERNMENT OF CANADA 6% JANUARY 15, 2028

BOND DISCOUNTED AT 8%

Present value of semi-annual interest payments	6,787.05
Present value of principal repayment	950.60
Total value of bond	$7,737.65

TABLE 2.8

CALCULATING A BOND'S PRICE

Particulars: Government of Canada 6% January 15, 2028
Start Date: 15-Jan-99

DATE	INTEREST & PRINCIPAL	PRESENT VALUE OF PAYMENTS AT 10%	PRESENT VALUE OF PAYMENTS AT 8%	PERCENT CHANGE IN PRESENT VALUE
11-Jan-00	300.00	272.11	277.37	1.93%
11-Jan-03	300.00	203.05	219.21	7.96%
11-Jan-06	300.00	151.52	173.24	14.34%
11-Jan-09	300.00	113.07	136.92	21.09%
11-Jan-12	300.00	84.37	108.21	28.25%
12-Jan-15	300.00	62.96	85.52	35.83%
11-Jan-18	300.00	46.98	67.59	43.86%
11-Jan-21	300.00	35.06	53.41	52.36%
11-Jan-24	300.00	26.16	42.21	61.36%
10-Jan-27	300.00	19.52	33.36	70.90%
10-Jan-28	300.00	17.71	30.85	74.20%
10-Jan-28	10,000.00	562.12	988.63	75.87%

Table 2.8 and Figure 2.2 provide more insights into term to maturity. In Table 2.8, I have examined selected annual dates on which interest payments will be made and calculated the present value of the principal repayment. The payments have been discounted to their present value. In the second column the payment is

being discounted at 10%, while in the third column the payment is being discounted at 8%. The far right column shows the impact of a change in the discount rate on the selected terms to maturity.

For example, the semi-annual interest payment due on January 15, 2003, has a present value of $203.05 when discounted at 10%, and a present value of $219.21 when discounted at 8%. Which means that a 2% decline in interest rates pushes up the value of that payment by 7.96%.

FIGURE 2.2

PERCENT CHANGE IN PRESENT VALUE

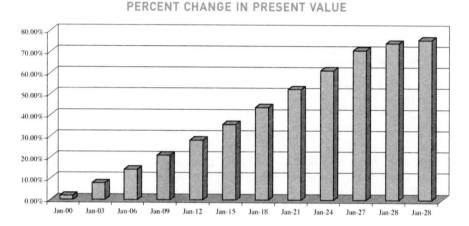

If you want to see how government bonds can be even more appealing to the aggressive investor, look at the semi-annual interest payment due on January 2028. Assuming the same 2% decline in interest rates, that payment rises from $17.71 to $30.85, an increase of 74.20%. That's an aggressive trade!

The final example is the principal repayment—the longest term to maturity—due on January 15, 2028. Discounted at 10%, the present value of the principal repayment was $562.12, or 5.62% of face value. The same principal repayment discounted at 8% was worth $950.60, or 9.56% of face value, an increase of 75.87%.

To make a staid government bond appeal to an aggressive investor, we need to strip away one of the semi-annual interest payments or the principal repayment and use it to make a bet on the future direction of interest rates. This gives you the best bang for your aggressive dollar.

THE STRIPPED-DOWN BOND

In recent years, bond desks have been doing just what the aggressive investor ordered: stripping away the components that make up a bond's total return. In Table

2.5, for example, 19 components make up that particular bond's total return: 18 semi-annual interest payments and one principal repayment.

Each of the components in Table 2.5 was also discounted to its present value. In other words, to buy any of those components—i.e., a stripped interest payment or the stripped principal repayment—we would simply pay the discounted present value of that amount.

The advantage of a strip bond is that it eliminates the re-investment risk. Earlier I talked about the yield to maturity as a theoretical concept, because it assumed that we could re-invest each semi-annual interest payment at the same discount rate.

With a strip bond, we have only one payment to contend with, made on a specific date. The one payment is discounted at the assumed rate. In the process, the yield to maturity for a strip bond is not only a theoretical concept but a real-world principle.

As shown in the previous tables, a strip bond will rise and fall more dramatically with each change in interest rates. As a rule of thumb, the value of a 10-year strip bond will rise or fall approximately 10% given a 1% change in the level of interest rates. Similarly, a 30-year bond will rise or fall approximately 30% for every 1% change in the level of interest rates. That's only a rule of thumb. As you can see from Table 2.8, the 30-year principal repayment actually moved about 37% for every 1% change in the current level of interest.

THE HYBRIDS

Hybrid securities have attributes associated with equity and debt. The most common hybrid is the convertible debenture. The convertible debenture can be exchanged at the convenience of the holder into shares of the underlying common stock. A convertible debenture has some of the attributes of a bond and some of the attributes of an equity investment. When the company's stock rises, so does the value of the convertible debenture. Conversely, when the price of the common stock declines, so does the value of the convertible debenture, but only to a point. And it is that "point" that makes the convertible debenture attractive as an aggressive trading instrument.

The convertible debenture is first and foremost a bond. Semi-annual interest payments are fixed for the life of the bond and must be paid before any dividends can be paid to shareholders. In the event of bankruptcy, the convertible debenture is considered part of the company's debt and therefore has a prior claim on the corporate assets.

The fixed interest payment provides a floor below which the convertible debenture should not trade. If the value of the company's stock falls dramatically because of an earnings downgrade, the convertible debenture will fall but probably not as far as the stock. That's because the fixed-income element of the bond will come into play and at some level support the price of the convertible debenture.

To make this explanation as painless as possible, we'll use a series of examples to explain the concepts. In our examples we'll use the hypothetical XYZ 5% January 2010 convertible security—that is, convertible into XYZ common stock at $50 per share. We'll assume that XYZ is currently trading at $40 per share, and the XYZ convertible debenture is trading at 95% of face value, or $950 per $1,000 face value.

In this example, the *conversion price*—the price at which the convertible debenture can be converted into the underlying common shares—is $50 per share. When a convertible debenture is first issued, it is usually priced anywhere from 15% to 20% above the conversion price.

The *conversion ratio* is the current price of the convertible bond divided by the number of shares into which the bond can be converted. The number of shares that can be purchased with each convertible debenture is based on a $1,000 face value for the convertible.

Using our numbers, each $1,000 face value of convertible debentures can be converted into the common stock at $50 per share. If we simply divide the face value ($1,000) by the conversion price ($50), we see that each XYZ convertible debenture can be used to purchase 20 shares of XYZ common. So the conversion ratio is 20.

The next definition is the *conversion value*. In this case, we want to calculate what the convertible debenture is worth if we convert it today into the shares of the underlying common stock. In this case, we simply multiply the current stock price by the number of shares each convertible debenture can buy: $40 per share × 20 shares per convertible = $800 conversion value.

The *conversion premium* is the amount by which the convertible debenture is trading above its conversion value. To calculate the conversion premium, we divide the conversion value into current price of the convertible: $950 current price of the convertible dividend by $800 conversion value based on current stock price = 1.1875. To convert that to a percentage, we subtract 1. The conversion premium then is 18.75%.

While there are other advantages for the aggressive investor, the primary reason for owning a convertible debenture is that it provides a higher income stream than the underlying common stock. Here's the income advantage from the convertible relative to the common stock:

Let's assume that XYZ common stock pays $1 per year in dividends. To compare the income from the convertible with the dividend of the common stock, we'll follow a three-step process:

> 1. In step one, we need to know how many shares of XYZ common stock we could buy with one convertible debenture at current prices.
>
> | | |
> |---|---:|
> | Current Price of XYZ Convertible debenture: | $ 950.00 |
> | Divide by current price of XYZ common | $ 40.00 |
> | Equals number of common shares per convertible | 23.75 |

2. In step 2 we multiply the number of common shares per convertible by the dividend per common share

Number of common shares per convertible from step 1	23.75
Multiply by annual dividend per common share	$ 1.00
Equals income per common share equivalent	$ 23.75

3. In the final step, we compare the annual interest income from the convertible and compare that with the dividends from the common stock. To calculate the income from the convertible we simply multiply the face value ($1,000) by the coupon rate (5%), for a total annual income of $50.

Convertible annual income	$ 50.00
Minus income per common share equivalent	$ 23.75
Equals income advantage for convertible	$ 26.25

The income advantage calculation leads us to the final calculation: the *break-even period*. The break-even period helps us measure the value of the income advantage against the cost of the conversion premium. In other words, we can determine how many years it will take to recover the conversion premium we are paying when we purchase the bond. There are two steps involved in calculating the break-even period:

1. In step 1, we need to ascertain the dollar value of the conversion premium. In our example, the XYZ convertible debenture was trading at $950 and its conversion value was $800. The dollar difference then is $150.

2. In step 2 we divide the dollar conversion premium by the income advantage to arrive at a break-even period in years.

Dollar conversion premium from step 1	$ 150.00
Divide by income advantage	$ 26.25
Equals break-even period in years	5.7 years

These calculations and definitions provide us with a set of rules that we will use when including convertible debentures as part of an aggressive investing strategy. For now, we simply need to understand the terminology and the basics of the calculations.

LEVERAGE

The final piece to the puzzle in this chapter is leverage—the idea that a few dollars can do the work of many. Leverage is what turns ordinary investments into aggressive investments. It is also the tool that raises the risk profile of all the aggressive trades discussed in this book.

The most common form of leverage is to borrow money to make or add to an investment. Brokerage firms will allow you to borrow against investments held in your account. However, you have to open what's called a margin account. Your margin limit is the percentage of assets in your account that a broker will allow you to borrow.

With blue-chip stocks, a broker will usually lend you up to 50% of the value of the shares. If you own 1,000 shares of XYZ—our blue-chip stock—at $40 per share, the broker will allow you to borrow 50% of the current value of your stock, or $20,000. The balance sheet for your account will look like Table 2.9.

TABLE 2.9

ACCOUNT STATEMENT

	CREDITS	DEBITS
Cost of stock		$ 40,000
Broker loan (50% of current value)	$ 20,000	
Net capital investment	$ 20,000	
Totals:	$ 40,000	$ 40,000

TABLE 2.10

ACCOUNT BALANCE SHEET

	CREDITS	DEBITS
Cost of stock		$ 40,000
Broker loan (50% of current value)*	$ 17,500	
Initial capital investment	$ 20,000	
Margin call	$ 2,500	
Totals:	$ 40,000	$ 40,000

* Broker will lend 50% of $35,000 current value.

Every day, the broker marks to the market the amount you can borrow. That means he or she determines the value of your holdings according to the current day's prices and calculates your margin limit based on that value. If the value of your holdings rises, so does your margin limit. If it falls, your margin limit falls too, and your broker will demand repayment of some or all of your loan, known as a margin call.

As an aggressive investor, you need to make certain that you do not over-leverage your position. The last thing you want is to make an aggressive trade and then have to exit prematurely because you can't afford to keep the position.

For example, suppose the value of your stock declines from $40 to $35 over the next week. Your account balance sheet would look like Table 2.10.

Notice in Table 2.10 the value of your debits (i.e., the cost of your initial investment) remains the same, but, because the value of your stock has declined, you no longer have enough assets to support the full $20,000 loan. Your broker will make a margin call of $2,500 to bring your account back into balance.

LEVERAGING COMMON STOCK

We've seen the downside of borrowing. What about the upside? Keeping the 50% margin, if we were to buy 1,000 shares of XYZ at $40 per share and borrowed half the cost, your net investment would be $20,000, as we saw in Table 2.9.

Assuming XYZ rallies to $50 per share over the next six months and the cost of borrowing is 5%, Table 2.11 compares the return on investment of buying the stock outright compared with buying the stock on margin.

TABLE 2.11

THE POTENTIAL OF XYZ STOCK

	MARGIN	NO MARGIN
Capital gains	$10,000	$10,000
+ Dividends or interest earned	0	0
= Net dollar return (step 1)	$10,000	$10,000
Net capital outlay	$20,000	$40,000
+ Cost of borrowing (5% over six months)	$ 1,000	0
= Total investment (step 2)	$21,000	$40,000
Return on investment (step 1/step 2)	47.6%	25.0%

The non-margin account returned 25% over six months—a good return by any stretch. But it pales in comparison with the margin account. After accounting for borrowing costs, the margin account returned 47.6% on invested capital over six months.

LEVERAGING CONVERTIBLE DEBENTURES

The returns from leveraging stock look great, but they're based on borrowing 50% of the cost of the stock. The loan value of other assets like convertible debentures is much higher. Most brokerage firms will lend up to 80% of the value of a convertible debenture. More leverage, more potential return.

In this case, we'll assume the convertible debenture produced a capital gain of $10,000 on an initial $40,000 investment. The initial outlay to buy the convertible on margin was 20%, or $8,000. In addition to the capital gain on this position, the convertible debenture pays interest at, say, 2.5% over the six-month period, which can help offset the 5% margin costs.

By now you get the picture of the impact of leverage on your bottom line. Obviously, it can work against you as well. A $10,000 loss in our convertible debenture would wipe out all your capital in very short order. This emphasizes why aggressive investors need to think about hedging their bets before entering any trade. "Live to invest another day" is the motto to follow.

TABLE 2.12

THE XYZ CONVERTIBLE DEBENTURE

	MARGIN	NO MARGIN
Capital gains	$10,000	$10,000
+ Dividends or interest earned	$ 1,000	$ 1,000
= Net dollar return (step 1)	$11,000	$11,000
Net capital outlay	$ 8,000	$ 40,000
+ Cost of borrowing (5% over six months)	$ 1,600	0
= Total investment (step 2)	$ 9,600	$ 40,000
Return on investment (step 1/step 2)	114.58%	27.5%

LEVERAGING GOVERNMENT BONDS

As you might expect, you can also borrow against bonds. The most secure asset in a brokerage account is of course a federal government bond. Brokerage firms recognize the low risk of a government bond and will lend a larger percentage against the value of the bond than they will against other types of investments.

For example, you can borrow up to 95% of the cost of 10-year Government of Canada bonds like the one we used in our earlier examples about bonds. That means that you can buy $100,000 in Government of Canada bonds for as little as $5,000 of your own money. The interest you earn on the bonds helps offset the cost of borrowing.

Now put on your aggressive investing hat and return to Table 2.8. Remember the principal repayment due in January 2028, which was priced at $562.12 when discounted at 10% and grew to $988.63 when discounted at 8%—a 75.87% return given a 2% decline in the level of interest rates. Such is the power of buying long-term strip bonds discounted to present day.

Long-term strip bonds are still government bonds—a stripped version maybe, but still backed by the federal government. As you can see, you can leverage those strip bonds by as much as 6 to 1. That is, you can put up only 15% of their value, and the brokerage will lend you the rest of the capital.

I would never advise anyone to borrow the maximum amount on a bond. But, just to add some real oomph to this discussion and to whet your appetite for the next chapter, let's look at the return on investment based on 5 to 1 leverage.

Assume the aggressive investor purchases $100,000 face value of the principal repayment. Assume too that interest rates decline by 2% and that the price of the principal repayment changes as per Table 2.8, but, because of the larger investment, it changes from $56,212 to $98,863. That's a capital gain of $42,651.

TABLE 2.13

THE GOVERNMENT OF CANADA STRIP

	MARGIN	NO MARGIN
Capital gains	$42,651	$42,651
+ Dividends or interest earned	0	0
= Net dollar return (step 1)	$42,651	$42,651
Net capital outlay	$11,242	$56,212
+ Cost of borrowing (5% over six months)	$ 2,810	0
= Total investment (step 2)	$14,053	$56,212
Return on investment (step 1/step 2)	303.5%	75.87%

The return from the margin account comes in at a staggering 303.5%: the kind of numbers that would have made Carl Sagan blush, but also the kind of numbers that are possible under the most aggressive types of positions.

To be fair, the strategies we'll use in this book will not generate such high numbers. Such strategies are too aggressive, and the potential, while great, is not worth the risk. We'll aim a little lower, but we'll also encounter a lot less risk.

CONCLUSION

The goal of this chapter was to introduce you to the equity and fixed-income assets that will form part of our aggressive investing strategies. Chapter Three will introduce you to options that offset some of the high-risk leverage discussed at the end of this chapter.

As you'll see in later chapters, the ability to trade one set of assets against another using leverage makes aggressive investing fun. It also provides the basis on which to invest aggressively and successfully.

3
EXCHANGE-TRADED OPTIONS

I've heard statistics that say 80% of all option contracts expire worthless. This probably overstates the case, but it dissuades new investors from venturing into the options market.

For aggressive investors, options will help manage the risks associated with the instruments discussed in Chapter Two. When you think about it, for every option buyer there has to be a seller. This means, presumably, the option contracts that expired worthless—whatever the percentage actually is—generated some decent profits for the sellers.

Option buyers have three things going for them: leverage, limited risk and flexibility. We know the impact leverage can have on a position. When you win, you win big. Limited predetermined risk means that you can define a worst-case scenario. For the option buyer, this means that the occasional big win can wipe out a number of smaller losing trades.

In terms of flexibility, option traders, unlike stockholders, are not limited by two-dimensional thinking: buying stock when bullish, selling when bearish. Option strategies can be used in a bullish, bearish or neutral environment. Equity options can protect your stocks against a price decline and can be used to generate additional income. Index options can be used to stake a claim on the overall market, eliminating the need to formulate an opinion about a specific stock. And all option strategies—bullish, bearish or neutral—can be structured with the risks clearly defined.

In this chapter and the next, you'll learn option basics and some option strategies—everything you need to know to implement the aggressive trading strategies in Part Four.

TERMINOLOGY

In the option business, it's hard to tell the players, even with a program. First, you need to understand the language—and the options market has a language all its own.

To begin, you can trade options on individual stocks, stock indices, interest rates, commodities, financial futures contracts, and probably tulip bulbs, which is enough to scare all but the most dedicated aggressive investor. Fortunately, all options, regardless of the underlying security, share similar characteristics.

Equally fortunate—since our preference is to avoid overkill—we need only look at options on stocks and stock indices, referred to as *equity options* and *index options*. What works for equity options usually works with index options. There are some subtle differences, which I'll explain soon. But most of the terms that apply to stock options apply to index options, as well.

There are two types of stock options—*calls* and *puts*.

A call gives you the right to buy 100 shares of an underlying stock at a specific price for a predetermined period. For example, if you buy a six-month call option on XYZ stock at $50, you've paid for the right to buy XYZ at $50 per share (that's the specific price we referred to) at any time over the next six months (that's the predetermined period). Option traders refer to the specific price (i.e., the $50 per share price in our XYZ example) as the option's *strike* or *exercise* price.

A put option gives you the right to sell 100 shares of the underlying stock at the put's exercise or strike price for a predetermined period. If you buy an XYZ six-month $50 put, you have bought the right to sell XYZ at $50 per share any time over the next six months. (We'll talk about strategies and why you might do that in the next chapter.) You usually buy a call option if you expect the stock to rise (i.e., you're bullish). You buy a put option if you think the stock will decline (i.e., you're bearish). The date the option expires, as you might expect, is called *the expiration date*. Options expire on the Saturday following the third Friday of the expiration month. The Saturday expiration simply allows the options clearing corporation to settle all expiring option contracts before the next trading day.

You can also sell options. This is referred to as *writing an option*. It works in much the same way as an insurance company writes a policy. The compensation an investor receives for writing an option—or the price an investor must pay to buy an option—is referred to as the *premium*.

At this point, we have set out the basics of the option market, to wit:

- *We have defined the two types of options—a put and a call.*
- *We know that a particular stock, index or other investment asset is defined as the underlying security.*
- *We know the expiration date, the date the option expires, which is actually the Saturday following the third Friday of the expiration month. Most important for us is the last day of trading, which is the third Friday of the expiration month.*
- *We know the strike or exercise price, being the price at which the underlying security can be bought or sold.*
- *We know the premium, being the price an option writer would receive and an option buyer would pay.*

Armed with these basic terms, we can now define, in one simple statement, all the facets of an option contract. When talking investments at a party, you can now say, "I just bought the XYZ June 50 call. We know, whether or not anyone else does, that we have purchased an option to buy (because we bought a call) XYZ (the underlying security) at $50 (the strike price) per share. The option will expire on the Saturday following the third Friday in June.

On the off chance that someone understood what you said, she might ask how much you paid for this option. You can answer $5 (trust me, that was the price), which would mean that the premium you paid would be $5 per share, or $500 per contract.

A bit of explanation is in order. Each XYZ call option grants the buyer the right to buy 100 shares of XYZ. Each equity option contract equals 100 shares. The premium for each index option contract must also be multiplied by 100. In our example, one XYZ June 50 call option contract is exercisable into 100 shares of XYZ. The premium for one option contract is 100 times the quoted per-share price ($5), which equals $500.

Now, if the person you're speaking with asks what implied volatility you paid, you might want to excuse yourself and go freshen your drink.

TRANSACTION COSTS

Not all brokers can trade options. They must be licensed. That means they have to meet specific regulatory qualifications. Ideally, you would like to deal with someone who actually understood the conversation from the previous section. It might also help if the broker could explain why an option didn't move as you might have expected given a specific price change in the underlying security, or why an option was exercised before the expiration date. And by the way, "Can I call you right back?" doesn't qualify as an appropriate answer.

Options trade on an exchange, just like shares of stock. The largest options exchange is the Chicago Board Options Exchange (CBOE). Others include the American Stock Exchange, which also lists a number of interesting derivative securities, and the Pacific Stock Exchange, best known for its handling of the very active Microsoft options.

Because options are listed on an exchange, you can buy and sell them before they expire, without having to go through exercise procedures. Just like any other financial instrument, you pay a commission when you buy, sell, exercise or assign an option. (If you buy the option, you have the right to exercise. If you sell the option, you have assumed an obligation and can be assigned an exercise notice.)

To some, option commissions seem high, and in some cases they are, especially when compared with the cost of buying stock. The commission for an option trade valued at $2,500 can be as high as $150, about 6% of the purchase price.

To be fair, however, you have to look at the cost of purchasing an option contract relative to buying a similar quantity of the underlying stock. For example, suppose you were buying 10 XYZ June 50 call option contracts at $500 per contract. Because each contract equals 100 shares of the underlying stock, you are effectively buying control of 1,000 shares of the underlying stock for a specified period. If we compare the cost of the option position with the cost of buying 1,000 shares of XYZ at $50, the commissions are not much different.

Obviously, discount brokerage firms will charge less than full-service brokers. But discount brokers don't provide advice or the support of a full-service firm. The point is, you should know the difference in cost, then decide for yourself whether you need the hand-holding that you get from a full-service options specialist or whether looking in the mirror gives you all the support you need to enter option orders with confidence.

THE ADVANTAGES OF EXCHANGE-TRADED OPTIONS

The CBOE opened for business in 1973. The opening of an options exchange radically changed the way options were traded. A central meeting place to transact business gave investors the ability, as we have already said, to close out an option position before expiry, without having to exercise the option.

What made this possible was the introduction of standardized option contracts. July options, for example, would all expire on the same date in July, whether it was an option on IBM, Intel or Microsoft—that is, on the Saturday following the third Friday in the expiration month.

Exchange-traded option contracts have similar multipliers. Stock-option contracts represent 100 shares of the underlying security, index options, 100 times the quoted per-unit premium. Standardized strike prices were also established by the exchanges, at appropriate and defined intervals. Standardization allowed traders to compare and contrast option contracts and, by extension, price them more efficiently.

Standardization facilitated next-day settlement of all contracts. You buy an option today, you settle the transaction tomorrow or the next business day (unlike stocks, which settle three days after the purchase or sale).

Don't look to receive your options certificates in the mail. They don't exist. Options are the truest form of trading computer blips. Buy and sell transactions are cleared through a central clearing house—usually the Option Clearing Corporation (OCC). The OCC guarantees the integrity of all option contracts, but it doesn't issue certificates.

The clearing corporation is the buyer and seller of last resort. The buck really does stop there. The OCC is responsible for matching all buy and sell orders. If you buy an option, someone has to sell it to you. The OCC makes certain that buy and sell orders match up at the end of the day. It doesn't want any loose computer blips hanging around.

Because an option contract expires, we need to further define buy and sell orders. Buy and sell orders are opening and closing transactions. If you buy the XYZ call option, then you have initiated a new position—an *opening* transaction. When you sell that XYZ call option, you have closed out your position or conducted a *closing* transaction. Opening and closing should appear on the transaction record you receive from the broker.

All option positions must eventually be closed out. That can be accomplished in one of three ways:

1. The option can be exercised by the buyer, assigned to the seller.
2. The option could expire worthless, which is, according to statistics, the most likely scenario.
3. The option can be sold or repurchased, depending on whether the opening order was a buy or sell transaction.

The OCC not only matches all buy and sell orders, it keeps a running total of all positions currently outstanding—i.e., all opening transactions that have yet to be closed out. Option traders refer to this as *open interest*. The open interest number is published in the financial press alongside the option quotations. In short, open interest defines the total number of outstanding contracts at a particular time. The number changes daily, reflecting new opening and closing transactions (see Table 3.1).

1. If an opening buy order is matched with an opening sell order, then open interest will rise.
2. If an open buy (or sell) order is matched with a closing sell (or buy) order, open interest will remain unchanged.
3. If a closing buy order is matched with a closing sell order, open interest will decline.

The open interest speaks to the issue of liquidity. Obviously, if we're trading aggressively in and out of positions, we want to use option contracts that we can trade easily, not so much because we want to execute the trade, but because we want to receive or pay a reasonable price when selling or buying. Liquidity helps to keep the spread between the option's bid and offered price tight, and that allows us to trade in multiple contracts with little problem. Liquidity is not as big an issue if we're using options to counter a stock position, which we'll do in many of our aggressive trades. In such a case, we may establish a position and leave it until expiry.

There are options available on literally thousands of companies. But of that number, fewer than 100 offer the kind of liquidity that will work with aggressive in and out trades.

TABLE 3.1

TYPICAL TABLE FOR OPTION QUOTATIONS

	XYZ $50 STRIKE	LAST SALE	OPEN INTEREST
Mar	45	6 1/4	1000
Mar	45P	1 1/4	1200
Mar	50	3 1/4	3500
Mar	50P	2 3/4	3100
Mar	55	1 3/4	1700
Mar	55P	6 1/2	1300
June	45	7 3/4	650
June	45P	2 3/4	850
June	50	5	2700
June	50P	4	2100
June	55	3	1350
June	55P	7	950

THE PRICE IS RIGHT—OR IS IT?

On the old television game show *The Price Is Right,* contestants tried to guess the actual price of a product. If you have trouble with that concept, imagine trying to value an option: "Am I paying too much?" "Maybe I'm not getting enough premium to justify selling an option."

A number of option books spend a great deal of time showing the reader how to value an option. I don't purport to be able to do it as well as other authors, especially when they tell you how easy the formula is.

Fortunately, the price of an option is visible. Because it trades on an open market, we know that its price is, if nothing else, based on a consensus of buyers and sellers making informed decisions based on all publicly available information.

That being said, we still need a rudimentary understanding of the factors that drive an options price, of which there are six:

1. current price of the underlying security
2. the strike price of the option
3. the time remaining until the expiration date
4. volatility (risk) of the underlying stock
5. the risk-free interest rate (i.e., 90-day Treasury bills)
6. the dividend payout

These six factors are plugged into the Black-Scholes option pricing model. Using the aforementioned inputs, the option model calculates a theoretical fair value for the call and the put. The model works as follows:

BLACK-SCHOLES FORMULA

Used to calculate a theoretical option price (TOP):

Fair Value = $pN(d_1) - se^{-rt} N(d_2)$

Where

$$d_2 = \frac{1n\left(\frac{P}{S}\right) + \left(r + \frac{v^2}{2}\right)t}{v\sqrt{t}}$$

and

$d_2 = d_1 - v\sqrt{t}$

The variables are:

P = Stock price

S = Strike price

t = time remaining until expiration, expressed as a percent of a year

r = Risk free rate of interest

v = Volatility measured by the annual standard deviation

$1n$ = natural logarithm

e = exponential function

$N(x)$ = cumulative normal density function

You may understand all the pieces of this model. Personally I need to translate the math into something I can relate to. The following is how I approach the option pricing model:

INPUTS FOR CALCULATING FAIR VALUE

• *Stock Price*
• *Strike Price*
• *Time to Expiry*
• *Risk-Free Rate*
• *Dividends*
• *Volatility*

= *Fair Value*

Two of the three professors who contributed to the model—Myron Scholes of Stanford University and Robert Merton of Harvard University—were awarded the Nobel Prize for economics in October 1997. Fischer Black, a former partner at Goldman Sachs in New York and the other contributor to the model, died in 1995. The model is essentially a heat transfer formula: basic calculus and first-year physics. What makes it noteworthy is its acceptance within the investment community, first as a model to value options and, more recently, as a tool to value other financial assets, including stocks, bonds and even the value of crop insurance.

According to Black-Scholes, the fair value of a stock option is based on the six factors discussed above. We know with certainty most of the variables. The price of the stock and the strike price of the option are visible. We know with certainty the time to expiration and the risk-free rate of interest payable on short-term treasury bills. Dividends are not certain, but they are transparent. The only variable that is, well, variable is the volatility of the underlying stock, volatility being the tool of choice to measure risk.

The theoretical fair value defines what the option should be worth based on the numbers used in our model. If the theoretical fair value is higher than the current price for a particular option, then the option is said to be undervalued. If the current price of the option is more than its calculated theoretical fair value, then the option is said to be overvalued. In theory, based on the theoretical fair value concept, which is based on theoretical inputs, you would buy—theoretically—undervalued options and sell overvalued options. You might not make any money doing this, but over time, presumably, you would be putting the odds on your side. However, I'm not certain the effort is worth the reward, unless you're the type of person who would bend over to pick up a nickel.

We still need to understand the pricing model, or at least the basics. Specifically we need to understand the interplay of the six factors and how some are more relevant than others at a particular time. Further, we will examine *delta*, which is a useful tool when trying to figure out where an option's price will be, given various assumptions about the underlying security.

Don't worry if these points are not crystal clear by the end of this chapter. As you get into Part Four of this book, you will see how we intend to use this information in the context of aggressive investing strategies. And you don't have to worry about calculating the Black-Scholes model or writing a program in your computer spreadsheet. You can download the model or use it straight from the Internet at any of a number of sites including www.cboe.com/tools/optcalcu.htm.

CURRENT PRICE OF THE UNDERLYING SECURITY VERSUS THE OPTION'S STRIKE PRICE

The relationship between the option's strike price and the current price of the underlying security is considered the most dynamic element in the model. Indeed, if the price of the underlying security is substantially above or below the strike price of the option, other factors have little influence. Moreover, on the last day of trading, the option's price will be exactly equal to the difference between the price of the underlying security and the strike price of the option.

You will notice that all profit and loss charts used throughout this book are based on the prices of the underlying security on the day the options expire. That might seem strange, given that most options are bought and sold prior to expiration. But, when you think about it, profit and loss tables help us ascertain the potential rewards and risks of any strategy. By looking at prices on expiration day, we know for certain what the option will be worth, given a price for the underlying stock. There are no other external factors to consider. On expiration day, the only factor that will affect the price of the option is the relationship between the strike price of the option and the current price of the underlying security.

Given that position, it's important that we clearly understand the relationship between the stock's price and the option's strike price. For example, assume that XYZ is currently trading at $50 per share. What would you be willing to pay for each of the following call options?

- *the XYZ 100 call option that expires in 60 days $_____*
- *the XYZ 25 call option that expires in 60 days $_____*

While neither option would appeal to most traders, extremes often make the best case studies. With XYZ trading at $50, common sense will tell us that the XYZ 100 call—with only 60 days to expiry—will have little if any value. What price would you attach to an option when, to make a profit, the price of the underlying stock must more than double within the next 60 days? That's simply not a realistic prospect and, if that was your opinion, then why not buy, say, an XYZ call with a $55 or $60 strike price? Or a lottery ticket?

On the other hand, the second option would appear to have tremendous value. Simple arithmetic—i.e., subtracting the current stock price from the option's strike price—tells us that the XYZ 25 call should be worth at least $25. (Note: That's the per-share value. Each contract would be worth $2,500.)

However, in the real world, the value of an option is based on what someone is willing to pay for it. Yes, the option would be worth at least $25 per share ($2,500 per contract), but ask yourself, "Would I pay $2,500 for a call option contract?" Most investors would answer no, if for no other reason than it is an inefficient use of money. After all, you could purchase 100 shares of XYZ on margin for only $2,500 ($5,000 × 50% = $2,500) and not have to worry about your position expiring.

An option that is deep in the money, as the XYZ 25 call is, offers the trader no leverage, and virtually no downside protection. In our example, the value of the XYZ 25 call will fall dollar for dollar with the price of the stock.

In reality, neither option would appeal to investors. The factors that would usually affect an option's price will have little or no impact on either of these options. The deep-in-the-money call (the XYZ 25 call) would, therefore, trade more like a stock substitute than an option. Similarly, the XYZ 100 call would be akin to a lottery ticket, and only a dramatic movement in the underlying stock would have any impact on the price.

TIME REMAINING UNTIL EXPIRATION

Looking back at the prices from Table 3.1, we see, with XYZ trading at $50 per share, the three-month (March) 50 calls are priced at 3 1/4 while the six-month (June) calls are trading at 5. When you think about it, the longer the time to expiration, the better the chance the underlying security will make the move you were anticipating.

What the prices tell us is that time is not a linear function. The June at-the-money (the XYZ 50 options being the at-the-money strike) option with 180 days to expiration is not worth twice what the March at-the-money options are worth, even though March options have only half the time before expiry of the June options.

At first glance, that may seem surprising. But ask yourself, is a stock likely to move twice as far simply because you give it twice as much time to do it? Stock prices are not that predictable. Time is important, but its importance is limited by other factors.

The key to understanding time is to recognize the speed at which the option's premium declines as the expiration date approaches. For instance, the time premium decays almost twice as fast in the last few weeks of the option's life (i.e., in the weeks immediately preceding expiration) than it does in the early stages.

For the mathematically inclined, the rate of decay is tied to the square root of the time remaining. Put another way, the time value of a three-month (90-day) option decays at a rate that is approximately twice as fast as a nine-month (270-day) option, the square root of 9 being 3. It also holds—in theory at least—that a two-month (60-day) option will decay at about twice the rate of a four-month (120-day) option, as shown in the time premium decay graph (Figure 3.1).

The risk-free interest rate is generally assumed to be the current interest rate available on government treasury bills. Generally, higher interest rates imply higher option premiums. However, changes in interest rates affect call and put options differently. Higher rates tend to push up call prices and push down put prices.

The risk-free rate is used for nearly all investments as a comparative measurement. For instance, if you are going to buy stock, you would expect a return higher than the one on a risk-free investment. After all, if the rewards didn't justify the additional risk, why not simply buy the riskless asset?

The same can be said for option premiums. Investors who buy stock and sell calls against that position—i.e., the so-called covered call write, which is a strategy we will explore in Chapter Four—want to receive sufficient premium from the sale of the option to justify holding the underlying stock until the option expires. And that potential reward, because the risk is greater, must be higher than the current risk-free rate.

FIGURE 3.1

TIME PREMIUM DECAY
THE RISK-FREE INTEREST RATE

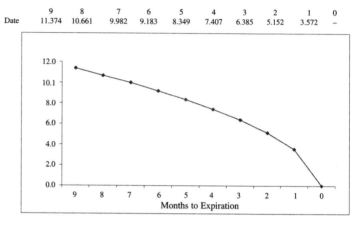

Date	9 11.374	8 10.661	7 9.982	6 9.183	5 8.349	4 7.407	3 6.385	2 5.152	1 3.572	0 —

THE DIVIDEND PAYOUT

In the overall scheme of things, the dividend payment is not considered a major factor in the price of the option. Obviously, in the case of a stock (or an index) where there is no dividend, it has no bearing at all.

Nevertheless, a dividend can be particularly important to the writer or seller of an option. If you sell a call option against stock you own, the dividends are payable to you (unless the call option buyer exercises the option prior to the ex-dividend date).

It stands to reason that if the stock pays a high dividend, you will demand less money for the call option. Suffice it to say that the higher the stock's dividend yield, the lower the call option premium, and the higher the put premium.

The fact that dividends and interest rates are opposing forces in the equation— i.e., they have different effects on the value of call and put premiums—is not something you need to be concerned about. Suffice it to say that interest rates and dividends work together when defining equivalent option strategies. Again, we will look at this in more detail in Chapter Four.

VOLATILITY (RISK) OF THE UNDERLYING STOCK

Option traders pay close attention to risk. To a professional options trader, understanding risk is as important as earnings estimates are to a securities analyst. Understanding the role volatility plays in the option-pricing equation explains why.

In Chapter One we looked at how volatility is calculated. Again, this is not something you'll have to calculate, because volatility numbers are available from the various option exchanges and the CBOE website at http://www.cboe.com. What you do need to understand is how you can translate volatility into a daily, weekly and monthly trading range for the underlying stock. That calculation was also discussed in Chapter One. In Chapter Five, we'll show you how to use volatility within the context of an option-strategy matrix. The option matrix will define how we approach each of our aggressive trading strategies.

Volatility is important in the pricing of an option because it provides the trader with some perspective on the market's assessment of the likelihood of the underlying stock moving above or below the option's strike price prior to expiration. If a stock can advance dramatically (i.e., if it's more volatile than the average stock), traders will bid up the price of the call and put options. The stock simply has a better chance of reaching or exceeding the strike price.

That also holds for the seller of an option. If the stock was particularly volatile, you'd want to receive a higher premium to help offset the risk of holding the stock until the option expires. In short, higher volatility means higher options premiums.

Volatility is also important because it must be estimated. Go back to the beginning of this section and take another look at the six components in the options price. We know for certain the current price of the stock, and the strike price of the option is part of the contract. The time to expiration is known, while the risk-free rate is assumed to be the rate available on Government T-bills. The only other component is the dividend payment, and, while that may not be a given, it is known with reasonable certainty.

Adding a volatility number to the formula means that traders must input their best guess about the stock's future price movement. Best guesses are usually formulated based on historical volatility patterns. But the past does not necessarily indicate the future. Past patterns do not tell with certainty what volatility the underlying stock will experience in the future. The stock could very easily move above its high price or hit a new low. And there's no guarantee that because the stock was extremely volatile over the past year it will continue to be so in the future.

In fact, volatility estimates are no different than earnings estimates. Security analysts examine past trends, look at the overall health of the economy, and then make their best guess about future earnings. How actual earnings compare with the estimates directly affects the value of the stock.

The accuracy of those earnings predictions also affects the volatility of the stock. Just look at what happens if a company misses or exceeds its quarterly earnings estimate. Even looking at the confidence with which security analysts make their estimates will affect the day-to-day volatility of a stock.

For example, the consensus earnings estimates for large-cap stocks usually remain in a relatively narrow range. You might see a company whose mean earnings estimate for the quarter is, say, 50 cents, with a variation among analysts between 45 cents and

55 cents. Companies with less predictable earnings patterns might have a mean of 50 cents, with a range from 25 cents to 75 cents. Stocks with less predictable earnings are more volatile, and that volatility, in turn, is reflected in the options premium.

Taking this concept further, the options market is assessing the risk associated with factors driving the underlying stock's price. If XYZ is a growth company whose stock price is primarily driven by earnings, then the premium on XYZ options will reflect the risk associated with those earnings estimates. If XYZ is a drug company awaiting FDA approval for some new miracle cure, then the option premium will reflect the risk associated with that event. The bottom line for the aggressive investor is that the option contract is a financial tool that can aid in the removal or enhancement of risk.

COMPARING YOUR VOLATILITY ASSUMPTION WITH THE MARKET'S

That volatility must be estimated raises another question: If you are using an option-pricing model to establish a fair value for a particular option contract, you must understand its limitations. Any variation between the price you calculate for an option and the current price on the trading floor simply means that your volatility estimate differs from the consensus estimate of the options market. Stated another way, the price of the option at any given time is merely a reflection of the market consensus of the underlying stock's current and future volatility.

Attempting to estimate volatility is more art than science. And for those of us who are neither artistic nor scientific, it begs the question: Why bother? Why not simply plug all the variables into the option-pricing formula (including the current price of the option) and ask the formula to calculate volatility or the so-called implied volatility. We will use this approach when examining different aggressive investing strategies.

Since most investors do not have the equipment necessary to plug variables into a mathematical model and then trade instantaneously based on that information, we have to accept the limitations of attempting any trade that is based on whether options are over- or underpriced at a particular time.

Still, traders should have some notion of whether they're paying too much or too little for a particular option contract. It's useful information when deciding on the appropriate option strategy, especially for aggressive investors.

SUMMARY

The interplay of these six variables within the option-pricing formula can be quite complex. A stock that is rising in price can exert upward pressure on the value of the call option at the same moment as the time-premium decay is driving the price lower. Or the price of the option may rise, even if the stock hasn't moved, because the market has increased its estimate of volatility.

Of course, it is also important to understand that these six factors are only assumptions and are useful only because the inputs can be quantified mathematically. In reality, there are other influences that cannot be readily assessed. Investor sentiment, as well as the supply and demand forces at work in the market, can both be significant influences. When traders are optimistic, they tend to bid up call premiums. In a panic-driven sell-off, traders will pay almost any price for a put. Psychological factors are usually short-lived but can create interesting short-term opportunities for aggressive investors.

THE OPTIONS DELTA

So now we have a basic understanding of how options are priced. The concept of over- and undervalued options was explored. And you are probably asking, "Is that all there is?"

Not quite. One of the benefits of pricing an option is the calculation of the option's delta or hedge ratio. Delta provides us with a tool to calculate how far an option might move given a movement in the underlying security.

For example, if you purchased the XYZ 50 call option when the stock was trading at $50 per share, the delta of the option would be approximately 0.50. That is, the XYZ $50 call option would be expected to rise by about 50 cents for every $1 increase in the shares of XYZ.

Delta is a dynamic number affected by changes in any of the factors in the option-pricing equation. For example, delta changes along with the time to expiration, when volatility estimates change, and when the stock price advances or declines over short periods. If, for example, XYZ were to advance from $50 to $58 per share, the delta on the XYZ 50 call option would rise as well, probably from 0.50 to 0.85.

We can use delta to estimate the price of the option given a preselected move in the underlying stock. If nothing else, this helps us to set trailing stop losses for aggressive trades. In the above example, if the original cost of the XYZ 50 call was $5 (with XYZ trading at $50), and you expected XYZ to advance to, say, $56, you could use the delta to approximate the price of the option. Assuming XYZ advanced by $6 per share, we could reasonably expect the XYZ 50 call (remember the delta is about .50) to rise from $5 to $8. In other words, the $6 increase in the stock would likely translate into a $3 increase for the option.

The delta has other uses as well. For one thing it can help us assess the risk in any particular strategy. To illustrate, let's return to the XYZ example. Remember that each call option contract gives you the right to buy 100 shares of the underlying stock (in this case XYZ).

If you were to buy the XYZ 50 call option (remember the delta was .50), each contract implies about the same risk as owning 50 shares of XYZ common stock (100 shares per call option × .50 delta = 50 shares). Now keep this perspective on risk firmly in your mind, for the next point I want to make is extremely important.

Understanding the risk in a position is one of the pillars of strategy selection. Let's assume that you have $15,000 to invest. In the above example, you have a choice. You could buy 300 shares of XYZ—$50 × 300 share = $15,000 (we're ignoring commissions for the sake of clarity). Or you could buy 30 call options (30 × 100 shares × $5 per share premium = $15,000). Or finally you could buy three call options and place the balance of the money in some riskless investment such as U.S. government treasury bills ($15,000 – $1,500 [cost of three option contracts] = $13,500 in T-bills).

The risk in the first choice is obvious. You are long 300 shares of XYZ stock. However, if you bought the 30 call options, you are long (from the standpoint of risk) 1,500 shares of XYZ stock (30 calls × .50 delta × 100 shares per contract = 1,500). The question you must ask is: Would you be comfortable in your current financial position owning 1,500 shares of XYZ? If not, then buying 30 call options is not a viable alternative.

Finally, you could opt for the call option/treasury bill combination. Using the call option in conjunction with a T-bill actually carries less risk than outright ownership of the stock (the risk of this position is about equal to 150 shares of XYZ stock). If you think about that for a moment, you will see that the call option/T-bill combination has the same characteristics as a convertible debenture we talked about in Chapter Two (i.e., interest income from the T-bill, plus a call on the underlying security).

THE RISE OF INDEX OPTIONS

Index options began trading on the Midwest Stock Exchange with the introduction of the Value Line Composite Index, back in 1981. But index trading didn't really take off until the CBOE introduced options on the S&P 100 index (symbol OEX) some six months later.

Since the introduction of the OEX, index option trading has dwarfed trading in equity options. Daily trading in OEX options often exceeds daily volume in all other equity options combined.

The CBOE took the concept another step forward when, in October 1997, it introduced options on the Dow. You can now trade options on the Dow Jones Industrial (symbol DJX), Transportation (symbol DTX) and Utilities (symbol DUX) averages.

The idea that Dow Jones—parent company of the *Wall Street Journal*—would allow investors to trade options on their famed indices was quite an about-face. For years the company had resisted the temptation to license their indices for such a speculative venture. With equity options you have an underlying stock certificate. But with no real economic value, because no tangible investment supported the option, index options were seen as examples of excess within the financial markets.

5 8

Much has changed. Today, index options are seen as valuable risk-management tools for portfolio managers, particularly managers who utilize asset allocation strategies and want to fine-tune their asset mix without making wholesale changes to their portfolio.

For speculators, index options are ideal because they eliminate two steps in the investment decision process. With equity options, investors have to:

1. predict the direction of the overall market
2. select specific industries that are expected to outperform
3. buy options on the best stock in that particular sector

With index options, investors need only be concerned about the direction of the market.

On the other hand, many investors think index options are more volatile than stock options—not surprising when 50-point moves in the DJIA are an everyday occurrence. However, in reality, index options are much less volatile. A diversified portfolio of stocks, which is what an index is, will be less volatile than any single stock. The 50-point moves on the Dow, while numerically large, are really quite small in percentage terms.

Options on the DJIA will be based on 1/100th of the value of the underlying index. DTX options will trade with a factor of 10 (i.e., 1/10th the value of the Dow Jones Transportation Average) and DUX options will track the actual value of the Dow Jones Utilities Average.

With options based on 1/100th of the value of the Dow Jones Industrial Average, and a standard industry multiplier of $100, each options contract will represent the market value of the DJIA, according to literature from the CBOE.

For example, when the Dow is at 9,000, options on the DJIA will be based on an index level of 90.00 (9,000 × 1/100th). Given the standard multiplier of $100, the underlying value for the options would be $9,000 (90.00 base index level × 100 the multiplier for an options contract = $9,000).

Options on the Dow indices, unlike the OEX, are European-style, which means they can be exercised only at expiration. The settlement value is calculated based on the opening prices of the component securities in the index on the business day prior to expiration. This value is calculated by Dow Jones & Company, Inc.

In terms of the calculation, the DJIA is a price-weighted index that consists of 30 large NYSE-listed blue-chip industrial stocks. Price-weighted simply means that the prices of the 30 stocks are totaled and then divided by a divisor.

The S&P 100 and S&P 500 indices, on the other hand, are capitalization-weighted. That is, each component stock within the index is weighted according to its market capitalization (i.e., the share price multiplied by the number of outstanding shares).

Historically, the DJIA, S&P 100 and S&P 500 index levels have all tended to move in the same direction at the same time. However, differences in index composition and weighting methods can cause the index levels to move in dissimilar ways, over short periods.

EUROPEAN VERSUS AMERICAN-STYLE OPTIONS

An option that allows you to exercise it any time prior to the expiration date is called an American-style option. For the record, all equity options and most index options are American-style.

There is another option, referred to as a European-style option, which has been gaining in popularity in recent years. The term European simply refers to the settlement procedures. Whereas the more common American-style options can be exercised by the holder or assigned to the writer at any time prior to expiration, European-style options can be exercised only on the last trading day.

European settlement, especially on index options, eliminates the problem of early assignment. Traders who prefer to use spreads know with certainty their maximum exposure. The S&P 500 index options traded on the Chicago Board Options Exchange are European style.

It is because of this interest among investors that we need to look specifically at index options and rationalize the advantages and pitfalls while explaining the unique aspects of this market.

THE UNIQUE CHARACTERISTICS OF INDEX OPTIONS

Most equity-option strategies can be applied to index options, with one major difference: the point at which an option is exercised. When you exercise an XYZ call option, you receive 100 shares of XYZ at the agreed upon price. However, if you exercise an index option, you would not want to end up owning all the stocks that make up the index. If that were how index options were settled, investors who exercised an OEX call option would end up holding shares in 100 different companies. Obviously, delivering the shares of all the companies that make up an index, in the exact quantities represented in the index, is not practical. So when you exercise an index option, the account is settled in cash.

In other words, if you exercised a call option, you would receive the closing value of the index that day, less the strike price of the option multiplied by 100. (Note that the multiplier for most stock-index options is the same as it is for a stock option). If an investor exercised a put option, settlement would be in cash for the difference between the strike price less the current value of the index.

Consider the following example: Assume that you owned an OEX 400 call option, and the value of the OEX at the end of the trading day was 405.75. If you exercise your option, you would receive the difference between the strike price of the call (400) and the current closing value (405.75) of the index times the underlying multiple (100).

$$405.75 - 400 = 5.75 \times 100 = \$575 \text{ cash per contract}$$
(less applicable commissions)

That $575 would be credited to your account the next business day.

THE RISKS OF CASH SETTLEMENT

While the cash settlement feature is a distinct advantage for the option buyer, it can be a burden to the investor who is short an index option. Suppose, for example, that an investor wanted to implement a spread trade.

DEFINITION OF A SPREAD

A spread involves the simultaneous purchase and sale of two options. Both the buy and sell order must include either calls or puts.

With the OEX at 400, one potential spread could entail the purchase of, say, an OEX 410 call at 5 and simultaneously sell an OEX 390 call at 13 for a net credit of 8 (13 credit minus 5 debit = 8 net credit). This particular strategy is referred to as a bear call spread.

Since the position is established with an $800-per-contract net credit, that's the most you can hope to gain. Ideally, you want both options to expire worthless. If the index closes below 390 on expiration day, both the OEX 390 call and the OEX 410 call will expire worthless. You lose $500 per contract paid for the OEX 410 call, but you keep the $1,300 credit from the sale of the OEX 390 call. In other words, at expiration, you pocket the $800 per spread net credit.

So much for your best case. In the worst case, the OEX is trading at, say, 450 on expiration day. In that case, you would have to close out both option positions. You would sell your OEX 410 call at $4,000 per contract (450 – 410 = 40 × 100 multiplier = $4,000) to close out that side of the trade. You would also have to buy back your short OEX 390 call at $6,000 per contract (450 – 390 = 60 × 100 multiplier = $6,000). Total cost to close out the position is $2,000 ($6,000 debit less $4,000 credit = $2,000). Your total loss on this trade is the difference between your close-out costs ($2,000) and your initial credit ($800). Total loss based on our worst-case scenario is $1,200 per spread.

Such is the risk-reduction aspect of spread trading. Your best-case scenario is defined, as is your worst-case scenario. Or is it?

Let's look at one potential problem with spread trading using American-style index options, which is what OEX options are. Suppose the buyer of that OEX 390 call (the one you sold as part of the bear call spread) decided to exercise it. You would be left with a much different position than you'd originally envisioned. To fully appreciate this, let's look at a specific example.

Suppose that, shortly after implementing your spread trade, the OEX moved up to 415. The OEX 390 call is exercised, and your account is assigned. You now owe the call buyer a cash settlement equal to the difference between the closing value of the index less the strike price of the call. That is, the difference between 415 (current value of the OEX) less 390 (the strike price of the short call option) times 100 (index multiplier) = $2,500 per contract (excluding commissions).

After the early assignment, you are now left with the long OEX 410 call, the other side of the initial spread position, which at the close of trading the previous day would presumably be worth at least $500 per contract (415 index value − 410 strike price × 100 index multiplier = $500). Since you now hold a long OEX 410 call, the position is bullish—remember the initial spread was a bear call spread—and that's diametrically opposed to your original intention. Originally you were bearish.

"So what's the problem?" you ask. With a stock option, you could exercise your long call and then deliver the stock against the exercise notice. With index options, that is not an option.

You can exercise the OEX 410 call (remember the index closed at 415.00) and take the difference between the closing value and the strike price. But you will be exercising the call against the closing value of the index the next night That means that the value you will receive for the OEX 410 call will be the difference between a different closing value of the index and the strike price of the call. There is no reason to assume that the index will close at the same value tonight as it did the night before.

In a worst-case scenario, let's assume that the OEX fell sharply the next day and closed at 400. You can no longer exercise your OEX 410 call, because the strike price is well above the current value of the index. Since exercising the long OEX 410 call is not a reasonable alternative, you are left with the frustrating task of attempting to sell the option after the market has opened.

The spread strategy is designed to limit risk. However, if the short side of an index spread is assigned early, the investor is left with a position far removed from the initial intent, which takes us back to the issue of European- versus American-style exercise. If we are doing spreads, keep in mind the concept of European settlement. Eliminate the risk of early assignment before it becomes a problem.

LEAPS

In the last five years, option exchanges have introduced a new option concept: so-called Long Term Equity AnticiPations or LEAPs. Essentially, LEAPs are long-term options that have more than nine months to expiration. So why not simply call them long-term options? Why not indeed? I think the term LEAPs is meant to satisfy the exchanges' affinity for acronyms.

In any event, there are two types of LEAPs: call LEAPs and put LEAPs. Call LEAPs give you the right to buy 100 shares of a common stock within a period (referred to as the expiration date) for a specified price (known as the strike or exercise price).

For example, if you bought five two-year $50 call LEAPs on XYZ stock, you would have purchased the right (note: call buyers are under no obligation to exercise their option) to buy XYZ stock at $50 per share any time over the next two years.

Call LEAPs give you the right to buy the underlying stock at a specified price; put LEAPs grant you the right to sell 100 shares of the underlying stock at the strike price until the expiration date. You would buy call LEAPs if you expected the stock to rise (i.e., bullish), and you would buy put LEAPs if you expected the stock to fall (i.e., bearish).

THE BENEFITS OF LEAPS

Recall that the longer the option has before it expires, the greater the chance that the stock will move the way you want it to. Therefore, the longer the time to expiration, all other things being equal, the greater the value of the option.

Figure 3.2, much like Figure 3.1, demonstrates the nonlinear decay of time premium. The longer the period to expiration, the less important time is within the option-pricing equation. And there lies the advantage of LEAPs.

FIGURE 3.2

TIME PREMIUM DECAY—LEAPS

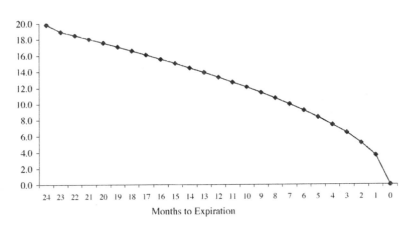

Months to Expiration

Simply stated, LEAPs reduce to some extent the importance of the strategic aspect of your investment decision. We suggested earlier that buying an option is a two-step process:

1. a view about the underlying security and
2. an evaluation of whether the option is over- or undervalued.

With LEAPs, the strategic part of the investment decision, while important, is less of an issue than it is with short-term options. If you buy LEAPs with two years to expiration, the value of those LEAPs will more closely mirror the performance of the underlying stock and will not be so dramatically affected by other factors within the option-pricing equation.

In short, the time premium decays faster in the last few weeks of the option's life (i.e., the weeks immediately preceding expiration) than it does in the early stages. Time is far less of a factor with LEAPs than for shorter-term options.

CONCLUSION

Chapter Three was meant to lightly enlighten. I wanted to introduce you to the language of options. Recognize that we are not talking about buy and hold with these investments. We are talking about opening and closing positions and how open-interest numbers give us a sense of the liquidity in a particular option contract.

I also wanted to provide you with a primer on how options are priced and, most importantly, explain the role of volatility in the options price. That becomes a major consideration with our aggressive investing strategies in Part Four. In the Appendix, I'll also show you where you can get option-pricing technology off the Internet.

Think of this chapter as setting the scene for the next chapter, a discussion of basic option strategies.

PART III

INVESTMENT TOOLS FOR THE AGGRESSIVE INVESTOR

4
THE PROFIT-AND-LOSS TABLE

In our efforts to characterize a particular option strategy, we will make liberal use of tables and charts—teaching aids that illustrate numerically and graphically the profit-and-loss characteristics of an option strategy based on the price level of the underlying security. Usually the price of the underlying security is assumed to be at expiration.

The profit/loss tables and charts serve another important purpose, especially the charts that give us a snapshot defining the biases of particular strategies. These can be useful when comparing equivalent option positions. All this will make more sense when we examine aggressive investing strategies. For now, we need only understand that any position we can implement with call options can be replicated with put options. These so-called equivalent positions share similar risk/reward characteristics and can help us establish the most efficient position at a particular time.

TABLE 4.1

BUY 100 SHARES OF XYZ STOCK

XYZ STOCK PRICE	CURRENT VALUE	COST OF PURCHASE	PROFIT / LOSS
30.00	3,000.00	5,000.00	–2,000.00
35.00	3,500.00	5,000.00	–1,500.00
40.00	4,000.00	5,000.00	–1,000.00
45.00	4,500.00	5,000.00	– 500.00
50.00	5,000.00	5,000.00	—
55.00	5,500.00	5,000.00	500.00
60.00	6,000.00	5,000.00	1,000.00
65.00	6,500.00	5,000.00	1,500.00
70.00	7,000.00	5,000.00	2,000.00

Getting back to the actual tables and charts, consider the following illustration. Assume you bought 100 shares of XYZ stock at $50 per share. If you sold that stock six months later at $60 per share, you would pocket a $1,000 profit ($60 – $50 × 100 shares = $1,000). The stock can also decline. If it falls to $40 per share and you sell it, you will suffer a $1,000 hit to your pocketbook, before commissions.

We'll ignore commissions for the moment. The goal here is to identify the specifics of the strategy, not its cost-effectiveness. With that in mind, Table 4.1 defines the profit-and-loss characteristics of a 100-share position in XYZ stock, at various price levels.

FIGURE 4.1

PROFIT/LOSS—LONG 100 SHARES XYZ STOCK

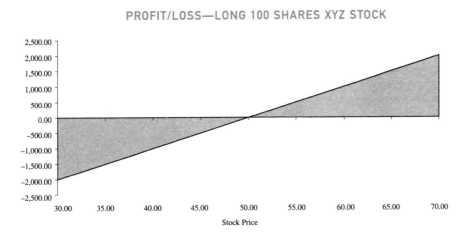

Notice how in Figure 4.1 that as the price of the stock rises from left to right along the bottom of the chart, the profit/loss line moves from negative to positive territory in a straight line. Straightforward, really! Buy 100 shares of stock, and your position gains or loses $100, for every $1 movement in the underlying stock.

THE LONG CALL

We know that the buyer of a call option profits if the underlying stock rises. And, since a stock can theoretically rise to infinity, the call buyer's potential profit, like that of the stockholder, is unlimited. Continuing with our XYZ example, then, assume that an investor bought one XYZ 50 call and paid a $5-per-share premium ($500 per contract).

Again, using the stock prices from our previous example, Table 4.2 provides us with a numerical study of the profit-and-loss potential from this position.

TABLE 4.2

P&L FROM ONE XYZ 50 CALL AT $5 ON THE LAST TRADING DAY

XYZ STOCK PRICE	PUT VALUE PER CONTRACT	COST OF XYZ CALL OPTION	PROFIT/LOSS	PERCENT
30.00	—	500.00	−500.00	−100
35.00	—	500.00	−500.00	−100
40.00	—	500.00	−500.00	−100
45.00	—	500.00	−500.00	−100
50.00	—	500.00	−500.00	−100
55.00	500.00	500.00	—	0
60.00	1,000.00	500.00	500.00	100
65.00	1,500.00	500.00	1,000.00	200
70.00	2,000.00	500.00	1,500.00	300

FIGURE 4.2

PROFIT/LOSS—LONG 1 XYZ 50 CALL

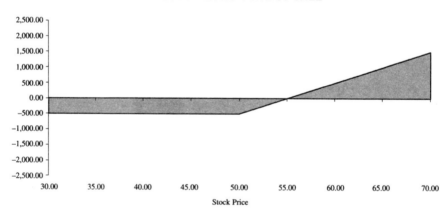

Note from Figure 4.2 that the profit/loss line crosses the breakeven axis further to the right, accounting for the cost of the call option premium. After crossing the breakeven axis, the profit/loss line follows a similar pattern to the long stock position, reflecting the unlimited potential of the underlying stock, whose value can, theoretically, rise to infinity. But notice how, below the breakeven axis, the chart truncates from right to left to the point at which the investor experiences the maximum loss. In this example, the maximum loss is capped at $500 per contract, telling us two things:

1. The maximum amount you can lose when buying a call is known.
2. You can lose your entire investment buying call options.

As well, with both the table and chart, we are looking at the value of a call option on the last day of trading. As such, the table assesses only the profitability of a strategy based on the option's intrinsic value. We define an option's intrinsic value as the difference between the market price of the underlying stock less the strike price of the call or, for a put option, the difference between the strike price of the put and the market price for the underlying stock. By looking only at intrinsic value, we can eliminate external influences like time from the illustration. We will discuss this in greater detail a little later in this chapter.

THE PUT

The put option profits if the underlying stock declines, so it stands to reason that profits will occur as the stock price falls. Although the stock can rise to infinity, the losses on the long put are still capped at the cost of the put. Table 4.3 and Figure 4.3 assume the investor purchased one XYZ 50 put at a cost of $4 per share ($400 per contract).

TABLE 4.3

P&L FROM ONE XYZ 50 PUT AT $4 ON THE LAST TRADING DAY

XYZ STOCK PRICE	PUT VALUE PER CONTRACT	COST OF XYZ CALL OPTION	PROFIT/LOSS	PERCENT
30.00	2,000.00	400.00	1,600.00	400%
35.00	1,500.00	400.00	1,100.00	275%
40.00	1,000.00	400.00	600.00	150%
45.00	500.00	400.00	100.00	25%
50.00	—	400.00	– 400.00	–100%
55.00	—	400.00	– 400.00	–100%
60.00	—	400.00	– 400.00	–100%
65.00	—	400.00	– 400.00	–100%
70.00	—	400.00	– 400.00	–100%

FIGURE 4.3

PROFIT/LOSS—LONG 1 XYZ 50 PUT

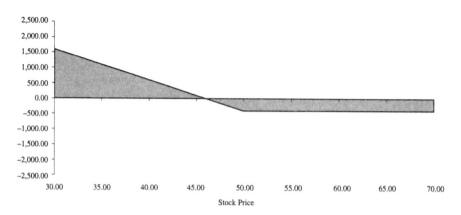

The profit-and-loss chart for the long put is the mirror image of the long call chart. Note in Figure 4.3 that the profit/loss line crosses the breakeven axis to the left of the point where the long stock position becomes profitable, which accounts for the cost of the put premium. Note also that the profit/loss line truncates from left to right along the chart, representing the maximum potential loss, which is the premium paid for the put.

BUYING CALL OPTIONS

It is nearly impossible to understand all there is to know about options after reading one chapter of one book. Indeed, there are many fine books that take the time to explain options from A to Z, so we won't attempt that here.

What we will do is focus on what's important to the aggressive trader and explain the role that options will play within the context of our aggressive positions. What options bring to the table is, in a word, flexibility.

With this in mind, let's revisit the first three profit-and-loss charts. Remember, these charts help us illustrate how different option strategies affect specific positions.

The most basic option strategy is buying calls. That's the strategy that was discussed in Figure 4.2. The advantages are relatively straightforward: The call option allows a few dollars to do the work of many. In our example, we control 100 shares of XYZ at $50 per share, yet had to invest only $5 per share ($500 per contract), another example of leverage.

From Table 4.2, should the stock rise to $70 per share, the option would be worth $20 per share ($2,000 per contract), which translates into a $15-per-share ($1,500-per-contract) profit. In that scenario, your $500 investment triples in value.

Compare that return with the stockholder whose $5,000 investment (i.e., the cost to control the same 100 shares of XYZ) returned $2,000 profit or a return of 40% over the same period.

That's the upside. What's the risk? Again, in Table 4.2, note that call buyers lose their entire investment if the stock falls below $50 per share. In fact, if the stock even stays at $50 per share, call buyers lose their entire investment. The risks of limited-time investments are high indeed.

This begs the question, How likely is it that the option will expire worthless? Well, if you buy the statistics mentioned at the beginning of Chapter Three, then up to 80% of such positions will not turn a profit by expiration.

Mind you, as with most investment concepts, there are two sides to the coin. The glass-half-empty position says that with call buying you can lose your entire investment. The glass-half-full scenario says that with call buying your risk is limited and predetermined.

Without belaboring the point, let's accept for the moment that call buying is a risky strategy.

THE PUT, THE STOCK, THE MARRIAGE

Most of the potential and risk associated with call buying also affect the put buyer. You have leverage, and you can lose your entire investment.

When you buy a put option, you make money if the underlying stock declines. According to Table 4.3, if XYZ declines to $30 per share, the $400 per contract invested in the XYZ 50 put option returns $2,000 per contract, or 400%. If XYZ stays at $50 per share, or rises in value, put buyers lose their entire investment. But again, the risk is limited and predetermined.

Puts are sometimes difficult to understand. Remember, a put option gives you the right to sell the underlying stock at a predetermined price. When you buy the XYZ 50 put, you have the right to sell XYZ at $50 per share until the option expires. Because of characteristics unique to the put option, many stockholders see put options as a valuable portfolio management tool, much like an insurance policy, with a deductible.

A common strategy is to purchase a put to protect a long stock position. For example, you could purchase 100 shares of XYZ at $50 per share and simultaneously purchase one XYZ 50 put at $4 per share ($400 per contract). This is referred to as the *Married-Put* strategy, the put presumably being married to the stock position, and never the two will part.

I'm not sure why anyone would buy a stock and then add some protection to the equation immediately. If you're that uncertain, why buy the stock in the first place? Still, I think we can all agree that the married put is a conservative strategy. Some might say ultraconservative.

With the stock + the six-month put option, you have protected yourself in the event the stock declines. If the stock falls to $30 over the next six months, you could exercise your put, and force the put seller to buy your stock from you at $50 per share. You would not lose anything on the transaction save for the initial $4 per share cost of the put. That's the deductible I talked about when referring to the put as insurance.

TABLE 4.4

PROFIT/LOSS: LONG XYZ STOCK + LONG 1 XYZ 50 PUT

XYZ STOCK PRICE	TOTAL COST STOCK + PUT	STOCK STOCK PRICE AT EXPIRY	PUT VALUE AT EXPIRY	PROFIT / LOSS
30.00	5,400.00	3,000.00	2,000.00	– 400.00
35.00	5,400.00	3,500.00	1,500.00	– 400.00
40.00	5,400.00	4,000.00	1,000.00	– 400.00
45.00	5,400.00	4,500.00	500.00	– 400.00
50.00	5,400.00	5,000.00	—	– 400.00
55.00	5,400.00	5,500.00	—	100.00
60.00	5,400.00	6,000.00	—	600.00
65.00	5,400.00	6,500.00	—	1,100.00
70.00	5,400.00	7,000.00	—	1,600.00

FIGURE 4.4

PROFIT/LOSS—LONG STOCK + 1 XYZ 50 PUT

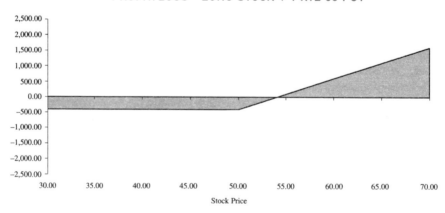

Figure 4.4 graphically illustrates the profit-and-loss characteristics of this position. Notice how the put protects your downside should the stock decline sharply. Remember, the put gives you the right to sell your stock at $50 per share.

Even if the stock falls to $30 per share, you have the right to force someone to buy the shares from you at the higher price. In a worst-case scenario over the next six months, this position loses only $400, while the upside potential is unlimited.

Take a good look at Figure 4.4. Notice how the graph truncates from right to left below the breakeven axis, the point at which the maximum loss occurs. Now return to Figure 4.2, which depicts the profit and loss from a long-call position. Notice the similarity between the charts.

The fact is, the married-put and the long-call position share the same profit-and-loss characteristics: limited loss to the downside, unlimited potential to the upside. Yet we refer to the cost of the put as the deductible cost for an insurance policy, while the cost of the call is the price of admission for speculators who want to bet on the outcome for XYZ—two perspectives for strategies with similar characteristics.

Why is it that two equivalent option positions have slightly different profit-and-loss characteristics at each price level, not in terms of direction, but in actual dollar terms? The married-put strategy loses only $400 in a worst-case scenario. The worst-case scenario for the long-call position is a loss of $500. Stay with me for a moment, and I'll explain the discrepancy.

Before doing that, however, we need to understand the psychology behind both strategies. When we talk about the long-call position, we talk about the potential of losing 100% of the initial investment. There are no such caveats when talking about the married-put strategy. We view the long-call position as a speculative high-risk trade. We look at the married-put strategy as an ultraconservative investment. Why?

Simple really: Think leverage! With the married-put strategy, the investor owns the underlying stock. The total investment was $5,400 ($5,000 for 100 shares of XYZ + $400 for one XYZ 50 put option). In a worst-case scenario, the married-put buyer will get back at least $5,000, or 92% of the initial investment.

With the call buyer, we assume the $500 was the entire investment. Lose $500 and you lose your entire investment. If the stock rises, you make double or triple your initial investment. We look at the married-put strategy as a package in which the put accounts for only a small part of the initial investment. The percentage return if the stock rises looks more like the returns the stockholder would achieve, not the potential double or triple return from the long-call position. Such is the reasoning behind two similar strategies viewed from different perspectives.

Back to the differences in the net returns at all price levels: To fully grasp the similarity between the strategies, we need to turn the long-call position into a low-risk alternative to the married-put strategy. To do that, let's revisit the long-call position, only this time we'll assume the investor has $5,400 to invest—the same amount of money that is tied up in the married-put position.

Now, let's take $500, buy an XYZ 50 call and invest the remaining $4,900 in a six-month treasury bill. Let's assume the treasury bill yields 4% per year. The treasury bill, then, will earn about $96.08 for a six-month holding period. Table 4.5

looks at the profit and loss from a long call + a six-month treasury bill. As you can see from the far right column, the profit-and-loss characteristics from this position are virtually identical to the married-put strategy.

TABLE 4.5

LONG XYZ 50 CALL + SIX-MONTH T-BILL

XYZ STOCK PRICE	TOTAL COST CALL + T-BILL	VALUE T-BILL AT MATURITY	CALL VALUE AT EXPIRY	INTEREST EARNED	PROFIT/ LOSS
30.00	5,400.00	4,900.00	—	96.08	– 403.92
35.00	5,400.00	4,900.00	—	96.08	– 403.92
40.00	5,400.00	4,900.00	—	96.08	– 403.92
45.00	5,400.00	4,900.00	—	96.08	– 403.92
50.00	5,400.00	4,900.00	—	96.08	– 403.92
55.00	5,400.00	4,900.00	500.00	96.08	96.08
60.00	5,400.00	4,900.00	1,000.00	96.08	596.08
65.00	5,400.00	4,900.00	1,500.00	96.08	1,096.08
70.00	5,400.00	4,900.00	2,000.00	96.08	1,596.08

And as mentioned in Chapter Three, the combination of a call and a T-bill looks a lot like a convertible debenture, the call providing exposure to the underlying stock, the T-bill representing the fixed-income component of the position.

MORE BASIC OPTION STRATEGIES: THE COVERED CALL WRITE

Covered call writing is probably the most common option strategy used by individual investors. With this strategy the investor owns the underlying stock and sells a call option against the shares. When selling the call option, you are agreeing to deliver the underlying stock to the call buyer at a predetermined price.

For example, suppose you owned 100 shares of XYZ at $50 per share. You sell the XYZ six-month 55 call for a net premium of $2 per share ($200 per contract). In this example, you have agreed to sell your 100 shares of XYZ to the call buyer at $55 per share until the option expires. For agreeing to this, the call buyer will pay you $3 per share in premium. The premium is yours to keep no matter where the stock ends up in six months.

Does this sound familiar? It's the strategy we looked at in Chapter One with Electronics for Imaging. In that case we bought the stock in January and agreed to sell it at a predetermined price in April.

Because you own the underlying shares in this strategy, the covered writer should be mildly bullish, or at the very least neutral on the prospects for the underlying stock. You should never write call options on a stock that you expect to fall in price. If you are bearish on that stock, sell it!

Now three things can happen from this position:

1. The stock can rise above $55 per share in six months. In that event, the call will be exercised, the call buyer will pay you $55 per share, and you will deliver your 100 shares of XYZ to the call buyer.

2. The stock can remain unchanged for the life of the option. In this case, the call option will not be exercised and will in fact expire worthless. Another call option bites the dust. As the seller of the call option, you will no longer be under any obligation to sell your stock at $55 per share. You still own the 100 shares of XYZ, the $3 premium received when you sold the call option is yours to keep, and you move on.

3. Finally the stock can decline below $50 per share between the time you sold the call option and the expiration date. In this case, you will be better off than the investor who never sold the call. Why? Because the initial $3 per share premium received can be applied against the purchase price of the stock. In other words, the premium reduced your cost by $3 per share.

TABLE 4.6

PROFIT/LOSS—XYZ COVERED CALL WRITE

XYZ STOCK PRICE	TOTAL COST STOCK CALL	STOCK PRICE AT EXPIRY	CALL VALUE AT EXPIRY	PROFIT/ LOSS
30.00	4,700.00	3,000.00	—	−1,700.00
35.00	4,700.00	3,500.00	—	−1,200.00
40.00	4,700.00	4,000.00	—	− 700.00
45.00	4,700.00	4,500.00	—	− 200.00
50.00	4,700.00	5,000.00	—	300.00
55.00	4,700.00	5,500.00	—	800.00
60.00	4,700.00	6,000.00	− 500.00	800.00
65.00	4,700.00	6,500.00	−1,000.00	800.00
70.00	4,700.00	7,000.00	−1,500.00	800.00

With a covered call write, then, you establish limits. In this example, you have limited your upside potential to the strike price of the option, plus the $3 premium ($55 + $3 = $58). At the same time, you have reduced the cost base of the stock by the premium received. In this case the net cost to buy XYZ stock was reduced from $50 to $47. Remember, covered call writing doesn't eliminate your downside risk, it merely helps offset some of the decline.

Keeping with the profit-and-loss theme, Table 4.6 examines the profit-and-loss potential from the XYZ covered call write at different price levels. Again, the prices quoted are assumed to be for the last trading day for XYZ options.

Figure 4.5 characterizes the covered call write in graphic form. Note how the profit/loss line truncates from left to right above the breakeven axis. Further, note how the call reduced your risk. As the price of the stock declines, so does the size of your wallet. But as a consolation prize, at each price level, you lose less than the investor who holds the stock but did not sell a call option against the position. That is depicted in the chart, in which losses occur to the left of where they would with the long-stock position in Figure 4.1.

FIGURE 4.5

PROFIT/LOSS—LONG STOCK SHORT XYZ 55 CALL

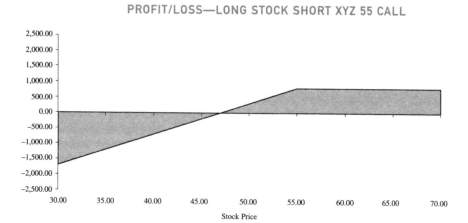

Stock Price

WHAT TO LOOK FOR

A successful covered write is one in which you can balance potential capital appreciation with downside protection. At what price are you willing to sell the underlying shares? How much downside protection do you require to give up your stock at the strike price of the option?

Many option advisory services promote covered writing solely on the basis of the rate of return over a specific period. The most attractive covered call write is the one with the highest rate of return if the stock remains unchanged until the expiration date.

Evaluating the potential of a covered call write on the basis that the stock price remains unchanged until expiration is valid. By doing so, we remove any hidden biases about where the stock may be going between now and expiration.

However, the notion that a covered call write is attractive because it offers a high rate of return if the stock remains unchanged is misguided. We need to understand why the rate of return is so high.

For example, in December 1985, Texaco was trading at $32 1/4. The Texaco April 35 calls (only four months to expiry) were trading at 4 1/4. A covered write at that point was yielding better than 29% on an annualized basis (assuming the price of the stock remained unchanged). Why? At the time, Texaco was vulnerable. Pennzoil had sued Texaco and, in December 1985, it had just won its first battle, convincing a Texas jury that its lawsuit against Texaco was well founded.

On a rate-of-return basis, the Texaco position was attractive. In fact, this particular covered call write would have been profitable. But you had to understand the risks associated with the Pennzoil lawsuit. How much downside should Texaco lose, what was the upside assuming the court ruled in Texaco's favor, and how long before any real judgment or appeal would be heard?

Bottom Line: If a covered write looks attractive—on a rate-of-return basis—it means that professional traders expect the underlying stock to be particularly volatile over the near term, which emphasizes the role that volatility plays in the option's price.

CALCULATING RATE OF RETURN

Obviously, before considering any covered write, we need to be certain we are comfortable holding the underlying stock. Having gained a measure of comfort with a particular stock, we can then examine the position from a rate-of-return perspective. This leads us into the realm of the aggressive investor and the potential strategies that can flow from the covered call write.

Table 4.7 examines a potential covered call write, using a covered call writing worksheet. A worksheet will provide you with all the necessary information to appraise the merits of any covered call write.

In this example, we assume the trader bought 100 shares of ABC at $28 per share. The shares were purchased in late January. The investor then sold an ABC July 30 call against the stock position. There are 138 days to expiry. Commissions were not included, although we have left space to incorporate commission costs into the worksheet, since they will have an impact on the rate-of-return calculation.

Returns from a covered call write should always be annualized. In other words, if the six-month rate of return is 10%, the annualized rate of return would be approximately 20%. Annualized returns allow us to make apples-to-apples comparisons with other investments over different periods.

TABLE 4.7

COVERED CALL WRITE WORKSHEET

NET INVESTMENT CALCULATION

		PRICE PER SHARE	NUMBER OF SHARES	TOTAL COST
Buy	ABC	28.00	100	2,800.00
Sell	ABC July 30 calls	2.00	100	(200.00)
Plus	Transaction Costs			
Equals	**Net Investment**			**$2,600.00**

RETURN IF STOCK CALLED AWAY

		RECEIPTS PER SHARE	NUMBER OF SHARES	NET RECEIPTS
Sell	ABC	30.00	100	3,000.00
Plus	Dividends Received	—	100	—
Less	Net Investment			(2,600.00)
Equals	**Net Return**			**$400.00**
	Percent return if called away	**15.38%**		
	Annualized rate of return	**33.03%**		

RETURN IF STOCK UNCHANGED

		VALUE PER SHARE	NUMBER OF SHARES	NET VALUE
	ABC	28.00	100	2,800.00
Plus	Dividends Received	—	100	—
Less	ABC July 30 calls	—	100	—
Less	Net Investment			(2,600.00)
Equals	**Net Return**			**$200.00**
	Percent return if unchanged	**7.69%**		
	Annualized rate of return	**5.13%**		

DOWNSIDE BREAKEVEN

		VALUE PER SHARE	NUMBER OF SHARES	NET COST
	Net Investment			2,600.00
Less	Dividends	—	100	—
Equals	Total stock cost to expiration			2,600.00
Divide	By number of shares held		100	
Equals	**Breakeven price per share**			**$26.00**
Equals	**Percent downside protection**			**7.14%**

For example, assume that the rate of return for a three-month covered write was 4%, while the return on a six-month covered write was 6%. On an annualized basis, the first covered write is equivalent to 16% (4 × 4% = 16%), while the second situation equals only 12% (6% × 2 = 12%). Based on that comparison, the first covered write appears to be the more attractive alternative.

However, simply extrapolating the return over a full year does not guarantee that the annualized result is actually obtainable. After all, as in the first example, it's not prudent to assume that the return for the next three months will be the same as for the first three months.

As a general rule, when appraising the minimal acceptable return (assuming the stock remains unchanged), you should only consider covered writes that offer at least twice the rate of interest (after factoring in commissions) available on treasury bills. For instance if the return available on T-bills is 8% annualized, you should get at least a 16% annualized return for the covered write. Obviously, more volatile stocks will offer greater returns and provide higher return numbers for the aggressive investor.

In the end, using this rule of thumb as a foundation and the covered write worksheet, you will be able to analyze any covered write option within the context of risk and reward.

WRITING CALL OPTIONS AGAINST CONVERTIBLE DEBENTURES

As mentioned in Chapter Two, convertible debentures combine the fixed-income attributes of a bond and the capital-gain potential of common stocks. As the name suggests, convertible debentures can be exchanged, at the option of the holder, for the common shares of the underlying company.

The exchange privilege makes the convertible debenture attractive to an aggressive investor. Since the convertible security has a call on the underlying common shares, it can be used to cover the sale of call options.

We would expect, based on an analysis of the convertible debenture, that its value will rise and fall with any movement in the underlying common shares. The fixed-income—i.e., annual interest payments—side of the convertible debenture gives it an investment value, which helps to support its price during a market decline. In other words, the convertible debenture would not likely decline so far or so fast as the underlying common stock. At some point, the convertible would begin trading as a straight bond, and the yield would support its price.

For the aggressive investor, the support mechanism is an attractive feature. The convertible debenture will be less volatile than the underlying common stock, and that can be an asset to the covered writer. The volatility assumption factored into the option's price will reflect the risk associated with the underlying common stock, not that of the convertible debenture. In other words, whereas the price of the options may be reasonable relative to the volatility (remember option traders quantify risk in terms of volatility) in the underlying common stock, they may be overpriced in terms of the volatility in the convertible debenture.

Of course, convertible debentures are only preferable when their yield is higher than the dividend payout on the underlying common stock. If we assume a yield advantage over the common shares, the returns from a covered-writing program should improve. In fact, given that the convertible debenture carries less risk than the common shares, the risk/reward trade-off should also be more attractive.

But there's another interesting side to yield advantage. Take, for instance, the investor who is concerned about current income. Many option traders in that situation tend to write covered calls against stocks with high dividends. But there are drawbacks to that approach. Most important, from the perspective of the covered writer, is that stocks with high dividends tend to have low call-option premiums.

Covered writers who use convertible debentures (because of income requirements) rather than a high-dividend-paying stock are not penalized with lower call premiums, because the calls reflect the dividend payout on the underlying stock and not the yield on the convertible debenture.

Perhaps the best situation is one where the underlying common stock doesn't pay a dividend and is reasonably volatile. In that case, the convertible debenture will:

1. be less volatile

2. have a distinct yield advantage. You will be able to write calls that have attractive premiums.

WRITING NAKED PUTS

Like the naked city, there are a thousand horror stories about selling naked puts. Most of them are true!

When you sell a put option, you agree to buy the underlying stock at a specific price. For example, suppose you sold an XYZ 50 put for a premium of $4 per share ($400 per contract). Having sold the put, you immediately receive $4 per share in premium income. That's yours to keep regardless of the outcome over the next six months.

In this example, you are obligated to buy XYZ anytime over the next six months at $50 per share. As with all option strategies, one of three things will happen: The stock will rise, fall or remain unchanged. If the stock remains unchanged, the put will expire worthless, and you will keep the $4 per share premium.

If the stock rises in value, the put will also expire worthless. Here's why: The investor who owns the put has the right to make you buy his stock at $50 per share. But if his stock is trading at a price higher than $50 per share, there is no incentive for the owner of the put to exercise it. Why should the owner of the put make you buy his stock at $50, when he can get a higher price selling in the open market?

Finally the stock can decline in price, in which case you will be forced to buy XYZ at $50 per share. It is the last possibility that strikes fear in the heart of traders.

What happens if the stock should decline to zero? With this question in mind, traders have pointed out that put writing, with its limited upside potential and significant downside risk, appeals only to investors with a propensity for tax losses. In the case of XYZ, the potential risk is $50 per share (in a worst-case scenario) for the chance to earn a maximum $4 per share.

Option traders will also regale you with countless stories about investors who were wiped out during a market meltdown, for instance in October 1997, when the U.S. stock market fell 500 + points in one day. All of which leads me to think that this is an interesting strategy, particularly for aggressive investors. You'll see how we can use it later in this book.

When you think about it, most of us have used the concept of put writing at some point in our investment careers. Have you ever phoned your broker and placed an order to buy 100 shares of stock at a specific price—the so-called limit order? Rather than pay the market price for the shares, you set a specific price: buy XYZ with a limit of $49 when the stock is trading at $50. Now I ask you, is that any different from writing a put? With the put, however, you earn a fee for committing to the order.

So how did such a basic strategy get such a bad reputation? In a word, leverage. When you enter a limit order you must have the money set aside to buy the stock. Too many investors selling naked put options use it as a trading strategy, never expecting to get assigned.

If you are over-leveraged, and the underlying stock gets whacked with bad news—as happened with the Electronics for Imaging story in Chapter One, put writes get hit with a double whammy. The value of the put is rising because:

1. the stock is declining
2. volatility is increasing

Think of it this way: When a stock falls sharply on bad news, holders of that stock scramble to buy puts as insurance and will usually pay any price, much as you would pay any price to buy fire insurance if your house were burning down.

The volatility component of the option-pricing formula simply quantifies that rush to the exits and factors it into the put option's price. Naked put writers who are over-leveraged have to close out their positions, usually with huge losses, all because they cannot afford to buy the underlying stock should the put be assigned. Aggressive investors cannot put themselves into a position in which they would have to close out their option trade prematurely.

ANOTHER NAKED PUT EXAMPLE

Having talked about how other investors feel about writing naked puts, let's look at it objectively, breaking down the strategy into its component parts. We begin by looking at the profit-and-loss tables and charts.

In this example, we will use the same strike price as we used with the XYZ covered write example in the previous section. That is, we will sell the XYZ 55 put for a net premium of $7 per share.

Table 4.8 looks at the profit-and-loss characteristics for the investor who sells one XYZ 55 put for $7 per share.

TABLE 4.8

PROFIT/LOSS FROM SALE OF XYZ 55 PUT

XYZ STOCK PRICE	PUT VALUE AT EXPIRATION	PREMIUM RECEIVED	PROFIT / LOSS
30.00	2,500.00	700.00	−1,800.00
35.00	2,000.00	700.00	−1,300.00
40.00	1,500.00	700.00	−800.00
45.00	1,000.00	700.00	−300.00
50.00	500.00	700.00	200.00
55.00	—	700.00	700.00
60.00	—	700.00	700.00
65.00	—	700.00	700.00
70.00	—	700.00	700.00

FIGURE 4.6

PROFIT/LOSS—SHORT XYZ 55 PUT

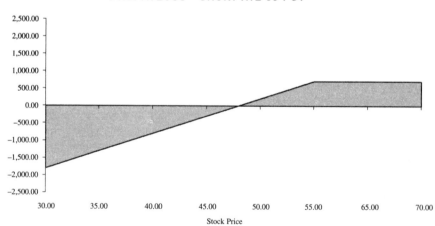

Figure 4.6 illustrates the profit-and-loss characteristics of the naked put write using the numbers from table 4.8. Note how the chart truncates from left to right

above the breakeven axis, indicating the limited potential return from the strategy. Note also how the potential downside is unlimited, except of course that a stock cannot fall below zero.

Now return to Figure 4.5—the covered call write—and note how the profit-and-loss charts for the naked put write and the covered call write are identical, meaning that we are looking at yet another equivalent position.

In the covered call example, we bought the underlying stock at $50 per share and sold an out-of-the-money call, the XYZ 55 call. With the naked put, we sold the same strike price and placed the balance of cash into a short-term treasury bill. The interest earned on the treasury bill accounts for the slight difference in return between the two positions.

The first question you might ask is, "What happens if the stock declines to zero?" To which I would answer, the same thing as would happen if the stock in the covered call write were to drop to zero. The loss from either position would be the same.

So again, we have a position—the naked put write—that is viewed from one side of the table as a risky proposition while, on the opposite side, an equivalent position is seen as conservative and low-risk. Bottom line: Option strategies by themselves are not risky. The degree of leverage an investor uses dictates the riskiness of any option strategy at any time.

THE COMBINATION/STRADDLE

We've looked at options from the perspective of buying and selling calls and puts. But in all cases, we've looked at positions that are based on some view of the underlying stock. You buy a call because you are bullish, you buy a put because you are bearish. And the beat goes on.

What about those times when you are not certain about direction? Or the times you would normally sit on the sidelines waiting for the market to make a new high or, better yet, go through a mild correction to create a buying opportunity?

In these moments the straddle or combination strategy can be most useful. A straddle is defined as the simultaneous purchase (or sale) of both a call and a put with the same strike price. A combination is defined as the simultaneous purchase (or sale) of both a call and a put with different strike prices.

For example, with XYZ at $50, we could buy a six-month XYZ 50 call (trading at $5 per share) and a six-month XYZ 50 put (trading at $4 per share) for a net debit of $9 per share. Note we purchased both the call and the put, both at the $50-per-share strike price.

Now think about this for a moment: Since we bought both options, we will make money if the underlying stock goes up or down. If XYZ declines, the put will rise; if XYZ rises, the call will make money. Seems like the perfect strategy, don't you think? A no-lose proposition.

Well not quite. The problem is you are paying two premiums when you buy both the call and the put. To make money on this position, the stock has to move more than $9 per share from its current price over the next six months. At expiration the stock has to be above $59 per share or below $41 per share for the long straddle to be profitable. In this example, we don't care which direction the stock goes, only that it moves dramatically over the next six months (see Table 4.9 and Figure 4.7).

TABLE 4.9

PROFIT AND LOSS ON LONG XYZ 50 STRADDLE

XYZ STOCK PRICE	STRADDLE NET DEBIT	PUT VALUE AT EXPIRATION	CALL VALUE EXPIRATION	PROFIT/ LOSS
30.00	900.00	2,000.00	—	1,100.00
35.00	900.00	1,500.00	—	600.00
40.00	900.00	1,000.00	—	100.00
45.00	900.00	500.00	—	– 400.00
50.00	900.00	—	—	– 900.00
55.00	900.00	—	500.00	– 400.00
60.00	900.00	—	1,000.00	100.00
65.00	900.00	—	1,500.00	600.00
70.00	900.00	—	2,000.00	1,100.00

FIGURE 4.7

PROFIT/LOSS—LONG XYZ 50 STRADDLE

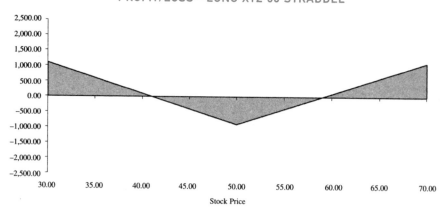

Stock Price

It is unlikely you will lose your entire $9-per-share premium with this position. For that to happen, both the call and the put would have to expire worthless, which would mean the stock would have to close at exactly $50 per share on expiration day—not a very likely scenario.

With a long combination, however, you could lose your entire premium. As we said, the combination has many of the same characteristics as the long straddle, in that you buy both a call and a put. But with the combination, you use different strike prices. For example, with XYZ at $50 per share, you might buy the six-month XYZ 55 call (trading at 3) and the six-month XYZ 45 put (trading at 2 1/4) for a net debit of 5 1/4.

TABLE 4.10

PROFIT/LOSS FOR LONG XYZ 45/55 COMBINATION

XYZ STOCK PRICE	STRADDLE NET DEBIT	PUT VALUE AT EXPIRATION	CALL VALUE EXPIRATION	PROFIT/ LOSS
30.00	900.00	1,500.00	—	600.00
35.00	900.00	1,000.00	—	100.00
40.00	900.00	500.00	—	– 400.00
45.00	900.00	—	—	– 900.00
50.00	900.00	—	—	– 900.00
55.00	900.00	—	—	– 900.00
60.00	900.00	—	500.00	– 400.00
65.00	900.00	—	1,000.00	100.00
70.00	900.00	—	1,500.00	600.00

The advantage of the long combination is a lower up-front cost. The disadvantage is that the underlying stock has to move more dramatically to make money. At expiration, XYZ would have to be above $60 1/4 ($55 call strike + 5 1/4 = $60 1/4) or below 39 3/4 ($45 put strike – 5 1/4 = $39 3/4) for the position to be profitable. As well, you could lose your entire net investment if the stock were to close between the two strike prices—i.e., between $45 and $55 per share at expiration.

You can also sell a straddle or combination. You would do that if you felt the underlying stock was unlikely to move beyond the trading range as defined by the strike prices + the option premium. For example, with the straddle, we were looking at the XYZ 50 call at $5 and the XYZ 50 put at $4. If we collect those two premiums, the stock has to remain between $41 and $59 for the position to be profitable. Think of that as the implied trading range for XYZ.

In the real world, that trading range tells you a lot about the cost of XYZ options. Recall in Chapter Three, when we talked about the impact of volatility on

FIGURE 4.8

PROFIT/LOSS—LONG XYZ 45/55 COMBINATION

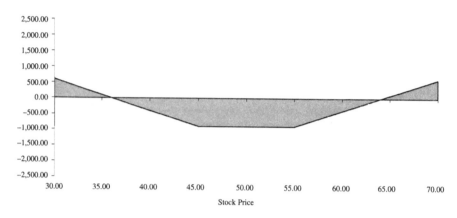

the price of an option. Higher volatility means higher option premiums. Recall also that volatility is simply a way of quantifying the risk in the underlying security. How far is the underlying stock likely to move over the prescribed period? We also talked about taking the current option premium, plugging that into the option-pricing formula, and then asking the model to solve for volatility, the result being the implied volatility.

Implied volatility was of course a percentage. And that, by itself, doesn't always tell investors what they really need to know, such as the implied trading range of the stock and the period. The straddle and combination help us put implied volatility into perspective.

The straddle and combination are really volatility trades. If we're buying a straddle or combination, we're not concerned about market direction, only about the underlying stock moving dramatically. If we're selling the straddle or combination, then we want the stock to remain within the trading bands defined by the option premiums.

Which takes us to the next step in this discussion. If we are willing to buy the six-month straddle on XYZ, then by definition we are saying that the option premiums are understating volatility. In other words, the XYZ options are underpriced.

On the other hand, if we are willing to sell the six-month straddle on XYZ, we are by definition saying that the option premiums are overstating volatility. In other words, the XYZ options are overpriced.

Whether you ever trade a combination or straddle, it can be a useful tool in defining whether the options you are looking at are overpriced or underpriced. And that will have an impact on the type of strategy we will use with our aggressive trades.

We would most likely look at option writing strategies if we thought premiums were overstating volatility. We would tend to look at option-buying strategies if we thought premiums were understating future volatility.

For example, if we were bullish on the prospects for XYZ, but felt that the options were overstating volatility, we would look at bullish strategies where we could write the options and collect the premium. We could look at covered writing and naked put writing as two potential strategies.

If we were bullish on the prospects for XYZ and believed, based on the implied trading range, that the options were understating volatility—i.e., the stock could breach either end of the trading range before the option expired—we would look at bullish option buying strategies. In this case, we could buy calls or buy the stock plus a put.

CONCLUSION

You now have an overview of some basic option strategies. Whether bullish, bearish or neutral, there is an option strategy that fits your view on the underlying stock. The neutral strategies help us define whether the option is over- or underpriced, and that helps us choose the strategy that makes the most sense given a particular view about the underlying security.

In this chapter, we made liberal use of examples, emphasizing our fictitious XYZ stock. Of course, most of the basic option strategies work equally well with indices. And in most cases we can use LEAPs (discussed in Chapter Three) as a longer-term option substitute.

5

TECHNICAL ANALYSIS AND THE AGGRESSIVE INVESTOR

Is a picture really worth a thousand words? Technical analysts think so. And so, too, should aggressive investors, the picture in this case being the chart patterns of specific stocks and indices.

When you think about it, there are two basic ways to analyze stocks and the stock market. You can follow a fundamental approach, poring over financial statements and assessing growth prospects, formulating a top-down analysis of the economy, trying to ascertain which sectors should do well based on that analysis, and then getting down to stock picking.

This is not a bad approach for the long-term investor, who does not shift gears frequently. In fact, aggressive investors should have at least one ear to the tracks listening for any oncoming trains. Fundamental analysis makes for good background information, and you should do it before entering any aggressive trading strategy. You don't want to take an aggressively bullish short-term stance on a stock or the stock market if the company has no good long-term prospects or if the stock market is about to get hit with a hike in interest rates.

The problem with using fundamental techniques as an analytical approach comes down to timing. For the most part, information gleaned through fundamental analysis seeks to make judgments about earnings one, two and three years hence. Over any three-year period, aggressive investors could be in and out of a position 40 times.

Because of the shorter-term focus of aggressive investment strategies, technical analysis is a more useful analytical tool from a number of perspectives. It allows you to define the primary trend—i.e., up or down—and to spot when that trend is about to change. The use of trend lines and moving averages can be particularly helpful in determining trends, and those are tools of the technician.

Trend lines can also be useful tools when attempting to establish short-term trading ranges for the underlying security. The trading range is defined by support and resistance points.

And for good measure, we'll add some of our own unique tools to the process, something to overlay on the traditional high-low-close chart. Specifically we'll add trading bands that are defined by the options market. Within those trading bands we define four sectors. Within each sector we define an optimum option strategy, based on our view about the underlying market. We'll even show you how to gather this information on the World Wide Web, through my association with E-trade Canada. Together in one place you'll find all the tools necessary to help you trade aggressively and successfully.

But we're a little ahead of ourselves. We first need to explain how the tools work and then how to apply them. Let's crawl before we walk before we run.

READING THE PAST TO PREDICT THE FUTURE

Charts allow us to display the ebb and flow of the financial markets. They paint a nice picture, but tell us very little about where the market is going. For charts to add value, we need to translate chart patterns into some meaningful information about the future. We do that by taking pages from history—pages and pages of charts, that is—working on the assumption that past patterns tend to repeat themselves. They don't always do this precisely, mind you, but within reasonable limits.

No one ever said that technical analysis was an exact science. In fact, most would concede that it is more art than science. This is why technicians spend so much time trying to confirm their findings with other tools, like confirming a movement in the Dow Industrial Average with a move in the Dow Transportation Average, confirmed again by the trend in the broader market, confirmed again by the advance/decline line, confirmed again by the number of new highs versus the number of new lows—and the beat goes on. It goes on to the point where some nonbelievers suggest that, by the time you get a confirmed signal to actually do something, the move has already taken place.

So much for the technical preamble. Let's assume that great technicians can tell you that this or that chart pattern usually leads to this or that result. Let's also concede that great technicians are about as hard to find as the holy grail, a needle in a haystack, or a stockbroker who doesn't like to trade. But that's okay. To be an aggressive investor, using the aggressive trading strategies discussed in this book, you don't need to be a great technician or even an average technician. Just understand the basics, and apply the discipline. We'll teach you both.

HOW NOW DOW THEORY?

The granddaddy of technical analysis was Charles Dow, the man who began the *Customers' Afternoon Letter*, later renamed the *Wall Street Journal*; the man who began the Dow averages, dating back to 1884; the man who introduced Dow theory and demonstrated how one could use it with the Dow averages.

The first Dow average included 11 stocks, nine of which were railroad companies, a good starting point, since most of the blue-chip companies of the late 1880s were railroads. That original average, by the way, eventually became the Dow Transportation Average.

The Dow Industrial Average debuted in 1896, some 12 years later. The original Dow Industrial Average included 12 smokestack stocks, the industrial and manufacturing companies of the day.

Armed with an industrial and a transportation average, Charles Dow went to work explaining his theory, which he later published in a series of *Wall Street Journal* articles between 1900 and 1902.

At that time, Dow was using the averages to help him forecast the business climate—a sort of capitalist sermon from the mount. Today, Dow theory is used to forecast the direction of the stock market—a sort of multimedia presentation on how to read the wiggles and squiggles within a chart pattern.

There are six basic tenets underlying the Dow theory. The first says that the averages discount everything. That's a reasonable proposition, which has, in fact, gained widespread support from the academic community. Effectively, we are saying that a stock's price or the value of the stock market index reflects everything that is known (i.e., all relevant public information) about the company, the market, and by extension the economy.

That's a reasonable tenet, when you consider that any new information is evaluated quickly and assimilated into the stock's price or the market's value. If you question that position, consider how quickly a stock's price reacts to a poor earnings release or how quickly the market can fall when hit by an unexpected rise in interest rates or, as happened in October 1997, after coming in contact with the Asian flu.

Taking that view to the macro level, it stands to reason that all relevant information about the economy is priced into an index. The market averages reflect and discount all known inputs. They represent the cumulative view of all active stock market participants, which makes for an interesting academic exercise.

But before we get caught up in the notion that professors at Harvard or MIT are embracing technical analysis as a formula for successful investing, think again. Aside from the discounting mechanism of the market, academics and technicians have very little else in common. Most academics believe that you cannot use information that has been discounted by the market to forecast the future direction of the market. Technicians believe you can.

The second tenet in the Dow theory says that the stock market is made up of three basic trends: a primary trend, a secondary trend, and a tertiary trend. The latter reflects daily fluctuations in the index, which for the most part are considered noise.

The primary trend is either bullish or bearish and usually prevails for at least 12 months, but can last several years. The current bull market is an example of a multiyear primary trend.

Primary trends are defined by specific chart patterns. With a bullish pattern, successive highs and lows are higher than previous highs or lows. In a bearish pattern, the market records progressively lower highs and lower lows. Technicians constantly seek to pick up on changes in the primary trend.

Secondary trends are considered short-term corrections. Usually lasting from one to three months, these secondary trends frequently retrace between one-third and two-thirds of the previous move. To put that in perspective, let's assume the market rises 300 points as part of the primary trend. A secondary corrective trend might see the average fall between 100 (one-third) and 200 (two-thirds) points. If that were the extent of the correction, it would be considered, well, a correction, not a change in the primary trend. Anything more than a 66% retracement, and technicians begin to seek out confirming signals.

Tertiary trends can last from one day to three weeks. Think of them as a trading range. They're not of much use as a forecasting tool. Basically, technicians operate on the premise that stock prices can be susceptible to short-term manipulation, which tells us nothing about the trend. Fortunately, such manipulation cannot be sustained over longer periods, and the primary trend will eventually assert itself.

The next tenet states that primary trends have three distinct subphases. The initial phase of a primary trend is believed to include aggressive buying by so-called informed investors, those who are buying in anticipation of an economic turnaround, positive news about a company, a favorable earnings report. This is based not necessarily on inside information, but rather a top-down assessment by informed investors about the health of the economy and the impact that will have on a company's earnings. (This is how fundamental analysis relates to technical analysis.)

In the second phase, corporate earnings will increase while the overall economic picture improves. An increasing number of investors participate at this point. The market improves, and prices rise.

In the third phase we often see record corporate earnings and excellent economic conditions. Sound familiar?—anxiety-free investing, as individual investors enter the market and trade with no fear. Unrealistic expectations underpin this surge in buying, which can be a dangerous time for investors. But this is also a phase which can last for long periods.

The fourth tenet says that the Dow averages must confirm each other. (We had to bring the averages in at some point.) The idea that the Dow Transportation Average must confirm a move in the Dow Industrial Average is also grounded in some fundamental logic. If the economy begins to slow, then orders for manufactured goods will start to drop off. The industrial companies that would fill those orders make fewer shipments, which ultimately affects the transportation companies.

The impact on the transportation sector is felt a little later in the business cycle, but it is felt nonetheless. If transportation stocks begin to lose value at the same time as the industrials, then investors believe the slowdown is real, and the impact may be felt for some time to come. A change in the primary trend?

Conversely, if orders begin to pick up, industrial companies have to order more trucks ands railroad cars, to transport the goods. If the stock of industrial companies begins to rise, we look for a confirmation from the transportation sector—i.e., higher prices for transportation stocks. And the primary trend may again change.

To summarize the fourth tenet, if the industrial average fell to a new low, we would look to see if the transportation average also fell to a new low. Similarly with new highs—always, looking for one to confirm the other.

Next comes volume. Although Dow theory relies on price action first and volume second, the activity during any trading day is certainly important. Volume is particularly useful in confirming uncertain situations (as if there were any certainty in the financial markets). Look for high and expanding volume during a primary trend: new highs on high volume, new lows on high volume. When the Dow averages make a new high on low volume, or a new low on low volume, then the move is suspect.

The sixth and final tenet—at least for now—states that a trend remains in place until the technician receives a definitive reversal signal. To reverse a bullish primary trend that includes higher highs and higher lows, we need to see at least one lower high and one lower low.

Similarly, with a downtrend, lower lows and lower highs are the norms. The trend reverses only when the market sees at least one higher high and one higher low, preferably on high volume. If a primary trend reversal is signaled in both the Industrial and Transportation Averages (i.e., both confirm the same price action), it is highly likely that a new trend is now in place.

Like it or not, the Dow theory is the first coherent western technical analytical theory. Nothing before or since has had such a profound influence on technical analysis as has Dow theory. It is important to understand, because virtually all technical tools are grounded in some way in the Dow theory.

THE TREND IS YOUR FRIEND

We know Dow theory holds that there are three trends: primary, secondary and tertiary. We also know that a trend is in effect until a definitive change in trend has been registered. The primary trend defines the long-term bias; secondary trends are corrective phases that retrace from 33% to 66% of the primary trend; tertiary trends are noise.

Now let's put some of that theory to work. Suppose XYZ stock went from $10 per share to $16 per share over a six-month period. If the stock peaked at $16 and then fell back to, say, $12 per share, it would have retraced $4 of the initial (i.e., primary) $6 move to the upside. The $4 retracement represents 66% of the initial move to the upside. If XYZ can hold support at $12, we assume the primary trend remains intact and the $4 correction, while painful, is simply a secondary correction within a primary trend.

If the stock continues to fall below the $12 per share price—i.e., more than a 66% retracement—then the technical analyst might see that as a reversal of the primary trend, particularly if the move was confirmed by higher volume. That would then define a change in the primary trend and the beginning of a new primary trend.

So in the very preliminary stages of this discussion, a retracement of more than 66% of the initial move to the upside is a dangerous signal, whereas a retracement of anywhere from 33% to 66% is actually healthy and, presumably, lays the foundation to move to even higher prices.

In Figure 5.1, the rise from point A to point B, over a period of six months, represents the primary trend. The decline from point B to point C, over, say, a period of three months, represents the secondary trend. Assuming XYZ stock can hold support at point C, then the stock will begin another primary trend from point C to point D. And the cycle continues.

FIGURE 5.1

CONTINUATION OF THE PRIMARY TREND

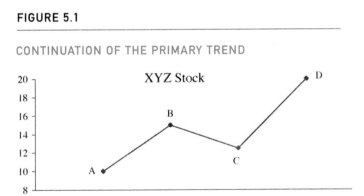

Figure 5.2 looks at the same concept, only using Dell Computer as a real-life example. Note how the stock began to rise in December 1997. Once the stock broke through $45 per share, you can see that it retraced more than 66% of the previous downtrend from the peak in mid-October 1997 to a bottom in early November 1997. When the stock finally broke $45 per share in January 1998, it had established a new primary trend to the upside. That trend continued to a peak in mid-May 1998. The stock has begun to retrace some of its move from the $45 to its high $98 1/2. That's a $53 1/2-point increase in the stock's price in less than five months.

With the stock at $83 1/2 (price at the far right), it has retraced 15 points of the 53 1/2-point increase, clearly not enough to change the primary trend.

FIGURE 5.2

DELL COMPUTER

Source: www.bigcharts.com

THE GENERAL AND THE ARMY

Obviously a change in the primary trend can have a significant impact on your investment portfolio. Your investment philosophy must change. But turning from a bull to a bear or vice versa is not an easy transition. If you do make a major transition and find you are wrong, you can be whipsawed. You go from a bull to a bear. You sell stock and raise cash, because the primary trend changed. Or so you thought. It turns out you were wrong, and now you have to buy back your stock at higher prices. Whipsaws like that have been known to cost portfolio managers their jobs.

Before technicians are willing to declare a change in the primary trend, they make every effort to confirm their findings. You want to make certain that the signals you are reading are correct.

Martin J. Pring addressed the issue of trend reversals and how one goes about confirming them in his book *Technical Analysis Explained*. As one confirming signal, Pring writes, "Generally speaking, the fewer the number of issues that are moving in the direction of the major averages, the greater the probability of an imminent reversal in trend." The troops following—or not following—the General theory.

The General in this case is the Dow Industrial Average. That's the bluest of blue-chip stocks traded on U.S. stock markets. The big names in industry. If they're moving higher, that's good. It's not so good if the big-cap stocks—as in the Generals—are moving higher, but the rest of the market—i.e., the troops—are not following.

The key is to make sure the army (i.e., the overall stock market) stays in step with the General (the Dow Industrial Average). When both are moving in the same direction, that confirms the current trend. On the other hand, if there is divergence between the Dow and the rest of the market, technicians get concerned about the validity of the trend.

Technicians use a couple of approaches to confirm whether the troops are following the lead of the Generals. We refer to this as measuring the breadth of the market. Breadth is simply a measure of stocks rising versus stocks declining over a given period. For example, if the Dow Industrial Average rises 50 points today, with 1,250 stocks rising, 1,000 stocks declining and 500 stocks unchanged on the day, that's a pretty good sign.

You would not want to see the Dow Industrial Average up, say, 100 points, with only 1,000 stocks advancing, 1,250 declining and 500 unchanged. That's called a divergence, which simply means that the Dow is going one way and the rest of the market is not really following.

The most common indicator to measure breadth is the advance/decline (A/D) line. The A/D line tracks the number of stocks advancing vs. the number of stocks declining over a given period. The technician is really interested in the cumulative affect on the A/D line rather than any particular movement on any given day.

When more stocks are rising than falling, the number of stocks moving up is added to the previous total; conversely, when more stocks are declining than are rising that difference is subtracted from the previous total. What you want to see is the A/D line rising when the Dow Industrial Average is rising.

In Figure 5.3, we have a two-year chart of the Dow Industrial Average. The A/D line is the thinner line on the chart. Note that the A/D line was rising along with the Dow Industrial Average from early January 1998 to the early part of April 1998. At that point, however, the A/D line began to fall, even while the Dow Industrial Average was still rising—in fact, moving to a new record high. The point, however, was that, in this case, the troops were not following the General.

Another way to measure breadth is to track the number of stocks making new 52-week highs vs. the number of stocks making new 52-week lows. When, say, the Dow Jones Industrial Average hits a low (in this case we mean a low within the context of the most recent move, not an all-time low) while the number of individual stocks making new lows stays the same, a turnaround may be imminent.

Conversely, when a market index like the Dow Industrial Average is rising without a corresponding rise in the number of new highs, a correction may be looming. For the record, technicians believe that the measure of new 52-week highs to new 52-week lows cannot be viewed in a vacuum but on a relative basis— relative in this case to recent levels. What we're really saying is to look for confirmations and be aware of potential divergences.

FIGURE 5.3

DOW INDUSTRIAL AVERAGE WITH ADVANCE/DECLINE LINE

Source: www.bigcharts.com

RELATIVE STRENGTH

One final technical tool (this is by no means an exhaustive discussion on the subject) is relative strength, which measures how an individual stock is performing relative to the overall market. Technicians believe that changes in a stock's relative strength tend to precede changes in the stock's trend.

Relative strength is easy to calculate: It is simply the price of the stock divided by the price of a market index. If, for example, you wanted to compare the performance of Dell Computer with the Dow Industrial Average, you would simply divide the closing price of Dell by the closing value for the Dow. The technician tracks the stock's relative strength over a period, looking for a divergence between the current stock price and its relative strength rating.

If relative strength is rising, it shows that the stock is outperforming the market over time. When relative strength is declining, it means the stock is underperforming the market index. Most technicians believe that a stock is most attractive when its relative strength has improved for four months or longer. However, that being said, you have to be careful, as with any technical indicator, not to view results in a vacuum. For example, you should not necessarily buy the stock with the highest relative strength. Stocks that reach the relative strength pinnacle may already have gone too far too fast.

Relative strength also works in a down market. A stock may be declining, yet its relative strength is rising. That is simply evidence that the individual stock is declining less than the market index.

Technicians also use relative strength to identify attractive industry sectors. The idea here is to measure the performance of a specific industry relative to the overall market. In this case, the technician seeks out strong industry sectors, and then proceeds to select individual stocks.

TECHNICAL TOOLS FOR THE AGGRESSIVE INVESTOR

THE TRADING RANGE

One of the keys when trying to pinpoint buy-and-sell decisions is to determine a security's trading range. In that sense, technical analysis can be quite useful. The trading range is defined as the range between the support and resistance points.

In many cases, stocks will go through periods when they seem to be stuck in a range between a high and low price. These stocks will experience huge selling pressure at the top of the range and significant buying support at the bottom of the range. In such instances, you should take notice when a stock regularly moves say, between 20 and 30. In that case, you might consider buying at 20 and selling at 30, or more likely buying in the low 20s and selling in the high 20s.

In these types of situations, stocks tend to remain in a trading range for some time, and that can be quite healthy. The longer the stock remains in a trading range, the stronger will be the price move when it breaks free of that trading range. When a stock breaks through to the upside—the upside being $30 on our example—then that resistance point now becomes the support price.

For example, if the stock broke above 30 and then rallied to, say, 35, the new support would be at 30. You would be concerned if the stock began falling and broke through the 30 support level. Breaking support in this type of pattern would be considered a serious setback.

SUPPORT AND RESISTANCE

At this point we should define support and resistance. When we talk about support and resistance, we are referring to price points at which the security or index changes direction. Support defines a point at which the price of the stock or index stops declining and resumes its upward trend. At that price there are more buyers than sellers.

Resistance defines the point at which the security or index stops rising and begins to fall, usually the result of there being more sellers than buyers. Technicians put a lot of emphasis on the point at which a security or index breaks through upside resistance or fails to hold downside support. Generally when that happens, it signals a change in direction.

Again in the case of XYZ stock, suppose that it fell below $10, which represents more than a 66% retracement from the previous high. Technical analysts would see that as a breaking of the support line, which could lead to a trend reversal, ultimately leading to still lower prices (see Figure 5.4). I, on the other hand, see that as an opportunity for the aggressive investor.

FIGURE 5.4

BREAKING THE TRENDLINE

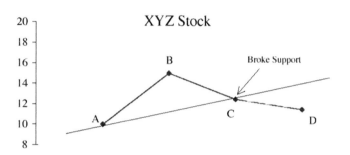

Note that the secondary trend continued beyond point C where the stock should have received buying support. By breaking through that support level, the price continued to decline to point D.

Now for the 64-dollar question: At what point would XYZ now be expected to find support? If you said zero, you might be right, depending of course, on the fundamentals for the company. Logically, though, the next support point would be $10 per share, which in this case is the point where the primary trend began.

The third basic element of technical analysis is the tertiary trends, defined as the day-to-day movements in the price of the stock. Most technicians see that as noise in the market, and don't attach much value to those moves in determining the current trend or changes to the current trend.

TRENDLINES

The charts we have viewed so far are all high-low-close charts. A high-low-close chart simply defines the range of price movement for the underlying stock or index during the course of trading on any given day. The top of the line represents the highest price traded on a given day; the bottom of the line represents the lowest point for the day, and the tick mark on the high-low line represents the price at which the stock or index closed. The volume is shown on the lower part of the chart.

Technicians draw lines on the high-low-close chart to depict the current trend. Referred to as trendlines, they connect the price points along the trend. In an upward-moving chart pattern, the trendline provides a quick and dirty support line.

An example of an upward-sloping chart pattern can be seen in Figure 5.5, where the trendline is defined as the line connecting the low points on a two-year chart ending June 1998 for the Dow Industrial Average.

FIGURE 5.5

DOW JONES INDUSTRIAL AVERAGE + TRENDLINE

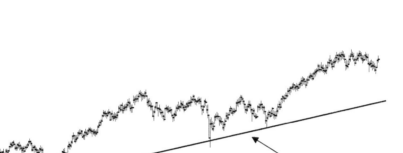

January 1997–June 1998

Similarly, a trendline can be used to connect the high points of a stock price or index value, when the primary trend is down. In this case, the trendline would basically reflect points of resistance, through which the stock would have a difficult time breaking. Figure 5.6 shows an example of a trendline that defines resistance points for Philip Morris stock.

The objective is to look for price points that present an opportunity to move into or out of a stock. If, in the case of Philip Morris, the trendline were to break through the $40 resistance level—especially on high volume—that might signal a change in the primary trend, in which case it could move substantially higher before it met new resistance. The next price level that should provide serious resistance would be the two peaks on the chart about halfway between the $45 and $50 price points.

Generally speaking, when a stock breaks through a resistance point it presents a buying opportunity. Similarly, a sell signal is registered if a stock breaks through a support level.

FIGURE 5.6

PHILIP MORRIS + TRENDLINE

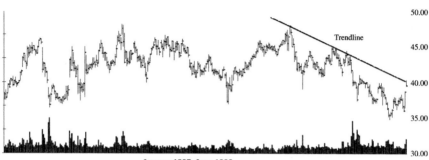

January 1997–June 1998

THE POSSIBILITIES AND THE PITFALLS

As with any aspect of security analysis, you can find chart patterns that have followed the script to the letter when breaking either support or resistance. You can also find just as many charts where the stock price has not done what you might have expected given a particular pattern.

Some points to consider: If you buy a stock that rises in price and then changes direction, the trendline can provide a snapshot of where you should expect to find some buying support. That can add a measure of comfort to your stock position, since you at least have some idea of what to look for.

The trendline that defines the stock's resistance can also be useful as a tool to establish a price at which you might consider selling the stock, assuming you purchased it at much lower prices. For example, if you buy Philip Morris at $40 per share and you believe the stock will meet significant resistance at $47.50 per share, that is what you would use as your selling price.

MOVING AVERAGES

Another way of evaluating a trend—aside from connecting the dots on a chart—is through the use of a moving average. The moving average, as the name suggests, is an average of a stock's price over a period. The notion that the average moves simply reflects the fact that stock prices change daily.

If you were to calculate a 10-day moving average for XYZ stock, you would begin with the closing prices of the previous 10 days, add them together and divide by 10. On day 10, as seen in Table 5.1, the average of the previous 10-day closing prices was $10.49. On day 11, the 10-day moving average rises to $10.61. That's because, in the calculation of the average, we added the closing price from day 11 (i.e., $11.25) and dropped the closing price from day 1 (i.e., $10). Hence the name moving average.

TABLE 5.1

CALCULATING THE MOVING AVERAGE

DAY	DAILY PRICE	MOVING AVERAGE
1	10.00	
2	9.50	
3	9.75	
4	10.00	
5	10.50	
6	10.75	
7	11.00	
8	11.25	
9	11.00	
10	11.13	10.49
11	11.25	10.61
12	11.38	10.80
13	11.50	10.98
14	11.25	11.10
15	11.50	11.20

There are almost as many moving averages as there are stocks to watch. The 200-day moving average is one of the more common measures used by technicians. It is thought to define the long-term trend in the underlying stock and to be most representative of the primary trend. Figure 5.7 is the same chart as Figure 5.5, except in this case we have replaced the trendline we drew with a 200-day moving average.

In theory, if the index or a specific stock whose primary trend is up breaks downward through the 200-day moving average, it is said to have broken support. Similarly, if an index or stock in a primary downtrend breaks upward above the 200-day moving average, it is said to have broken through resistance. Presumably, a breakthrough in the 200-day moving average means a change in the primary trend, especially if the breakout comes on heavy volume.

But theory doesn't always translate into reality. Note from Figure 5.7 where the Dow Industrial Average broke through the 200-day moving average in October 1997.

FIGURE 5.7

DOW JONES INDUSTRIAL AVERAGE + 200-DAY MOVING
AVERAGE

Source: www.bigcharts.com

That was the day when the Dow Industrial Average declined by 554 points. For the record, the 200-day moving average is really a 142-trading-day moving average representing the number of trading days in the previous 200 calendar days.

Note also the spike in volume on that day: The Dow broke the 200-day moving average, and it was confirmed with high volume. So we have a confirmed breakout to the downside, a change in the primary trend. But as has happened so often with the great bull market of the 1990s, the October collapse turned out to be a correction in the primary trend. It snapped back the next day in breathtaking fashion. This supports the view that theory doesn't always work in reality.

For short-term trendlines, technical analysts will simply use shorter moving averages. We will focus on two specific moving averages: the 10-day moving average for our index trades and the 50-day moving average, which we will use for our option-strategy matrix. For the record, both the 10- and 50-day moving averages are based on actual trading days, not calendar days.

Because the moving average trails the actual daily price changes in the stock, shorter-term moving averages tend to be more volatile. This means that the underlying stock or index will break the moving average more frequently, presumably creating more trading opportunities and, if we have done our homework, more profit potential. Figure 5.8 shows the Dow Industrial Average together with a

50-day moving average. Note that it broke the 50-day moving average in mid-October, well before the October 1997 sell-off.

FIGURE 5.8

DOW INDUSTRIAL AVERAGE + 50-DAY MOVING AVERAGE

Source: *www.bigcharts.com*

SENTIMENT INDICATORS

With the need to confirm signals, it is not surprising that technicians rely on a number of sentiment indicators to judge the mood of the market. There are a number of such indicators: the breadth, which we already talked about, along with daily new highs and new lows.

I find particularly interesting the *Elves Index* made famous by Louis Rukeyser of *Wall Street Week,* one of the most-watched shows on public television. Mr. Rukeyser refers to technicians as elves, and his Elves Index is made up of 10 technicians who regularly appear on his show. Each week he asks each of the 10 technicians for their short-term view on the market: bullish, bearish or neutral.

The index simply reflects the consensus of the 10 technicians. If there are five bulls, three bears and two neutrals, then the index is a +2. Aside from its entertainment value, it does rate the mood of senior technicians. I'm not sure how investors should treat the results—whether they should view it as a contrarian index, which means that investors would do the opposite of what the majority are suggesting, or whether they should follow the consensus and trade with the majority. Fortunately for our work as aggressive investors, it doesn't matter.

There are two sentiment indicators that we will use with our index-trading strategies. The first is the so-called put-call ratio. The second is the volatility index.

THE PUT-CALL RATIO

The put-call ratio is simply the number of puts traded in a day divided by the number of calls traded on the same day. A high ratio indicates that more puts than calls have traded on a specific day. A low ratio means that more calls than puts have traded. To smooth out the day-to-day fluctuations in the ratio, the numbers are smoothed using a moving average. Technicians generally compare the daily put-call ratio with some moving average. The idea is to look for extremes in the measure.

There are two widely followed put-call ratios. The first is the put-call ratio on the S&P 100 index options (symbol OEX). The OEX is the most active index option contract. On any given day, trading in the OEX equals half the trading volume on the CBOE. Because the OEX is so popular among option traders, it provides a good proxy for the mood of the market, particularly the mood among individual option traders.

The second is the equity-only put-call ratio. In this case you calculate the put-call ratio on all stock options that trade on a given day on the CBOE. There is no running total for equity-only volume. We need to take the total put and call volume and subtract the index call and put volume, to arrive at the equity-only volume.

You don't need to subtract the put and call volume from all the index options, only the most active. The most active are the OEX, the S&P 500 index, the NASDAQ 100 index and the Dow Industrial Average. Options on all four of these indices trade on the CBOE.

Technicians use the put-call ratio as a contrarian indicator. Believing that, when too many investors are bearish and buying puts, the market is about to bottom. Similarly, when too many individual traders are bullish and buying calls, the market is about to make a short- to medium-term top. The OEX is particularly useful, because many technicians believe that individual investors most frequently use this index. It is generally believed that institutional investors, who presumably are professional investors, trade the options on the S&P 500 composite index.

The idea is to buy the market if the put-call ratio gets too high and short the market if the put-call ratio gets too low. The question is, How high is too high and how low is too low? That's where the moving averages can help. The idea here is to smooth out the daily put-call ratio with, say, a 10-day moving average. Too high is when the put-call ratio is twice the 10-day moving average; too low is when the put-call ratio is half the 10-day moving average.

The put-call ratio is an excellent tool to help gauge the mood of investors. However, it is widely followed and, because of that, isn't as accurate a forecasting tool as it once was. However, when we confirm the index put-call ratio with, say, the equity-only put-call ratio and some other tools we will demonstrate, the results can be quite good. Not perfect, but not bad either. We'll show you how to use the put-call ratio in conjunction with other aggressive investing tools when we look at index options in Chapter Nine.

THE VOLATILITY INDEX

The volatility index (symbol VIX, available from the CBOE) tracks the implied volatility on the OEX options.

The VIX debuted in January 1993. Even with its limited history, the VIX has been a useful tool for option traders attempting to gain an edge on stock-market activity. It is generally believed that the VIX is a contrarian indicator: When the index is trending higher—meaning higher option premiums—investors are paying more to buy options in the belief that the market is about ready to make a significant move. But, as often happens, the market does just the opposite of what individual investors anticipate. When option premiums reach the high end of a range, the market will often settle into a narrow trading range, meaning that it would have been a good time to write options and not a good time to buy options.

Conversely, option premiums usually trend lower when the market has been stuck in a relatively narrow trading range. When the VIX reaches the low end of a range, that often precedes a market explosion. The problem, of course, is that the VIX only helps us ascertain when an explosive move is likely to occur. It doesn't usually tell us anything about direction.

On the other hand, there have been times when the VIX can be very useful in picking the direction of the market. Note, for example, from Figure 5.9 the spike on the VIX in October 1997. That spike occurred on the day the stock market fell 554 Dow points.

Remember Figure 5.7, where we saw the Dow Industrial Average break the 200-day moving average on the same day in October 1997? It was a classic example of the market breaking a primary trend on heavy volume, which would normally translate into a new primary trend. Of course, the market bounced back the next day and resumed its upward trend, an example of technical analysis falling down.

This is what makes the VIX numbers so interesting. Generally when the VIX spikes up and then quickly retreats, it is a sign that the market has bottomed and will soon turn around. In this case, the VIX predicted the market bottom and provided a counter position to the crossing of the 200-day moving average.

The VIX is useful as a tool to gauge the general level of option premiums. It can also be useful in selecting the right option strategy. As a rule of thumb, when the VIX is rising, that tends to precede a period of market stability, making option-writing strategies attractive. When the VIX falls to an extremely low level—meaning option premiums have contracted—that often precedes a sharp explosive move in the stock market, either up or down. Option-buying strategies now make more sense. And finally, when the VIX spikes up and then quickly retreats, that is often a sign of a market bottom.

FIGURE 5.9

OEX DAILY CHART AND VIX DAILY

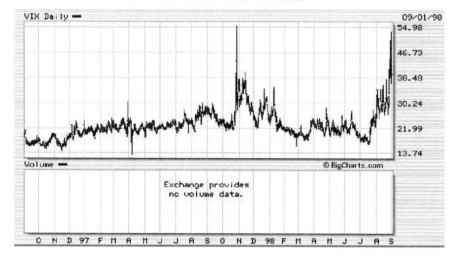

Source: *www.bigcharts.com*

BRINGING VOLATILITY INTO THE EQUATION

In Chapter One we introduced the concept of standard deviation and volatility. Early on, we wanted to focus on this subject. I view volatility as the amount the underlying security is likely to move around a trend (unlike other observers, who define volatility as the degree the underlying security is likely to move about its current price). This is a subtle difference, perhaps, but an important distinction for the aggressive investor.

Let's assume that XYZ is trading at $100 per share and has a historical volatility of 10%. On a go-forward basis, most observers would say there is a 66% probability that XYZ will trade within one standard deviation of its current price over the next year. Remember, we are using the one-year historical number. That means that XYZ could trade as high as $110 (100 × 1.10) or as low as $90.90 (100/1.10) over the next year.

There is a 95% probability that XYZ will trade within two standard deviations of the current price over the next year—twice the trading range, which equals $120 (100 × 1.20) on the upside and approximately $83.33 (100/1.20) on the downside. Note the bias to the upside. But also note that the upward bias in no way reflects the position that a stock is more likely to rise than fall. Rather, it reflects the fact that a stock cannot fall below zero but could rise to infinity. The point is, to most observers, the volatility assumption provides us with a trading range about the current price. I don't think that is of much use to the aggressive investor.

I think it is more useful if we use volatility to provide us with a trading range about a trend. Back to the XYZ example. We know the current price is $100 per share. Let's assume the stock is in a primary uptrend and the 50-day moving average is $95 per share.

Using the same 10% volatility assumption, a one-standard-deviation trading range about the 50-day moving average becomes $104.50 ($95 × 1.10) and $86.36 ($95/1.10). The two-standard-deviation trading range is then $114 ($95 × 1.20) and $79.17 ($95/1.20). The difference in the trading ranges is attributable to how one selects the midpoint. Rather than using the current price, we use the trendline, which we define as the 50-day moving average.

IMPLIED VOLATILITY VERSUS HISTORICAL VOLATILITY

Note that in the previous example we used the stock's historical volatility. This is all right if we simply want to frame a set of trading limits based on a 50-day moving average. But for the aggressive investor we need more information.

Aggressive investors will use leveraged instruments to play their view on the underlying stock, the tool of choice being options. Because volatility is one of the major components used to value an option, our discussion around this subject takes on an extra measure of importance—even more so, when you consider that volatility is the only component in the option-pricing formula that must be estimated. It is the unknown. At the end of the day, then, the cost of an option reflects the market's view of how volatile the underlying stock or index is expected to be between now and when the option expires.

The cost of the option and what that option says about the volatility estimates for the underlying security provide the backdrop that allows us to select the most appropriate option strategy for each aggressive trading situation. (For more information on what I mean by that, see the option matrix at the end of this chapter.)

For now, let's accept the position that the option's price reflects the market's assessment of the underlying security's likely volatility. Instead of using historical volatility to establish trading bands that represent one and two standard deviations about the trend, we will use implied volatility—the volatility assumption that is factored into the option's price. You should think of the bands as an *implied trading range.*

Implied volatility, like historical volatility, is annualized. In other words, if the volatility implied by options on the Dow Industrial Average was 18%, that reflects a potential trading range over the next year. And we know that a year represents approximately 252 trading days.

Options on all three Dow averages trade on the CBOE. As of June 1998, the volatility implied by the Dow Industrial options was 18%. Investors can calculate implied volatility using an option calculator available on the CBOE web site.

If we want to translate the annual volatility number into a more useful trading range, we need to adjust it to the period in question. And since we are using the 50-day moving average as our midpoint, I am most interested in calculating a 50-day implied trading range. We do that by multiplying the annual volatility by the square root of time:

$$18\% \times \sqrt{\frac{50}{252}} = 8.01\%$$

Almost done. We now know that the one-standard-deviation band will be 8.01% above and below the 50-day moving average. Figure 5.10 looks at the daily high-low-close on the Dow Industrial Average plus the 50-day moving average. We then transpose the trading bands about the moving average, the outer bands representing one standard deviation about the trend.

FIGURE 5.10

DOW JONES INDUSTRIAL AVERAGE + TRADING BANDS

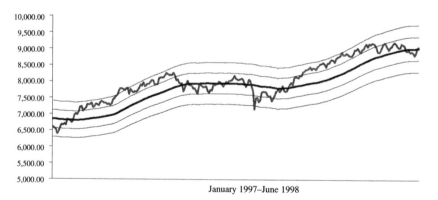

January 1997–June 1998

The trading bands provide us with a lot of information. We are establishing the bands on the basis of how volatile the market believes the underlying security will likely be over the next 50 days. We can expect about 66% of the time that the Dow Industrial Average will most likely remain within the limits of its implied trading range over the next 50 days. But that only gives us a reasonable expectation. We haven't yet found out how to make any money with this information. Which leads us directly into the Option Strategy Matrix.

THE OPTION STRATEGY MATRIX

We know that the four bands about the 50-day moving average represent a reasonable 50-day implied trading range. We can look at those bands as four specific sectors numbered, as you might expect, one through four. Sector one represents the lower quadrant, one standard deviation below the 50-day moving average, and sector four represents the upper quadrant, one standard deviation above the 50-day moving average.

Because we are using implied volatility to establish the implied trading range, we are by definition factoring into the selection process the cost of the option. Which means that if the underlying security or index is in the first sector, then specific option strategies make the most sense, depending on your view of the underlying security. The option strategy matrix simply helps us ascertain the best option strategy within each sector.

Table 5.2 defines the specific option strategies for each of the four sectors.

TABLE 5.2

OPTION STRATEGY MATRIX

SECTOR ONE	SECTOR TWO	SECTOR THREE	SECTOR FOUR
Buy Calls	Bull Pit Spread	Dollar Cost Averaging Option	Buy Puts
Bull Put Spread	Dollar Cost Averaging Option	The Event Spread	Bear Call Spreads
The Event Spread	The Event Spread		
Falling for Dollars			

Based on the information from Table 5.2, option-buying strategies are good choices when in sector one. So too are covered-call-writing strategies (note the Falling for Dollars strategy is a covered write) and option-spread strategies. Note that in no case would I ever recommend that readers use uncovered option positions. The risks are too great and, for each of our aggressive investing strategies, we want to make certain that we limit our risks. Spread strategies allow us to maintain a tight rein on the risk aspects of the portfolio.

CONCLUSION

This chapter is in no way meant to be an exhaustive look at technical analysis. At best, we have only scratched the surface. It is important that you simply understand the basics of technical analysis and gain some experience with the concept of an implied trading range. We will be using the material from this chapter to lay the foundation for each of our aggressive investments that begin in the next section.

So we have now come from a crawl to a walk. Time to begin running.

PART IV
INVESTMENT STRATEGIES FOR THE AGGRESSIVE INVESTOR

6

AGGRESSIVE STRATEGY #1: FALLING FOR DOLLARS

By the title you'd think our first aggressive strategy is one that's designed to profit by going short—selling a stock with the expectation of buying it back at a lower price. That might be your first impression, but simply selling stock short is not what falling for dollars—or aggressive investing—is all about.

As aggressive investors we need to seek out strategies with risk we can define and potential for profit slanted in our favor. More importantly, we need to clearly define a position that provides a reasonable risk–reward trade-off.

Short selling involves a high degree of risk that cannot comfortably be evaluated. For example, a stock can rise to infinity, which obviously is a more theoretical risk than a real-world concern. But in the real world a stock can spike up sharply in the event of a takeover or even on the rumor of a takeover, a risk that can't be quantified mathematically.

Profit potential is also a problem. You can profit if the stock declines. But the odds of the stock declining within an efficient market are about the same as the odds of the stock rising. This means that you have about a 50-50 chance of earning a profit, not good enough for the aggressive investor. Our strategies need to tilt the odds in favor of the aggressive investor. In this respect, short selling falls short.

A COMPANY-SPECIFIC EVENT SELL-OFF

Falling for dollars is a strategy that makes money even if the stock remains within a relatively narrow trading range. The goal is not so much to predict direction but to take advantage of a situation after the market has taken its pound of flesh out of a company. In many cases, these are good large-cap companies, in solid industries, that have just experienced a sharp sell-off for any of a number of company-specific reasons.

When aggressive investors speak about company-specific issues, they're talking about events that can affect a company but may not have an impact on the rest of the market. A rise in fuel costs can negatively affect an airline company, but it may have a positive effect on an oil company. That would be a company-specific event, affecting companies in different industries in very different ways.

A market event is something quite different. It's an event that will affect almost all stocks. For example, if the U.S. Federal Reserve should decide to raise interest rates, that will affect all stocks, especially if a rise in interest rates catches the market off-guard. In that case, we would likely see a major sell-off, and the value of most stocks would fall along with the general trend in the market.

Again, however, this is not the kind of situation that lends itself to the falling-for-dollars strategy. When the stock market falls, it rarely has anything to do with a specific company, but rather is symptomatic of a change in investor psychology. Stocks, like boats on an ocean, rise and fall with the tide. That doesn't mean you couldn't use this strategy during such an event. But normally I prefer to use strategies associated with index options when tracking market-driven events. We'll discuss these in more detail in Chapter Nine.

There are many reasons why a stock might get slammed by the market. Failure to meet the consensus estimate for quarterly earnings is one. In recent years, there has been a trend to announce earnings shortfalls well before the release date, making the actual earnings release anticlimactic.

There are other potential events that can be just as damaging. A drug company might fail to win approval for a new pharmaceutical from the Food and Drug Administration (FDA). Especially if the market were expecting the drug or new treatment to be approved, the company's stock would fall. The anti-trust case against Microsoft is another example, although Microsoft stock has never fallen as much as we might have expected. Tobacco litigation has been a significant event for tobacco companies. When tobacco giants lose a court battle, they lose big-time in the financial markets. Philip Morris, for example, was one of a number of U.S. tobacco companies whose stock was hit hard when courts awarded compensation to long-term smokers.

Company-specific events that produce sharp sell-offs can sometimes open the door to an aggressive trade. Under the right conditions, which I will clearly define, aggressive investors can catch a falling star and put profits in their pocket.

When a stock falls sharply as the result of a company-specific event, a couple of things happen:

> • *The company-specific event that caused the decline grabs headlines at least in most daily financial publications. Assuming it is a relatively well-known company, its stock will be on the most-active list on the day of the decline. The stock will also be one of the biggest*

*movers or—perhaps more appropriately—losers of the day. The point
is, you'll never have a problem finding potential candidates for the
falling-for-dollars trade. And it certainly beats sifting through a
database of stocks to catch the next big move by discovering
something the rest of the market may have overlooked. In this case,
all the information is available, and you do not have to make
judgments in a vacuum.*

• *Management will be quite willing to talk about their company after
having cold water splashed on their corporate face. In fact, after the
decline comes the cleansing process, when management will attempt
to put their best face forward to the media, shareholders, and their
own board of directors. More importantly, management will often be
quite forthright about their short-term problems—assuming they are,
of course, short-term problems—in an attempt to get all the bad news
into the open at the same time. Believing that the market has already
pounded the stock, management will try to air all its dirty corporate
laundry while the stock is down and find some breathing space so the
company can begin the rebuilding process.*

So why should you buy into a company when so many others are running for the
exits?

Using the falling-for-dollars trade, you are not required to forecast an event.
Think about this for a moment. If you're looking at a drug company, isn't it easier to
examine its merits after the FDA has announced a major decision rather than before,
when you don't know what the FDA thinks? If you're looking at a tobacco company,
isn't it easier to assess the company after a jury reaches a decision in a lawsuit for
damages rather than before? Isn't it easier to assess a company after rather than
before it announces its quarterly earnings?

All of us would like to predict the performance of a stock based on our
expectations of a future event or based on some chart pattern. But even
professionals have difficulty with predictions, so how much chance does the
average individual investor have?

With the falling-for-dollars strategy, not only do you avoid making predictions, you
can also find plenty of stocks to choose from. Every day you can find several stocks
that have been slammed by the market. Not all of them will meet our strict criteria for
this particular strategy, but you certainly will have a list to look at every day.

In particular, we should pay attention to management's reaction to a company-
specific, event-driven sell-off. Management's reaction can give us a great deal of
guidance in assessing the merits of a specific trade.

We should determine, for example, that the company has not made a major
change in direction or that the company is not wrestling with an industry-wide

issue, such as the anti-tobacco campaign, that could have long-term implications for the whole industry.

Likewise, I wouldn't buy into a technology company, for example, that failed to meet its quarter because an anticipated big order never materialized. A company's future should not depend on a single big order. Nor would I buy into a drug company whose future depended on FDA approval of a single drug.

All these details become apparent from management's comments after the decline in the share price. You should pay close attention, particularly over the two-week period immediately following the sharp sell-off. Management will usually discuss openly the company's current and long-term condition.

Assuming the company operates in a growth industry, management can often provide interesting insights into why the stock was slammed. During this so-called cleansing process, look for management to disclose other potential short-term problems. Management is entrusted with the interests of shareholders, and such honest appraisals after a company-specific event sell-off will not have as much impact on the stock's price as they would before the decline. That doesn't mean the stock can't continue to fall. But further declines will usually be driven by frustrated investors. They may be angry, but usually they're not selling in a panic. So after a major sell-off, look for more bad news followed by more bad news, and down days followed by more down days.

The trick to this trade is finding the right entry point. Finding the right entry point is obviously more art than science. The best we can hope to do is provide the right tools, show you how to stack the odds in your favor, and then roll the dice, bearing in mind that aggressive investing, while risky, is not a zero-sum game.

SIZE DOES MATTER

Speaking of stacking the odds in your favor, we begin with the underlying company. In the falling-for-dollars trade, size is important. Remember we are talking about a company whose stock price has just been slammed by the market, and there were probably good reasons for the sell-off.

I don't argue with the marketplace. Equity markets are efficient, and a stock's price accurately discounts all relevant public information about a company. But additional information usually becomes available shortly after the stock has fallen, especially if the stock fell because of disappointing earnings. Before I invest, I want to make certain that the company is large enough to withstand detailed investor scrutiny and will eventually recover from its quarterly earnings shortfall.

Smaller companies don't always recover. In fact, most companies that run into further problems after an initial earnings-related meltdown are small-cap companies. After a couple of quarters in which losses are greater than expected, these companies resemble a drowning victim going down for the third time. I'm not interested in aggressively buying into a company that may be going down for the count. I don't like the odds!

To be fair, some of these small companies will recover. And when they do, the turnaround can be dramatic. Some of them make interesting and exciting long-term investments. But we're looking for an aggressive short-term trade, not a long-term roller-coaster ride. The falling-for-dollars trade does not require a stock to make a major turnaround, only that it remain afloat, move up slightly or remain in a narrow trading range. That may not be easy with a small-cap company; with a big-cap company, it's a lot more certain.

So here's one simple rule for applying our falling-for-dollars strategy: Don't buy small-cap companies.

Consider Oracle Corporation. Oracle is a leading developer of database management systems software, which allows many computers on a network to use the same data at the same time. Oracle provides a critical product for today's corporate environment, and it's not likely other companies will displace Oracle anytime soon.

On December 10, 1997, Oracle's share price fell sharply after an earnings shortfall caused by the slowdown in Asia. This was a concern to be sure, but were the problems in Asia likely to bring Oracle to its knees? Possibly, but not likely.

Intel is another example. It fell sharply on March 5, 1998, after a similar story— a pre-announcement of an earnings shortfall related to the slowdown in Asia and a build up in computer inventories. Yet Intel has billions of dollars in cash. Its microprocessors are used in 90% of all desktop PCs. The market cap for Intel is $100 billion, and the company has a profit margin of more than 40%. Its main competitors, Advanced Micro Devices and Cyrix, have margins below 10%. Does it appear that Intel will never recover? Possibly, but not likely.

Both Oracle and Intel operate in the technology sector. The industry in which a company operates is important. You want to see long-term growth potential that can be clearly defined. In the longer term, analysts expect the technology industry to grow at double-digit rates into the next century. Perhaps the demand for high-end computers won't be as strong—which may have a slight impact on Intel—but you still have to like the long-term prospects for the industry. You still have to believe that the computer industry is healthy and will remain vibrant into the foreseeable future.

So Oracle and Intel, as part of the computer industry, will continue to expand over the long term. In some industries, however, the growth prospects are not so clearly defined, and neither is the potential for blue-chip stocks within those industries.

Take Philip Morris, an excellent example of a good company in a troubled industry. Philip Morris is a blue-chip large-cap company, one of the 30 companies in the Dow Industrial Average. However, Philip Morris earns nearly half its revenue from tobacco sales. The other half comes from food. Because the company continues to be mired in tobacco-related liability issues, it's a nonstarter for the aggressive investor.

Why? Looking at the two-year chart on Philip Morris (Figure 6.1), it seems as though it might actually be a good bet. Clearly it has been locked in a narrow trading range for some time. But a narrow trading range is not the only criterion for the falling-for-dollars trade. For all aggressive trades, we want some edge, something to stack the odds on our side of the table. In the falling-for-dollars trade, an edge is critical. The edge in this case comes from the option premium.

FIGURE 6.1

TWO-YEAR CHART OF PHILIP MORRIS

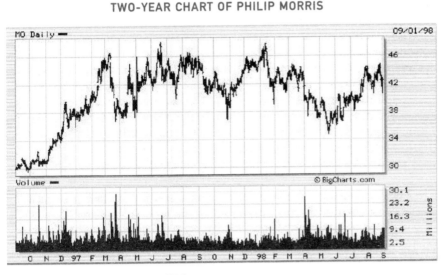

Source: www.bigcharts.com

We want to be able to sell a covered call option for more than it's worth. Or put another way, we want to sell a call option at a price that we think is higher than it should be. To do that, we need to know something the market doesn't.

With Philip Morris, what do we know that the market doesn't? Yes there's little downside at this point. The market has pushed the price of Philip Morris so low that the tobacco-litigation settlement has already been factored into the equation. But the market already knows that. The market also knows that until a definitive settlement is reached to limit liability, the stock will remain locked in a narrow trading range. The point is, investors expect the stock to remain in a narrow trading range, and the options are priced accordingly. Where's the edge?

A LESSON FROM THE PAST

To add some substance to this discussion, return with me for a moment to Monday October 19, 1987, and the great stock market crash. I know, another digression. But trust me, it's important. On Black Monday, the U.S. stock market as measured by the

Dow Industrial Average fell 508 points in one day. More importantly, that amounted to a 23% sell-off (the October 27, 1997, sell-off we talked about earlier was 7.2%), a panic-driven sell-off by any definition.

In Chapter Four we discussed volatility and its impact on an option's price. If option traders believed that the market—as measured by the Dow Industrial Average—was likely to move 500 points up or down on any given day, then option prices would reflect that concern, just as option traders who believe that Philip Morris will remain fixed in a narrow trading range will contract option premiums to reflect that bias. On Tuesday, October 20, 1987, options on the major stock market indices were priced so high their premiums implied that a 20% upward or downward movement in the market was expected, not a realistic long-term assumption.

Here's my own experience with the October 1987 crash: In August 1987 General Motors was trading at $83 per share. I purchased a November 85 call for $1.375 per share ($137.50 per contract). I was expecting General Motors to go to $100 per share before the end of the year, so this was a short-term speculation. I had a three-month option that gave me the right to buy General Motors stock at $85 per share, just $2 above where the stock was trading.

Along comes Black Monday. General Motors falls sharply and closes at $60 per share. (Bear in mind these were the prices at that time. General Motors has since split 2 for 1. If you look at long-term charting packages, General Motors shows as closing on October 19, 1987 at $30 per share.) I still own the November 85 call on October 19, 1987, now some $25 out of the money. With less than a month to go before expiration, what's the option worth?

You would think it would have no value. How likely is it that the stock of a company as large as GM would rise $25 per share over the next 30 days? Nevertheless, the GM November 85 call was trading at 0.875 cents per share ($87.50 per contract) on October 20, 1987.

That's a classic example of an option that's worth more than it should be. And that's what I mean when I talk about selling an option for more than it's worth—the edge that makes the falling-for-dollars trade work.

When a stock declines sharply, the options on that stock will be priced on the premise that it will continue to fall just as fast, just as hard. The market thinks that the underlying stock will continue to decline; we think the stock will settle into a reasonable trading range. That's what we know—or think we know—that the market doesn't.

That's not the case with Philip Morris. We think Philip Morris stock will remain in a relatively tight trading range, but so does the option market. The option premiums are priced accordingly. So where's the edge?

Another consideration with Philip Morris is the company it keeps. Like it or not, the company is a leading player within a troubled industry. The company will survive on some level over the longer term, but the industry itself faces some fundamental long-term problems. Even if tobacco sales grow, which is not a foregone conclusion, the industry will continue to face restrictions and legal challenges. Long-term exposure to huge costs cannot be good for the industry or for any company within that industry.

So what we have is three companies—Oracle, Intel and Philip Morris—that meet our condition of being big-cap blue-chip names. We also know that Oracle and Intel reside in a healthy industry with positive long-term growth potential. Philip Morris has a solid food business, but the tobacco half of the company is in some jeopardy. So Philip Morris does not meet our criterion for a healthy growing industry.

Before we set up the falling-for-dollars trade, let's define two fundamental rules that must be met before we will consider any aggressive trade using stocks:

1. The underlying company must be a large-cap blue-chip stock. We'll set the minimum market capitalization at US$5 billion. Market cap is defined as the number of shares outstanding multiplied by the market price for those shares. With Intel, for example, there are 1.696 billion shares outstanding. At US$70 per share, its market cap is US$118.72 billion.

2. The company must be in an industry that has long-term growth prospects and in which there has been no fundamental change in industry direction.

Armed with these criteria, let's look at the road leading up to a falling-for-dollars trade.

CONDITIONS FOR THE FALLING-FOR-DOLLARS TRADE

As aggressive investors we cannot commit to a falling-for-dollars trade the day of, or the day after, a major sell-off. We need to allow for a cleansing period when management lays more cards on the table. Don't worry about missing the trade. The stock is not likely to turn around quickly. Financial markets don't drive a stock lower based on a company-specific event and then, a week later, say "Whoops!"

At this point we need to look at how the stock reacts to more bad news. Does it slide further? If so, how much further? Does it find solid support and, if so, at what price? We're not looking for the stock to stage a major rebound. We simply want the stock to rise slightly, or to remain in a relatively narrow trading range for the duration of the falling-for-dollars trade. We want the stock to find a price level where it has solid support. If that happens, this trade makes good money.

Figure 6.2 is a 52-week chart on Oracle. Note the sharp one-day decline in Oracle's stock in late October 1997. (Just to the left of the circle.) Note at the bottom of the chart that there was no real variance in the volume pattern for that day. That's not surprising, because that was the day the market-driven sell-off took place, on October 27, 1997, and the day the Dow Industrial Average fell 554 points. Oracle fell with the rest of the market.

Moving further to the right, note the dramatic crack in Oracle's share price in December 1997. (Circle marks the spot.) The company's stock gapped lower on December 12, 1997, because of a pre-announcement of an earnings shortfall blamed on the Asian crisis. Note also the spike in volume on that day.

A gap takes place when a stock opens for trading at a price significantly higher or lower than the previous night's close. Trading gaps are particularly evident when you look at high-low-close charts as seen in Figure 6.2. There is simply nothing—as in the stock's high, low or close price—connecting the previous night's close with trading activity on the following day.

FIGURE 6.2

DAILY ONE-YEAR CHART ON ORACLE CORPORATION

Source: www.bigcharts.com

Technicians believe that stocks will eventually fill a gap. In other words, if a stock gaps higher, it will often fall back to that level at some point in the not-too-distant future. The same thing will happen when a stock gaps lower. The stock will often rally back to that point and fill the gap. For example, Oracle filled the December 12, 1997, gap in mid-March 1998, some three months later.

Filling a gap does not mean that a company has necessarily begun a new trend. In fact, we can say that the gap itself will probably be a strong support or resistance point in the marketplace. Or you might just look at a gap as one of those quirky things that can happen to a stock's price.

Intel provides another interesting case study on gaps. Looking at the one-year chart on Intel (Figure 6.3) we see that the stock has gapped lower on three occasions:

• *The first on October 27, 1997, was the result of the market-driven sell-off.*

• *The second, on March 5, occurred when the company announced that quarterly earnings would fall short of expectations.*

• *The third, a small gap in June, was filled within a couple of days.*

FIGURE 6.3

DAILY ONE-YEAR CHART OF INTEL CORP

Source: www.bigcharts.com

Because the falling-for-dollars trade is driven by company-specific events, we often see such stocks gap to the downside. Not that a gap by itself provides an entry point to this specific aggressive trade. It does, however, provide a starting point.

In the two examples we've talked about, Oracle is a candidate for a falling-for-dollars trade, but Intel is not. We'll see why after reviewing a hypothetical falling-for-dollars trade using XYZ.

THE FALLING-FOR-DOLLARS PROLOGUE

We'll use XYZ to examine the falling-for-dollars strategy and the follow-up action you might take in case things go wrong. Then I'll follow the hypothetical example with a case study of an existing company.

XYZ is a large blue-chip company with a long-term track record. The company operates and maintains a strong position within a healthy growth industry. XYZ is an option-eligible security. The options normally trade with an implied volatility of 35%.

After the close of trading on December 11, 1998, XYZ announces that it will not meet analysts' quarterly earnings target. In actual fact, XYZ is acting as many companies do in the current market environment, pre-announcing an earnings shortfall. It's worth pointing out that XYZ does not report a loss or that it will lose more than the street expected. XYZ simply says it won't earn as much as analysts had been expecting.

The market reacts in a straightforward manner. On December 12, 1998, investors panic. At the opening bell the stock drops sharply and option premiums expand quickly. The stock falls 25% in value, from just over $89 per share to $67 per share. At the end of the day, XYZ options are trading with an implied volatility of 50%.

All of the ingredients are in place to begin the falling-for-dollars aggressive trade. Figure 6.4 is a chart of XYZ the day the dust settled. Included in Figure 6.4 is a 50-day moving average for XYZ. Note how the stock fails to break up through the 50-day moving average in the weeks preceding the one-day collapse. For a good technical analyst, this might have raised some concern. That's not our role in this trade. We're looking at the situation after the fall, using the 50-day moving average to define short-term support and resistance levels.

FIGURE 6.4

XYZ + 50-DAY MOVING AVERAGE

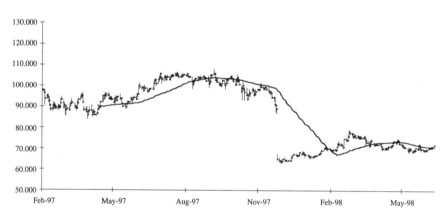

The options are trading with an implied volatility of 50%, up from the 35% volatility implied before the pre-announcement. Table 6.1 lists the available XYZ options and their premium at various strike prices.

TABLE 6.1

XYZ CALL PREMIUMS — DECEMBER 12, 1998

Stock Price: $64.875
Implied Volatility: 50%

STRIKE	MARCH	APRIL	JUNE
60.00	8.625	10.250	12.000
65.00	6.000	7.750	9.625
70.00	4.000	5.750	7.625
75.00	2.615	4.250	6.000
80.00	2.125	3.000	4.625

The next step is to look at the movement in the stock's price relative to the four trading bands we discussed in Chapter Five. Recall that the four trading bands represent one standard deviation about the 50-day moving average. The width of the trading bands is defined by the volatility implied by the XYZ options (see Figure 6.5).

FIGURE 6.5

XYZ WITH OUR FOUR TRADING BANDS

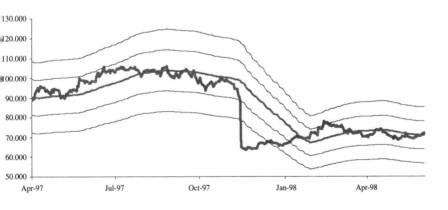

The falling-for-dollars strategy is triggered when a stock drops sharply. Look for a decline of at least 10% as a starting point, but only as a starting point. If we assume the stock is a blue-chip large-cap company in a strong and growing industry, there are three rules that the position must meet to qualify as a falling-for-dollars trade:

1. The stock must fall to a level that places it below band #1. Below trading band #1, it has fallen into what I call no-man's land, more than one standard deviation below the 50-day moving average, as defined by the XYZ option premiums. At this point, the odds suggest that the stock is oversold.

2. The option premiums must be higher than the historical normal for the underlying stock. Given the degree of the move, I would expect option premiums to expand dramatically.

3. We must allow time for the stock to work its way through the cleansing process. We want to allow time for the stock to cross back above trading band #1 before we enter the falling-for-dollars trade.

In this case the share decline in XYZ stock was the direct result of a company-specific event: the pre-announcement of an earnings shortfall. The XYZ press release was straightforward. The company said it was experiencing weaker-than-anticipated demand, and profit margins would have to be cut. Earnings would suffer as a consequence.

In fact, management was quick to point out that it was not expecting these problems to be long-term in nature. Mind you, that's what you'd expect as initial commentary.

Analysts usually respond quickly and cut earnings estimates to come into line with management's guidance. Some analysts would go so far as to suggest that next year's earnings would need to be trimmed, say, by 20%. This is typical of the cleansing process—bad news on top of more bad news.

Such discussions strike fear into the heart of investors. The fact is, analysts are in business to protect their reputation. In this case, it's much better to err on the side of caution. But usually such a cautionary stance acts as a catalyst that causes prices to fall still lower—down days followed by more down days!

At some point one brave analyst will step up to the plate and suggest that the stock has fallen too far, too fast, based on the information that's currently available. It's now at a point where investors can buy. That's when we usually get our first legitimate upgrade to a buy recommendation. It's not unusual to see this happen within the two-week period following the initial decline.

To review, XYZ is a large-cap blue-chip company whose value has fallen sharply, the result of an earnings surprise. The stock has fallen below trading band #1, which represents one standard deviation below the 50-day moving average.

The 50-day moving average is defined as our short-term resistance point, which for XYZ we will peg at $97 per share as of the day of the decline. Of course as the stock price consolidates, the 50-day moving average will decline quickly. By the time XYZ crosses back above trading band #1, the 50-day moving average for XYZ was about $90.

We know that XYZ operates in a strong industry, but has been hit with short-term problems. The option premiums have expanded, because investors perceive higher risk in the stock. All the ingredients are here for an aggressive trade. Or, more specifically, it has passed the requirements necessary to put the stock on a watch list. The watch list is just as it sounds. I follow the stock until it moves back above trading band #1. During that period I expect to see more bad news about the company. Too often a stock already damaged is susceptible to further hits. The question is, how many additional hits, and how bad are they likely to be?

Remember, trading band #1 is one standard deviation below the 50-day moving average. And the standard deviations—i.e., the band width—are defined by the volatility implied by the options market. Under these assumptions, the stock can break above trading band #1 in one of three ways:

1. the stock can rise in value,
2. the volatility implied by the options may contract, or
3. the stock can remain in a narrow trading range as the 50-day moving average converges with the stock's price.

Looking at a stock after such a decline goes against almost all investment literature. To breach so many investment rules, aggressive investors have to allow time for the stock to consolidate. I'm not looking for an opportunity to enter a position for the long term. In that sense, the falling-for-dollars strategy is not a pure contrarian play. I simply want to exploit a period in a stock's life when there is very little downside and when the option premiums are high.

The falling-for-dollars trade is designed to take advantage of a period of consolidation. The stock does not have to bounce back to new highs. The market does not have to admit making a mistake, driving the stock too low too fast. We simply want to initiate a short-term trade on the expectation that there is little risk to the downside. Assuming that option premiums are still well above the norm for that stock, this is contrary to what the market is saying.

If option premiums are still at high levels, then the market thinks there's a very good chance that the stock will continue to fall—hard!—just like our GM example after the 1987 stock market crash. That's why we need to go through this cleansing period—to put as many of the odds on our side before entering the trade. What we don't want is a period of consolidation to turn into a rout on the stock. We don't want XYZ to fall from $67 per share to, say, $30 per share.

This reflects our rules that require us to look only at big-cap companies with a long profitable history behind them in an industry that continues to grow. The time to step up to the plate is when the downside seems to be limited, but when the option premiums are still high enough to take advantage of an aggressive trade.

INITIATING THE FALLING-FOR-DOLLARS TRADE

Falling for dollars is really an aggressive covered call write. (We discussed covered call writing in Chapter Four.) Covered call writing involves the purchase of the underlying stock and the sale of a call.

We know covered call writing is a relatively conservative strategy on the surface. It works best as an aggressive strategy if we can get a higher-than-expected premium from the sale of the calls. And we can further enhance the covered call write through the use of leverage—margining the stock purchase, for example, in an attempt to earn double-digit returns over a short period.

With XYZ at $67 on December 12, 1997, we wait to see if:

1. the stock remained in a relatively narrow trading range;
2. the stock was able to cross back over trading band #1;
3. the stock reacted well on days when more bad news came out, and
4. the option premiums are still trading with a higher-than-normal implied volatility. They don't have to be as expensive as they were on the day the stock fell, but I want the implied volatility to be higher than the norm for that particular stock.

In this example, during the cleansing period, XYZ remained in a relatively tight trading range. There was more bad news, but investors took the news in stride. There were no really big down days. It took 19 trading days before XYZ finally breached trading band #1 (see Table 6.2 and Figure 6.5).

Finally, we want to make certain that we can get enough premium when we sell the XYZ call options. Table 6.3 looks at the option premiums on January 9, 1998, when XYZ crossed over trading band #1. On that day, we'll assume the options were trading with an assumed 45% implied volatility. The premiums have declined slightly, but are still well above the average for this stock, which gives us everything we need to enter the falling-for-dollars trade.

Given the information, we enter a trade on January 9. To keep the numbers consistent, we will buy XYZ at the closing price of $68.063 and sell the April 70 calls for $5.625 per share. Because we are taking advantage of a relatively tight trading range, my approach is to sell an at-the-money call or, more specifically, a call with a strike price just above the price at which the stock is trading.

We also know from Chapter Four that option premiums decline most rapidly in the last three months prior to expiration. I could have used the March calls, but I prefer to balance downside protection with upside potential. The April call provides a better balance. The March option is not a bad trade either; it just depends on the individual stock and how comfortable you are with the downside breakeven price. Using the prices from Table 6.3, we can plug the numbers into the following covered-call-writing worksheet.

TABLE 6.2

XYZ DAILY PRICES DURING THE CLEANSING PROCESS

DATE	HIGH	LOW	CLOSE
12-Dec-97	67.250	64.500	64.875
15-Dec-97	65.781	63.750	64.063
16-Dec-97	64.750	63.875	64.125
17-Dec-97	64.500	63.188	63.625
18-Dec-97	63.813	62.875	63.813
19-Dec-97	65.000	63.500	64.938
22-Dec-97	65.750	64.063	64.625
23-Dec-97	64.750	64.000	64.125
24-Dec-97	64.500	64.000	64.063
26-Dec-97	64.375	64.125	64.313
29-Dec-97	64.625	64.125	64.188
30-Dec-97	65.875	64.250	65.750
31-Dec-97	66.875	65.625	66.625
02-Jan-98	67.750	66.875	67.188
05-Jan-98	67.750	66.688	66.938
06-Jan-98	66.938	66.375	66.500
07-Jan-98	67.188	66.500	66.625
08-Jan-98	67.000	66.406	66.875
09-Jan-98	68.063	66.625	68.063

TABLE 6.3

XYZ CALL PREMIUMS—JANUARY 9, 1998

Stock Price: $68.063
Implied Volatility: 45%

STRIKE	MARCH	APRIL	JUNE
60.00	10.125	11.125	12.750
65.00	6.875	8.000	9.125
70.00	4.500	5.625	6.875
75.00	2.750	3.875	5.000
80.00	1.625	2.625	3.500

COVERED CALL WRITING WORKSHEET

NET INVESTMENT CALCULATION		PRICE PER SHARE	NUMBER OF SHARES	TOTAL COST
Buy	XYZ Corporation	68.063	500	34,031.50
Sell	XYZ April 70 calls	5.625	500	(2,812.50)
Plus	Transaction Costs			
Equals	**Net Investment**			**$31,219.00**

RETURN IF STOCK CALLED AWAY		RECEIPTS PER SHARE	NUMBER OF SHARES	NET RECEIPTS
Sell	XYZ Corporation	70.00	500	35,000.00
Plus	Dividends Received	—	500	—
Less	Net Investment			(31,219.00)
Equals	**Net Return**			**$ 3,781.00**
	Percent return if called away			**12.11%**
	Annualized rate of return			**48.44%**

RETURN IF STOCK UNCHANGED		VALUE PER SHARE	NUMBER OF SHARES	NET VALUE
	XYZ Corporation	68.06	500	34,031.50
Plus	Dividends Received	—	500	—
Less	XYZ April 70 Calls	—	500	—
Less	Net Investment			$(31,219.00)
Equals	**Net Return**			**$ 2,812.50**
	Percent return if unchanged			**9.01%**
	Annualized rate of return			**36.04%**

DOWNSIDE BREAKEVEN		VALUE PER SHARE	NUMBER OF SHARES	NET COST
	Net Investment			31,219.00
Less	Dividends	—	500	—
Equals	Total stock cost to expiration			31,219.00
Divide	By number of shares held		500	
Equals	**Breakeven price per share**			**$62.44**
Equals	**Percent downside protection**			**8.26%**

Based on the information from the worksheet, this XYZ trade will return 12.11% if the stock is called away in April. That's a three-month rate of return. On an annualized basis, that's more than 48%, with most of it coming from the option premium.

If the stock price remains the same until the April expiration, then the rate of return is 9.01% and you still own the stock.

Finally, the downside breakeven is 8.26% below the stock's current price. In this example, XYZ can fall to $62.44—well below trading band #1—and the position still breaks even.

Before going any further, we need to examine how this fits within the context of the trading bands in place for XYZ Corporation. As the stock was consolidating, the 50-day moving average was falling. By the time we were ready to enter this trade, the 50-day moving was about $85 per share, well above the maximum profit line for this trade (i.e., $70 strike price + $5.625 option premium). This corresponds nicely with the objectives of the strategy. We're not looking for a major bounce to a resistance point, just a relatively tight trading range, with not too much downside risk.

As for the downside, we can secure this position with a downside breakeven price that's lower than the lowest price for the stock on the day of the sell-off. In terms of our trading bands, the downside breakeven price is below trading band #1, meaning that the breakeven price is more than two standard deviations below the 50-day moving average, the best an aggressive investor can hope for and a nice balance between downside protection and upside potential.

LEVERAGING THE FALLING-FOR-DOLLARS TRADE

We know what kind of potential return and downside protection you receive when initiating the XYZ covered write on a cash basis—i.e., when we put up the money to buy the stock—and we do not borrow from the brokerage firm.

If we use a portion of the margin available from the brokerage firm, we can borrow to buy the XYZ shares. I suggest that you never use more than 35% leverage. Canadian investors can borrow up to 70% of the value of option-eligible stocks, so margining only 35% means that you're using only half the margin available. You'll be investing at least 65% of the value of the initial purchase price.

There are a couple of reasons for being a bit cautious:

>   1. You don't want to be hit with a margin call if the stock suddenly falls. A further sudden decline would cause a margin call if we were fully margined at the point of entry, forcing us to exit the position prematurely.

>   2. With all aggressive trades there are ways to follow up on a position that hasn't worked as well as you might have expected. But again, I would prefer to have the time to implement the follow-up strategies without being prematurely forced into the situation because of a margin call.

Having assessed why it's important not to over-leverage, let's plug the numbers into a second covered-call-writing worksheet that factors margin into the equation. In this example, we use 35% margin, and we'll assume for simplicity that your borrowing costs are 10% per annum.

COVERED CALL WRITING WORKSHEET—MARGIN

NET INVESTMENT CALCULATION	PRICE PER SHARE	NUMBER OF SHARES	TOTAL COST
Buy	XYZ Corporation	68.063	500	34,031.50
Sell	XYZ April 70 calls	5.625	500	−2,812.50
Borrow	35% of the purchase price			−11,911.03
Plus	Transaction Costs			
Equals	**Net Investment**			**$ 19,307.98**

RETURN IF STOCK CALLED AWAY	RECEIPTS PER SHARE	NUMBER OF SHARES	NET RECEIPTS
Sell	XYZ Corporation	70.00	500	35,000.00
Plus	Dividends Received	—	500	—
Less	Net Investment			−19,307.98
Less	Interest charges on margin *			−293.70
Less	Repayment of margin principal loan			−11,911.03
Equals	**Net Return**			**$ 3,487.30**
	Percent return if called away			**18.06%**
	Annualized rate of return			**72.25%**

RETURN IF STOCK UNCHANGED	VALUE PER SHARE	NUMBER OF SHARES	NET VALUE
	XYZ Corporation	68.06	500	34,031.50
Plus	Dividends Received	—	500	—
Less	XYZ April 70 calls	—	500	—
Less	Net Investment			−19,307.98
Less	Interest charges on margin *			−293.70
Less	Repayment of margin principal loan			−11,911.03
Equals	**Net Return**			**$ 2,518.80**
	Percent return if unchanged			**13.05%**
	Annualized rate of return			**52.18%**

DOWNSIDE BREAKEVEN	VALUE PER SHARE	NUMBER OF SHARES	NET COST
	Net Investment			19,307.98
Less	Dividends	—	500	—
Plus	Interest charges on margin *			293.70
Plus	Repayment of margin principal loan			11,911.03
Equals	Total stock cost to expiration			31,512.70
Divide	By number of shares held		500	
Equals	**Breakeven price per share**			**$63.03**
Equals	**Percent downside protection**			**7.40%**

By leveraging your covered call write with 35% margin, you increase your rate of return if called away to 18.06% over three months or better than 72% annualized. You receive 13.05% if the stock remains unchanged or nearly 52% annualized. However, you do not have as much downside protection, although, at 7.4% of the initial investment, it's not bad. The downside breakeven price on the margined covered call write is $63.03.

FOLLOW-UP ACTION

As you can see from Figure 6.5, XYZ did eventually climb above $70 per share by the April expiration. In this trade, you would have earned your maximum return (i.e., return if called away) over the three-month period.

Not all aggressive trades fare so well, and we need to know how to deal with trades that don't. What happens if the position goes bad and the stock declines much further than expected? Perhaps additional reports lead you to think that there's a distinct change taking place in the industry and that the worst for this company is far from over.

Should that happen, you need to re-evaluate the situation. The decline may have been caused by more bad news coming to the table. The fact we waited for two weeks before entering the trade should have given us enough time for any additional news to come out. But the unexpected can always occur.

Now we have to have a plan of action, and we have to know when to put it into effect. First, we need to look again at Figure 6.5. Note the four bands around the 50-day moving average.

I would consider follow-up action in the falling-for-dollars trade only if the stock falls below the breakeven price of the original covered call write. Even then, I might refrain from taking any quick follow-up action if the stock is still above trading band #1. If the stock is below the breakeven price and has breached the lower trading band, I would look at some follow-up action.

Again, trading band #1 is significant because it is one standard deviation below the 50-day moving average. At that point we get into statistical aberrations, the 1-in-3 occurrence during which a stock just can't get off the floor. We have to be concerned at that point, because we're using the option premiums to define the width of the trading bands and, by extension, the floor price. At this point we need to admit that perhaps the market knows something we don't.

Assuming the stock breaches the lower trading band, there are three strategies the aggressive investor can employ:

1. Close out the position by selling the stock and buying back the call option.
2. Roll down the covered call write.
3. Roll out the covered call write.

We will look at each of these responses and describe in detail how you can unwind a failed falling-for-dollars strategy.

Before considering any follow-up, aggressive investors need to change their mindset. When you decide to implement follow-up action, you're admitting that the initial aggressive strategy has failed. You're no longer trying to make a profit on the trade; you're looking for ways to minimize the loss.

With that in mind, we'll assume that XYZ over the next two months falls to $57. That's a decline of more than $11 per share from the price at which the trade was entered. The stock is now below trading band #1 and, of course, has slipped below the breakeven price. It is now March 1998, and the options are still trading with an implied volatility of 45%. Based on that information, we find the prices shown in Table 6.4.

TABLE 6.4

XYZ CALL PREMIUMS—MARCH 30, 1998

Stock Price: $57
Implied Volatility: 45%

STRIKE	APRIL	JUNE	SEPT
50.00	N/A	9.000	11.000
55.00	N/A	5.875	8.250
60.00	1.000	3.625	6.000
65.00	0.250	2.125	4.375
70.00	0.062	1.125	3.125

OPTION 1: CLOSE THE POSITION

The first choice is probably the most unappealing. There is no chance of recovering your losses. You have to admit the trade was a bust, and you need to regroup and move to the next aggressive trade—a difficult decision for even the most hardened stock trader. But it may also be the best follow-up strategy. At least you know exactly what your loss is, and that can be helpful as part of an ongoing cash-management program.

In this case, we would simply buy back the April calls at 6.25 cents per share or 1/16th. That's the lowest price an option can trade at. There likely will be no bid for the option, the 1/16th simply being the price other traders are paying to close out a position to free up margin. You'd make a profit on the April 70 call, based on the original sale price of $5.625 per share. To examine the trade in its entirety, it helps to construct a balance sheet that includes all the debits and credits involved in the trade along with commission costs.

In this case we initially bought 500 shares of XYZ and sold 5 XYZ calls. Our balance sheet looks like this:

PARTICULARS	DEBITS	CREDITS
Buy 500 shares XYZ @ 68.063	34,031.50	
Sell 5 XYZ April 70 Calls @ 5.625		2,812.50
Sell 500 shares XYZ @ $57.000		28,500.00
Buy 5 XYZ April 70 Calls @ .0625	31.25	
Totals	34,062.75	31,312.50

Note that the debits exceed the credits. You'll also pay commission when you implement any aggressive trade, so be sure to factor that into the price before you start. (We ignore commissions throughout this book for the sake of simplicity.) If, as in this example, the total debits exceed the credits, you have a loss on the position. By closing out this position, you take a loss of $2,750.25, which equates to an 8.1% hit on your risk capital. But on the positive side, you have sufficient capital to allow you to play again another day.

OPTION 2: ROLL DOWN THE COVERED CALL WRITE

The reason we take corrective action in the face of a declining stock price is to prevent a trade from eroding a significant amount of our capital. Covered call writing has the potential for a large loss should the stock actually decline to zero. Covered call writing also limits your potential upside. Your maximum profit occurs at the strike price of the short call.

With the rolling-down follow-up strategy, the original call is repurchased and another call with a lower strike price is written. In this case we would repurchase the April 70 call and write the April 60 call at $1.00. That will help us to reduce the cost of the initial position by 15/16th. (Note the cost to buy back the original April 70 call is 1/16th, and that has to be subtracted from the net premium received when writing the April 60 calls.)

If the stock rebounds to $60, you will lose the shares, and our balance sheet would look as follows:

PARTICULARS	DEBITS	CREDITS
Buy 500 shares XYZ @ 68.063	34,031.50	
Sell 5 XYZ April 70 Calls @ 6.625		2,812.50
Buy 5 XYZ April 70 Calls @ .0625	31.25	
Sell 5 XYZ April 60 Calls @ 1.000		500.00
Sell 500 shares XYZ @ 60.000		30,000.00
Totals	34,062.75	33,312.50

Note that we still lost money on the trade but, because we could successfully roll down our position, the loss was trimmed to $749.50 per share or 2.2% of our capital base. But remember, too, this assumes that the stock does bounce back to the $60 strike price. There is no guarantee this will happen.

On the other hand, if the stock simply stays at the $57 price point, this strategy may be preferable to option 1. If the stock does not rebound to the $60 price point by the April expiration, the April 60 calls will expire worthless, and we could then write the June 60 calls at $3.625. That would still tie up capital on a trade that we're simply trying to recover from. But by rolling out to the next month with the lower strike price, we could turn a losing position into a small profit—i.e., if the stock can rebound to $60 per share by the June expiration.

Assuming XYZ rallies to $60 and is called away in June, the balance sheet would look as follows:

PARTICULARS	DEBITS	CREDITS
Buy 500 shares XYZ @ 68.063	34,031.50	
Sell 5 XYZ April 70 Calls @ 5.625		2,812.50
Buy 5 XYZ April 70 Calls @ .0625	31.25	
Sell 5 XYZ April 60 Calls @ 1.000		500.00
Sell 5 XYZ June 60 Calls @ 3.635		1,812.50
Sell 500 shares XYZ @ 60.000		30,000.00
Totals	34,062.75	35,125.00

Note that in this case the total credits exceed the total debits. Therefore, this position is profitable. The total profit on this trade is $1,093.50, for a total six-month return of 3.1%, which is not very appealing, but remember we're talking about a strategy that's designed to minimize losses. Within that context, this would have been a successful follow-up.

OPTION 3: ROLL OUT THE COVERED WRITE

The final follow-up strategy involves the sale of a call with the same strike price but a longer time horizon. In most cases, unfortunately, this is the least effective strategy. That's because the stock has to return to the level you hoped for when you initiated the trade. And since we're implementing follow-up action to help reduce the loss on a busted trade, it might be overly optimistic to expect the stock to rebound to its former levels.

However, there may be times when you expect this to happen, in which case you'd usually wait for the April calls to expire and then write, say, a September 70 call. (Note the September 70 call is trading at 3 1/8th as of the end of March, assuming at the end of March the stock is at $57 per share.) Because I want to maintain an apples-to-apples comparison on the follow-up strategies, I'll assume that you repurchase the April 70 call at 1/16th and write the September 70 call. Your balance sheet would look as follows:

PARTICULARS	DEBITS	CREDITS
Buy 500 shares XYZ @ 68.063	34,031.50	
Sell 5 XYZ April 70 Calls @ 6.625		2,812.50
Buy 5 XYZ April 70 Calls @ .0625	31.25	
Sell 5 XYZ September 70 Calls @ 3.125		1,562.50
Sell 500 shares XYZ @ 70.000	35,000.00	
Totals	34,062.75	39,375.00

Should the stock rise to the $70 strike price by September, the shares would be sold and your total return would be $5,312.25 or about 15.6% on the initial investment over a nine-month period. In other words, you've made a decent profit on this trade, but you've done so over a longer period than most aggressive investors would prefer to work with. We've also made an assumption that the underlying stock can rebound to the initial strike price, which contradicts the reasoning behind the follow-up strategy.

SUMMARY

Executed with sufficient planning, these aggressive trades will often work without having to resort to any follow-up action. But no aggressive trade has a perfect track record. You have to be willing to take some losses along the road to some very healthy profits. Follow-up action helps you manage your cash flow if an aggressive trade doesn't work out.

The trick is to keep losses to a minimum, which will help you stay in the game. The longer you stay with the aggressive program, the better your chance for longer-term success. The only way to stay with the program is to manage your cashflow carefully and have follow-up strategies in place in case a trade doesn't go as expected.

FALLING FOR DOLLARS: A REAL-LIFE EXAMPLE

Having seen a hypothetical example of the falling-for-dollars trade, let's look at a real-life example, using real stocks—in this case Intel and Oracle.

Clearly the long-term fundamentals of both companies are sound. The market cap on Intel is more than $100 billion; on Oracle, around $22 billion. Both companies operate in an industry that continues to grow at double-digit rates. In terms of our initial screen, both companies pass the test.

Nevertheless, on March 5, 1998, Intel fell sharply after an earnings pre-announcement after the close of trading the previous day. The company said its earnings would fall short of expectations by some $600 million in the first quarter of 1998. The stock opened March 5 and immediately fell. (Actually it began falling sharply in after-hours trading on March 4, after the NYSE closed. But since charts track the price of a stock only during NYSE hours, the stock opened sharply lower on March 5.) When the dust settled, Intel had fallen 9 7/8ths in one day. In percentage terms, the stock fell 11.3%, from $86.65 to close the day at $76.75.

Needless to say the NASDAQ also fell sharply on March 5, down 35 points to 1,724.65 by the end of the day, reflecting industry-wide concerns about a pre-announcement from Intel. After all, if Intel couldn't meet its earnings expectations, who could?

The Intel press release was straightforward. The company said it was experiencing "weaker than anticipated demand," and profit margins would have to be cut. Short-term earnings would suffer as a consequence. It was a relatively straightforward commentary from management. It placed most of the blame on the slowdown in Asia, a problem that Intel management did not expect to last over the long term.

Analysts who follow Intel were not so kind or forgiving. Some noted quite correctly that Intel was down more than 22% from its August 1997 high of $102. They slashed 1999 earnings estimates by some 20%, and hinted that there were more problems to come. There were concerns about a huge backlog of unsold machines. Some said that nobody would buy computers in Asia. It was like the industry had suddenly shut down.

Such discussions are enough to scare even the most aggressive investor away. But such reports are typical of the cleansing process we mentioned earlier, a period when you hear bad news followed by more bad news and experience down days followed by more down days. In the middle of the cleansing process, you begin to understand just how difficult it is to pull the trigger on a trade, rushing in when so many are rushing to the sidelines, and when even more are sitting on the fence. It's the fence-sitters who will ultimately jump in when the stock begins to show some life, and that's what will trigger the next buying spree. Fortunately, fence-sitters are not generally short sellers—that is, they are not typical investors who wait for an opportunity to sell a stock short after it has already fallen dramatically.

Aggressive investors need another piece to this puzzle: How expensive were the Intel option premiums? As Table 6.5 shows, the March 5 sell-off did cause option premiums to expand rather dramatically, providing the edge we talked about earlier. At the close of trading on March 5, Intel options were trading with an implied volatility of 45%, up from an implied volatility of 36% just a week earlier. Table 6.5 provides a sampling of the approximate value of Intel call options using the 45% volatility assumption.

Let's review what we have: a large-cap blue-chip company whose value has fallen sharply, the result of an earnings surprise. But we know it operates in a strong industry and has been hit, for the most part, with short-term problems. We also know

TABLE 6.5

INTEL CALL OPTION PREMIUMS—MARCH 5, 1998

Stock Price: $76.75
Implied Volatility: 45%

STRIKE	JUNE	JULY	OCT
65.00	14.500	15.375	17.625
70.00	11.125	12.125	14.625
75.00	8.375	9.500	12.125
80.00	6.125	7.250	10.000
85.00	4.375	5.500	8.125

FIGURE 6.6

INTEL CORP. ONE-YEAR CHART PLUS TRADING BANDS

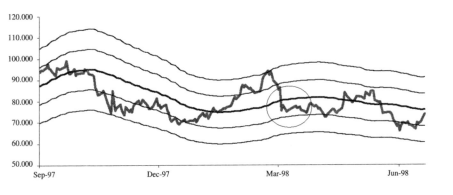

that the option premiums have expanded because investors perceive higher risk in the stock. But look at Figure 6.6, which is a chart of Intel plus the trading bands. Note that Intel was bumping up against trading band #4 before the sell-off, which means that Intel was in a different position than our hypothetical XYZ example.

With that in mind, let's review the falling-for-dollar trading rules and apply them to an Intel case study. Rule #1 states that the stock must fall below trading band #1. Intel never did. End of discussion.

WHAT ABOUT ORACLE?

Now let's apply the same rules to Oracle Corporation, specifically after the stock fell on December 10, 1997, sparked by a second-quarter earnings report that fell far short of analysts' expectations.

Oracle also blamed the shortfall on the turmoil in Asia and on currency fluctuations that made payments collected by Oracle in foreign currencies lose their value relative to the U.S. dollar. It was a reasonable commentary from Oracle's executives, because such a large percentage of Oracle's business comes from the Asia and the Pacific Basin.

But as might be expected, analysts were quick to jump on Oracle's case. Most had already built Asian weakness into Oracle's numbers. After all, the October 1997 stock market collapse was premised on weakness in Asia. It is not surprising that analysts would look through all the companies they follow and adjust earnings estimates based on the perceived slowdown in Asia. Clearly, Oracle management had not provided analysts with reasonable guidance as to the earnings outlook.

Oracle shares closed at $22.94 on December 10, down $9.43 on the day. More important, as Figure 6.2 shows, volume hit 172.5 million shares, the biggest one-day volume of any stock ever on NASDAQ.

Some analysts suggested that the record volume was more disconcerting than the actual drop in share price. That's an understatement. When volume is that large, investors have lost confidence in the stock, except for aggressive investors looking for an oversold situation.

As was to be expected, more bad news followed. It wasn't long before analysts pointed out that second-quarter sales in the United States, Canada and Latin America had fallen $50 million below estimates. Oracle missed that mark by more than they missed their mark in Asia. Clearly the problems at Oracle went far beyond Asia.

And the beat—or should I say beating?—continued. Observers said the composition of the shortfall was of greater concern than the shortfall itself, because it indicated a slowing of growth in Oracle's core businesses—database management and applications. The only part of the business that was growing was the service sector, which, unfortunately, happens also to have the lowest profit margin.

Then the other shoe dropped. Concern surfaced that Oracle may be vulnerable to inroads from Microsoft Corporation's SQL Server database product, perhaps not yet, since Microsoft's server can't handle the powerful tasks that made Oracle's name in this area, but certainly by late 1998 or 1999, when more powerful Microsoft versions would start chipping away at Oracle's core business. Investors were willing to stick with Oracle in the face of competition from Microsoft as long as Oracle continued to deliver on the earnings front. When that failed, investors rushed to the exits.

Further complicating the issue was Oracle's pursuit of the network computer (NC), a stripped-down machine that would power up from the Internet rather than from an operating system. With the NC, Larry Ellison, Oracle's flamboyant chairman, was taking clear aim at Microsoft's Windows operating system. But some analysts were becoming concerned that the NC was merely a distraction and that Oracle was taking its eye off the ball—its database and applications business. As one analyst said, referring to the company's substantial spending on the NC, "One hopes this financial setback will prompt a refocusing on the company's core business."

Most of this news came out over the next couple of weeks. If you read the headlines, you'd have had a hard time imagining anyone investing in this company. But while analysts were circling Oracle like vultures waiting for their prey to take its last breath, the stock remained in a tight trading range. Look at the prices from December 10 to December 31, 1997, as shown in Table 6.6.

TABLE 6.6

ORACLE PRICES

DATE	HIGH	LOW	CLOSE
10-Dec-97	23.88	22.75	23.44
11-Dec-97	23.44	21.75	21.94
12-Dec-97	22.97	21.94	22.75
15-Dec-97	23.44	22.81	23.19
16-Dec-97	23.56	23.13	23.31
17-Dec-97	23.75	22.38	22.63
18-Dec-97	23.00	22.00	22.00
19-Dec-97	22.19	21.00	21.63
22-Dec-97	22.75	21.63	21.75
23-Dec-97	21.88	20.94	21.03
24-Dec-97	21.38	21.00	21.06
26-Dec-97	21.44	21.06	21.44
29-Dec-97	22.00	21.44	21.75
30-Dec-97	22.38	21.75	22.38
31-Dec-97	22.50	22.00	22.31

Now take a look at Figure 6.7, a chart of Oracle Corporation plus the four trading bands. Note specifically how the sell-off on December 10 pushed Oracle's price below trading band #1, reflecting an oversold condition. In table 6.6, I've shown only the daily prices until December 31, 1997, when Oracle stock actually crossed over trading band #1.

FIGURE 6.7

ORACLE CORPORATION + TRADING BANDS

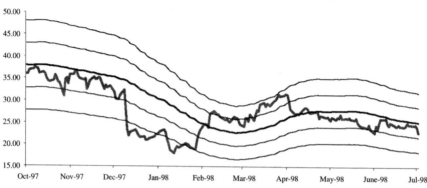

On December 31, options on Oracle were implying a 60% volatility, down slightly from the levels seen on the day of the sell-off, but well above the norms for Oracle and certainly high enough to justify entering a falling-for-dollars trade. The premiums are shown in Table 6.7

TABLE 6.7

ORACLE CALL OPTIONS ON DECEMBER 31, 1997

STRIKE	FEB	MARCH	JUNE
22.50	1.875	2.375	3.625
25.00	1.000	1.500	2.750
27.50	0.500	0.875	2.000

AGGRESSIVE TRADE #1: INITIATING THE FALLING-FOR-DOLLARS TRADE

We know Oracle fell to $22.94 on December 10, 1997. The stock closed below trading band #1, reflecting an oversold condition. We watched the stock during its cleansing period, as more bad news came out. We noted that the stock remained in a relatively narrow trading range. There was little reaction to the onslaught of bad news. The option premiums were still trading with a higher-than-normal implied volatility, not as expensive as they were the day the stock fell, but much higher than average for Oracle. On December 31, Oracle closed above trading band #1, and we initiated the trade.

To keep the numbers consistent, let's say we bought Oracle at the closing price of $22.31 and sold the March 22.50 calls for $2.375 per share. Because we're taking advantage of a relatively tight trading range, my approach is to sell an at-the-money call or, more specifically, a call with a strike price just above the price at which the stock is trading. We also know from Chapter Four that the option premium will decline most rapidly in the last three months prior to expiration. That is the rationale behind the March 22.50 call. Using the prices from Table 6.7, we can plug the numbers into the following worksheet.

ORACLE WORKSHEET—CASH

	NET INVESTMENT CALCULATION	PRICE PER SHARE	NUMBER OF SHARES	TOTAL COST
Buy	Oracle Corporation	22.310	500	11,155.00
Sell	Oracle March 22.50 calls	2.375	500	−1,187.50
Plus	Transaction Costs			
Equals	**Net Investment**			**$ 9,967.50**

	RETURN IF STOCK CALLED AWAY	RECEIPTS PER SHARE	NUMBER OF SHARES	NET RECEIPTS
Sell	Oracle Corporation	22.50	500	11,250.00
Plus	Dividends Received	—	500	—
Less	Net Investment			(9,967.50)
Equals	**Net Return**			**$ 1,282.50**
	Percent return if called away			**12.87%**
	Annualized rate of return			**51.47%**

	RETURN IF STOCK UNCHANGED	VALUE PER SHARE	NUMBER OF SHARES	NET VALUE
Plus	Dividends Received	—	500	—
Less	Oracle March 22.50 calls	—	500	—
Less	Net Investment			$(9,967.50)
Equals	**Net Return**			**$ 1,187.50**
	Percent return if unchanged			**11.91%**
	Annualized rate of return			**47.65%**

	DOWNSIDE BREAKEVEN	VALUE PER SHARE	NUMBER OF SHARES	NET COST
	Net Investment			9,967.50
Less	Dividends	—	500	—
Equals	Total stock cost to expiration			9,967.50
Divide	By number of shares held		500	
Equals	**Breakeven price per share**			**$19.94**
Equals	**Percent downside protection**			**10.65%**

Based on the information from the worksheet, this covered call write will return 12.87% if the stock is called away in March. That's a three-month rate of return, most of which has come from the option premium. Annualized, that works out to better than 50%.

If the stock remains the same until the March expiration, then the rate of return is 11.91% and you still own the stock. Finally, the downside breakeven is 10.65% below the stock's current price. In this example, Oracle can call to $19.94 and this position still breaks even.

Before going any further we need to examine how this fits into the context of the trading bands from Figure 6.7. Note that the $22.50 strike price is below the 50-day moving average, which I peg at $24.36 in March 1998. Effectively, if the stock is called away we would be selling just above trading band #2.

On the downside, the breakeven price is $19.94 per share. The low close for the stock was $18.06, which occurred in January after the position was established. Bottom line: $19.94 is below trading band #1 at the time the trade was executed. So I am comfortable with the balance between upside potential and the downside breakeven.

LEVERAGING THE FALLING-FOR-DOLLARS TRADE

We know what kind of potential return and downside protection you receive when initiating the Oracle covered write on a cash basis. That is, we put up the money to buy the stock and do not borrow from the brokerage firm.

If we use a portion of the margin available from the brokerage firm, we can borrow to buy the Oracle shares. As with the XYZ example, we'll borrow 35% of the purchase price and plug the numbers into the following covered call write worksheet. I'm assuming in this worksheet that your loan will cost 10% per annum in finance charges.

By leveraging your covered call write with 35% margin, you increase your rate of return if called away to 40.18% over three months and 18% if the stock remains unchanged. You do not have as much downside protection, although at 9.78% of the initial investment, it's not bad. The downside breakeven price on the margined covered call write is $20.13.

For your information, Oracle did rebound. In fact, the stock rallied quite nicely. By the time the March options expired, the stock closed at $28.94. Needless to say, the stock was called away, in March. You would have sold your shares to the call buyer at $22.50 per share and, in the process, earned the maximum return on this aggressive trade. That's cash in the till that's ready to be put to work on the next aggressive trade.

ORACLE WORKSHEET — MARGIN

NET INVESTMENT CALCULATION	PRICE PER SHARE	NUMBER OF SHARES	TOTAL COST
Buy	Oracle Corporation	22.310	500	11,155.00
Sell	Oracle March 25 calls	2.375	500	−1,187.50
Borrow	35% of the purchase price			−3,904.25
Plus	Transaction Costs			
Equals	**Net Investment**			**$6,063.25**

RETURN IF STOCK CALLED AWAY	RECEIPTS PER SHARE	NUMBER OF SHARES	NET RECEIPTS
Sell	Oracle Corporation	25.00	500	12,500.00
Plus	Dividends Received	—	500	—
Less	Net Investment			−6,063.25
Less	Interest charges on margin *			−96.27
Less	Repayment of margin principal loan			−3,904.25
Equals	**Net Return**			**$2,436.23**
	Percent return if called away			**40.18%**
	Annualized rate of return			**160.72%**

RETURN IF STOCK UNCHANGED	VALUE PER SHARE	NUMBER OF SHARES	NET VALUE
	Oracle Corporation	22.31	500	11,155.00
Plus	Dividends Received	—	500	—
Less	Oracle March 25 calls	—	500	—
Less	Net Investment			−6,063.25
Less	Interest charges on margin *			−96.27
Less	Repayment of margin principal loan			−3,904.25
Equals	**Net Return**			**$1,091.23**
	Percent return if unchanged			**18.00%**
	Annualized rate of return			**71.99%**

DOWNSIDE BREAKEVEN	VALUE PER SHARE	NUMBER OF SHARES	NET COST
	Net Investment			6,063.25
Less	Dividends	—	500	—
Plus	Interest charges on margin *			96.27
Plus	Repayment of margin principal loan			3,904.25
Equals	Total stock cost to expiration			10,063.77
Divide	By number of shares held		500	
Equals	**Breakeven price per share**			**$20.13**
Equals	**Percent downside protection**			**9.78%**

Assumes 10% annual interest on margin loans

CONCLUSION

I like to compare falling-for-dollars traders to firefighters: They enter burning buildings when everyone else is rushing to the exits. That's not unlike what you are doing here: buying a stock when so many others can't wait to get rid of it.

The firefighter rushing into the burning building has an edge: He or she is wearing protective clothing and carrying a hose. The covered call write provides similar protection with this trade, but only if the option premiums are higher than normal for the underlying stock.

7
THE DOLLAR-COST-AVERAGING OPTION

WHAT IS DOLLAR-COST AVERAGING?

Dollar-cost averaging is one of the oldest strategies in the investment business. It ranks up there with investment truisms like "buy low, sell high" or "the market will fluctuate," a phrase often associated with J.P. Morgan.

Simply stated, dollar-cost averaging is the process of investing a specific amount of money in a stock at regular periods. By investing the same amount of money each time, you can buy more shares when the stock price is low and fewer shares when the stock price is high. Over time, the high and low prices average out: Hence, dollar-cost averaging. What's appealing about dollar-cost averaging is its discipline. The approach forces you to invest when emotionally you may have second thoughts.

Another attribute that's psychologically appealing is the notion that dollar-cost averaging allows you to acquire stock at a bargain price. Or so it would seem. When you employ dollar-cost averaging, the average cost of the shares you acquire will always be less than the average price for the stock over the acquisition period. For example, suppose you decided to invest $100 each week in XYZ, using the following prices:

PERIOD	PRICE	INVESTMENT	# OF SHARES
Week 1	10	$100	10.00
Week 2	8	$100	12.50
Week 3	12	$100	8.33
Week 4	11	$100	9.09

At the end of the four-week period, the average price of the shares was $10.25 (10 + 8 + 12 + 11 = 4 1/4 = $10.25). Over the same period, you invested $400 and bought 39.92 shares. But you paid an average price of only $10.02 ($400/39.92 = $10.02). Voilà—average cost of your purchases was less than the average cost of the stock over that period. Hence the assumption that a bargain was had.

However, the average-price-average/cost debate is really a mathematical quirk. There is no magic to this part of the program. On the other hand, the mathematical quirk provides a measure of comfort for investors who want to buy, but think that the market may be a bit too high. Dollar-cost averaging means never having to say that you bought at the highest price.

The 1990s have provided us with an excellent environment in which to exercise a dollar-cost averaging program. Talk to most people, and they'll tell you that the stock market is expensive. Perhaps not overvalued, but clearly expensive. Yet despite the concern over valuations, the stock market keeps going and going and going.

Investors who don't want to be left on the sidelines often depend on strategies like dollar-cost averaging—something to motivate their decision to invest. I've even seen one advertisement about a mutual fund company that began selling a dollar-cost averaging fund that allows investors to enter the market systematically making equal weekly investments.

Market volatility is also a factor that attracts investors to the concept of dollar-cost averaging. The more volatile the market, the greater the spread between the average price of the shares over the acquisition period and the greater the perceived bargain. Allow me to explain:

Returning again to our XYZ example, suppose the following weekly closing prices occurred.

PERIOD	PRICE	INVESTMENT	# OF SHARES
Week 1	10	$100	10.00
Week 2	8	$100	12.50
Week 3	14	$100	7.14
Week 4	9	$100	11.11

The average price for XYZ over this four-week period is $10.25, just as it was in our first example. But this time you purchased 40.75 shares for an average cost of $9.81 per share. More shares were purchased at a lower average cost, even though the average cost of the stock over the four-week period was the same as it was in our first example. The difference, of course, is that the stock was more volatile, which leads marketing departments to suggest that, with dollar-cost averaging, volatility is your friend.

If you're nervous about the market being too high or too volatile, it's nice to know that there's a strategy that will let you avoid buying at the top. The average-purchase-price-versus-average-price mathematical quirk guarantees that.

Dollar-cost averaging in its traditional sense has very little value for the aggressive investor. However, when we venture beyond traditional views, dollar-cost averaging becomes an interesting concept for aggressive investors, especially if we can marry some of the positive attributes of dollar-cost averaging with the short-term biases of the aggressive investor.

DOLLAR-COST AVERAGING AND THE AGGRESSIVE INVESTOR

Let's begin with a couple of assumptions. Dollar-cost averaging is appropriate if:

1. you believe the underlying market or the specific underlying stock is expensive, and/or

2. the underlying market or stock is too volatile to allow you to comfortably enter a new position.

We know that the cost of an option—i.e., the option's premium—reflects the market's expectation of the future volatility of the underlying security. The higher the volatility assumption, the higher the option premium.

By combining options, whose price is inexorably linked to volatility, with dollar-cost averaging, a strategy that benefits from volatility, we should be able to create a more efficient approach to investing.

The trick is to understand both concepts and then apply a specific option strategy, with a specific goal in mind. This leads us into aggressive strategy #2, the dollar-cost-averaging option.

This strategy complements the falling-for-dollars trade. With the falling-for-dollars strategy, we look for stocks that have fallen from grace. With the dollar-cost averaging option, we look for stocks with strong positive momentum.

The dollar-cost averaging option is really a covered combination, a three-part strategy that involves:

- *the purchase of the underlying stock,*
- *the sale of a covered call, and*
- *the sale of a cash-secured put.*

By way of explanation, we'll use our hypothetical XYZ company. It's July 1998, and XYZ has rallied from $105 to $126 per share (circle marks the spot) over a period of three weeks. The reason: a quarterly earnings number that was much better than expected. At this point, XYZ has two positive factors going for it, in the context of our dollar-cost approach:

1. The stock has been extremely volatile, moving from $105 to $126.

2. The stock has positive momentum, not only in terms of the 20% rise during the first three weeks in July, but in terms of its performance since the beginning of 1998.

The next step is to examine the XYZ option premiums, the prices of which can be found in Table 7.1.

FIGURE 7.1

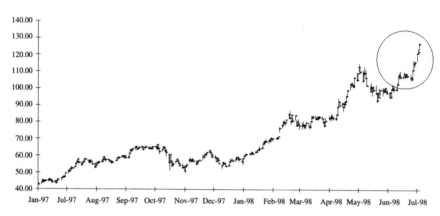

XYZ—ONE YEAR

TABLE 7.1

STRIKE PRICE	EXPIRATION	CALLS	PUTS
115.00	Oct	21.125	10.125
120.00	Oct	18.500	12.500
125.00	Oct	16.125	15.125
130.00	Oct	13.875	17.875
135.00	Oct	11.875	20.875

Implementing the dollar-cost-averaging option is a three-step process, although you should enter this trade as one order. Breaking the trade into its component parts, we begin by purchasing 100 shares of XYZ at $126, selling one XYZ October 130 call at $13.875 and one XYZ October 115 put at $10.125 (in the options market, this is referred to as a covered combination).

The sale of two options immediately nets $24 per share ($13.875 per share for the call + $10.125 per share for the put) in premium income. That's your upfront fee based on the current volatility of XYZ. The two option premiums effectively reduce your initial cost to buy 100 shares of XYZ from $126 per share to $102 per share. And since I want you to execute this trade as one order, you would ask your broker to buy the shares and sell the call and the put, for a net debit of $102 per share.

Placing this order using a net debit allows the broker to sell the call and the put at any price, as long as your total cost does not exceed $102 per share. For example, the stock may rise after the order is entered, and you might buy the stock at, say, $130 per share instead of $126. This is okay as long as you receive $28 in premium from the sale of the XYZ call and put. The bottom line is the total cost for your stock cannot exceed the $102 per share.

So what have we done? By selling the October 130 call, we are agreeing to sell the 100 shares of XYZ at $130 per share until the October expiration. Since you own the stock, this call is covered. If XYZ is above $130 per share in October, the call will be exercised. At that point, you will receive $130 per share for your stock. You will then deliver your 100 shares of XYZ to the call buyer.

That's the best-case scenario. Your total return is $130 per share less your net investment, which was $102 per share ($126 per share to buy the stock less $24 per share in option premiums). That's a 30% return over three months. If you can do that four times in a year, that's 120%!

Before you run to your broker with an order, however, let's understand the other side of this trade. Remember, we've also sold an October 115 put option. The put obligates us to buy an additional 100 shares of XYZ at $115 until the October expiry.

In order to be covered, you need to set aside sufficient capital to buy the additional 100 shares of XYZ should the stock be put to you. In fact some brokerage firms will not allow you to sell an uncovered put option without having all of the money necessary to buy the stock on deposit in the account. This means you need an additional $11,500 in your account—the cost of 100 shares of XYZ at $115 per share—before you implement this trade. By setting aside $11,500 to pay for the additional stock, you've met the definition of a cash secured put.

To review, if XYZ is below the $115 strike price by the October expiration, the put will be exercised, and you'll be required to buy an additional 100 shares of XYZ at $115 per share.

Here's where the dollar-cost averaging concept comes into play. If the put is exercised, your actual cost to purchase the additional 100 shares is $91 per share. Why? Because you received $24 per share in premium when you initially sold the two options. And you need to subtract that from the $115 per share purchase price for the second 100-share lot.

Here's the trade in its entirety:

> • *You buy the first 100 shares at $126.*
> • *If the stock falls below $115, the put is exercised, and you buy another 100 shares at a net cost of $91 per share ($115 strike price less $24 in premium income).*
> • *Should you end up with 200 shares, your average cost will be $108.50, which is about 16% below the current price of $126. And isn't that what dollar-cost averaging is all about?*

By the way, $108.50 in this example is your breakeven price, less any interest you might have earned on the capital set aside to secure the short put option.

Before going any further, let's look at the total return on this trade in a best-case scenario, assuming you pay for the initial 100 shares outright and maintain $11,500 in excess cash to support the purchase of the second 100-share lot if the put is assigned. Think of this as your cash-on-cash return. The covered combination worksheet is as follows:

XYZ MARGIN WORKSHEET

NET INVESTMENT CALCULATION		PRICE PER SHARE	NUMBER OF SHARES	TOTAL COST
Buy	XYZ	126.000	100	12,600.00
Sell	XYZ October 130 Calls	13.875	100	−1,387.50
Sell	XYZ October 115 Puts	10.125	100	−1,012.50
Deposit	Cash to secure short puts	—	100	—
Equals	**Net Investment**			**$10,200.00**

RETURN IF STOCK CALLED AWAY		RECEIPTS PER SHARE	NUMBER OF SHARES	NET RECEIPTS
Sell	XYZ	130.00	100	13,000.00
Plus	Dividends Received	—	100	—
Plus	Cash to secure puts	115.00	100	—
Plus	Interest on cash deposit *			—
Less	Net Investment			−10,200.00
Equals	**Net Return**			**$ 2,800.00**
	Percent return if called away			**27.45%**

RETURN IF STOCK UNCHANGED		VALUE PER SHARE	NUMBER OF SHARES	NET VALUE
	XYZ	126.00	100	12,600.00
Plus	Dividends Received	—	100	—
Plus	Cash to secure puts	—	100	—
Plus	Interest on cash deposit *			—
Less	XYZ October 130 Calls	—	100	—
Less	XYZ October 115 Puts	—	100	—
Less	Net Investment			−10,200.00
Equals	**Net Return**			**$2,400.00**
	Percent return if unchanged			**23.53%**

DOWNSIDE BREAKEVEN	VALUE PER SHARE	NUMBER OF SHARES	NET COST
Cost to buy first block of shares	126.00	100	12,600.00
Cost for second block if put exercised	115.00	100	11,500.00

continued

	DOWNSIDE BREAKEVEN	VALUE PER SHARE	NUMBER OF SHARES	NET COST
Less	Dividends	—	100	0.00
Less	Interest on cash deposit *			0.00
Less	Total Option Premiums Received			−2,400.00
Divide	By total number of shares		200	
Equals	**Breakeven price per share**			**$108.50**
Equals	**Percent downside protection**			**13.89%**

* Interest assumed to be 4% per annum.

Based on the cash-on-cash model, this trade returns 12.9% on the total capital investment during the three-month period, or 51.6% annualized. That assumes the stock rises and is called away. If the stock remains unchanged during the life of the trade, the static return is 11.59%, or 46.4% annualized.

The downside breakeven on this trade assumes that the other 100 shares are purchased. Downside breakeven then is the average price of the original 100-share purchase and the second 100-share lot, assuming the additional shares are put to us, less any dividends and interest earned on the cash. We're assuming that XYZ does not pay a dividend. Based on these assumptions, the downside breakeven is $107.93.

The next step is to look at this trade on a leveraged basis. By that I mean that we assume that cash is not set aside to buy the additional 100 shares of XYZ. In this example we pay for the original 100 shares of XYZ, but we do not then have a cash-secured put option.

XYZ CASH WORKSHEET

	NET INVESTMENT CALCULATION	PRICE PER SHARE	NUMBER OF SHARES	TOTAL COST
Buy	XYZ	126.000	100	12,600.00
Sell	XYZ October 130 Calls	13.875	100	−1,387.50
Sell	XYZ October 115 Puts	10.125	100	−1,012.50
Deposit	Cash to secure short puts	115.000	100	11,500.00
Equals	**Net Investment**			**$21,700.00**

	RETURN IF STOCK CALLED AWAY	RECEIPTS PER SHARE	NUMBER OF SHARES	NET RECEIPTS
Sell	XYZ	130.00	100	13,000.00
Plus	Dividends Received	—	100	—
Plus	Cash to secure puts	115.00	100	11,500.00
Plus	Interest on cash deposit *			115.00
Less	Net Investment			−21,700.00
Equals	**Net Return**			**$2,800.00**
	Percent return if called away			**12.90%**

	RETURN IF STOCK UNCHANGED	VALUE PER SHARE	NUMBER OF SHARES	NET VALUE
	XYZ	126.00	100	12,600.00
Plus	Dividends Received	—	100	—
Plus	Cash to secure puts	115.00	100	11,500.00
Plus	Interest on cash deposit *			115.00
Less	XYZ October 130 Calls	—	100	—
Less	XYZ October 115 Puts	—	100	—
Less	Net Investment			−21,700.00
Equals	**Net Return**			**$2,515.00**
	Percent return if unchanged			**11.59%**

	DOWNSIDE BREAKEVEN	VALUE PER SHARE	NUMBER OF SHARES	NET COST
	Cost to buy first block of shares	126.00	100	12,600.00
	Cost for second block if put exercised	115.00	100	11,500.00
Less	Dividends	—	100	0.00
Less	Interest on cash deposit *			−115.00
Less	Total Option Premiums Received			−2,400.00
Divide	By total number of shares		200	
Equals	**Breakeven price per share**			**$107.93**
Equals	**Percent downside protection**			**14.35%**

* Interest assumed to be 4% per annum.

   The leveraged model simply assumes that you do not set aside the capital required to buy the second block of stock should the put be assigned. The net investment calculation assumes that you pay for the original stock in full, less any option premiums received. There is no margin interest cost associated with this trade. Because you paid for the initial 100 shares, they can be used to cover the margin requirement, meaning you don't have to deposit additional capital when the trade is implemented.

   That being said, some brokerage firms will not allow you to trade an uncovered put that is not secured by cash. In such a case you can use the excess margin you may have available on other investments in your total portfolio.

   For example, suppose you have a $50,000 portfolio invested in a conservative mix of stocks, bonds and cash. That's in your conservative account. In your aggressive account you have a covered combination. Assuming you owe nothing on your conservative investment portfolio, you can use it as collateral to support the short put in your aggressive portfolio. Most brokerage firms will allow that type of cross-guarantee.

Based on the leveraged model, this trade returns 27.45% on the net capital investment during the three-month period or 109.8% annualized. That assumes the best-case scenario in which the stock rises and is called away, and it assumes that you could enter three other trades with similar return characteristics. If the stock remains unchanged during the life of the trade, the static return is 23.53%, or 94.12% annualized.

The downside breakeven on this trade assumes that the other 100 shares are purchased. Downside breakeven then is the average price of the original 100-share purchase and the second 100-share lot assuming the additional shares are put to us. Based on that assumption, the downside breakeven is $108.50. The only difference in the downside breakeven price between the cash and margin position is the interest earned on the cash set aside to secure the short puts.

THE APPEAL OF THE DOLLAR-COST-AVERAGING OPTION

This strategy will appeal to investors who are moderately bullish on the underlying stock. Whenever you buy an initial block of stock and agree to buy more at a lower price, you ought to be bullish. The dollar-cost-averaging option should also appeal to investors who have a basic understanding of covered call writing, because 50% of the combination strategy is a covered call write. Familiarity breeds comfort.

The covered combination, like dollar-cost averaging, is a disciplined approach to investing. The underlying stock is held when the put and call are sold. The sale of two options generates an upfront fee based on the volatility of the underlying stock.

Finally, the covered combination defines purchase and sale parameters at the time the strategy is initiated. Buying half now and, perhaps, half later should appeal to investors who preach dollar-cost averaging .

ADDING AN EDGE TO THE DOLLAR-COST-AVERAGING OPTION

So far, we've examined this strategy on the basis of its potential return in a best-case scenario and its downside risk. What we haven't done is establish a set of rules to enter the trade—our edge to help increase the odds of a successful dollar-cost-averaging option. Now we have to look under the hood of this high-powered trade to find out what makes it run.

We'll begin this trade with a review of the company's financials. Ideally, I look for a company that has a history of earnings, growing by at least 10% per annum. Ideally, I'd like to see the company's earnings growing at 1.25 times the rate of the industry in which the company operates. In other words, if I'm buying a software company, I want to make certain that my company is growing earnings at 1.25 times the rate of the average for the software industry. Assuming the company is growing earnings, has a long history of earnings and, as with all of our strategies, is a large-cap blue-chip company in a solid industry, then we have in place the proper fundamentals to begin our search for the right dollar-cost-averaging trade.

Assuming ABC meets our fundamental criteria, then it is probably a stock with positive momentum. It's also likely a company that's trading well above its 200-day moving average, which, as we've already defined in Chapter Five, is where we'd expect to see our strongest support.

Given that background, take a look at Figure 7.2, a chart of ABC company up to and including the second quarter of 1998. In this particular chart I've included the 200-day moving average for ABC. Since this stock has been one of the leaders in the market, the 200-day moving average is where I would expect to find it, well below the current price.

FIGURE 7.2

ABC CORP.

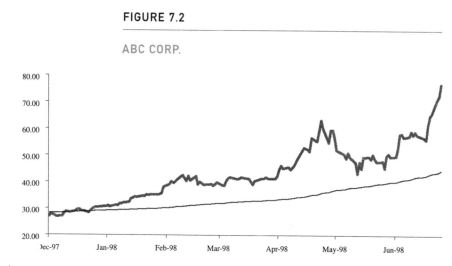

(As with all of our aggressive trades, I'm also interested in the 50-day moving average. The 50-day moving average provides the midpoint for our trading bands. Before looking at the trading bands for ABC, however, I want to know the price at which I'd expect the strongest support—the stock's 200-day moving average.)

I want to make certain that if I have to buy more shares of the stock, I'll be buying those shares below the 200-day moving average. We'll soon explain why.

Companies that are trading well above their 200-day moving average have, by definition, exhibited strong momentum. Presumably, the company has moved higher on the basis of good fundamentals. But now it has spiked sharply higher, driven for the most part by momentum investors.

Another way to look at this is through the stock's relative strength. I would expect a stock with positive momentum to rank among the top 20% of stocks in terms of relative strength—in this case, relative to some broad stock-market index. In fact, you could say that high relative strength is one of the best tools for screening potential dollar-cost-averaging candidates.

UNDERSTANDING RELATIVE STRENGTH

When I speak of relative strength, I'm looking at how a particular stock is performing relative to the overall market. How, for example, is ABC—a large-cap U.S. company—performing relative to, say, the S&P 500 composite index? What I'm looking for is a stock that's moving up faster than the overall market.

Think about that for a moment. It's one thing to have a stock moving higher. That tells us that it has positive momentum. But is the stock moving higher because the market is moving higher? Then the positive momentum probably has more to do with the market than the specific stock, like ships rising together with the tide. I'd rather not use such a stock as part of a dollar-cost-averaging trade. I'd prefer to employ an index-trading strategy and get a bigger bang for my aggressive dollar.

I want our dollar-cost-averaging ship to rise faster and farther than all the other ships, which brings relative strength to center stage. Relative strength is simply the price of a specific stock by the price of a broad market index. However, what I'm doing is comparing the 50-day moving average (remember a 50-day moving average encompasses the previous 35 trading days) for the stock in question, relative to the 50-day moving average of some broad measure of the stock market's performance. Table 7.2 compares ABC relative to the S&P 500 composite index.

TABLE 7.2

CALCULATING RELATIVE STRENGTH

DATE	RELATIVE STRENGTH	ABC 50-DAY	S&P 500 50-DAY
16-Feb-98	0.0322	31.51	979.91
17-Feb-98	0.0323	31.72	982.16
18-Feb-98	0.0325	31.94	983.85
19-Feb-98	0.0327	32.23	985.85
22-Feb-98	0.0329	32.54	987.77
23-Feb-98	0.0332	32.86	989.37
24-Feb-98	0.0334	33.16	991.82
25-Feb-98	0.0337	33.50	994.34
26-Feb-98	0.0339	33.85	997.17
01-Mar-98	0.0343	34.28	1,000.87
02-Mar-98	0.0345	34.65	1,004.26

continued

DATE	RELATIVE STRENGTH	ABC 50-DAY	S&P 500 50-DAY
03-Mar-98	0.0347	34.96	1,007.07
04-Mar-98	0.0350	35.32	1,009.44
05-Mar-98	0.0352	35.63	1,012.68
08-Mar-98	0.0354	35.98	1,015.39
09-Mar-98	0.0356	36.23	1,017.95
10-Mar-98	0.0358	36.50	1,020.91
11-Mar-98	0.0359	36.77	1,024.23
12-Mar-98	0.0360	37.01	1,027.52
15-Mar-98	0.0361	37.25	1,031.20
16-Mar-98	0.0362	37.47	1,034.62
17-Mar-98	0.0363	37.68	1,037.90
18-Mar-98	0.0364	37.89	1,041.18
19-Mar-98	0.0365	38.12	1,044.58

To calculate relative strength in the second column, we simply divide the 50-day moving average for the S&P 500 composite index on a daily basis into the 50-day moving average of ABC. On March 11, 1998, for example, the 50-day moving average for ABC was $36.77, while the 50-day moving average for the S&P 500 was 1,024.23. If we divide $36.77 by 1,024.23, the result is 0.0359.

FIGURE 7.3

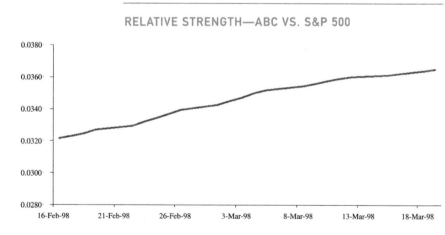

RELATIVE STRENGTH—ABC VS. S&P 500

The actual number is not important, only that the numbers are rising. Ideally, I like to see both the index and the stock price rising, although that's not critical to this particular trade. What's most important is that the stock is rising at a faster rate than the broad market as measured, in this case, by the S&P 500 composite index. Figure 7.3 graphs the relative-strength numbers from Table 7.2. Note how the line is rising from left to right.

LAYING THE GROUNDWORK

What we have to this point is a strong company that is growing earnings faster than the industry average. It has positive momentum and it's trading well above its 200-day moving average, with rising relative strength.

Finding such a company is not as difficult as you might imagine. It will be one of the strongest-moving companies on any given day and will often be setting new highs in a rising market. Analysts would look to companies like this for leadership in the broader market.

Always looking for an edge, we have as our next step to examine the option premiums. In this case, I look for stocks whose option premiums are well above average premium for equity options in general, although they do not have to be higher than the norm for the particular stock.

If, for example, the average equity option premium was implying a 30% volatility, and ABC options were implying a 40% volatility, then ABC options meet my criteria. In fact, the premiums on the ABC options will undoubtedly be higher than the average equity option, simply because ABC is rising faster than the average stock. Remember our relative-strength analysis: Ideally, I look for a stock whose options are in the top two quintiles (i.e., quintile 4 or 5) for all equity-option implied volatilities.

This strategy works best when the underlying stock has had a good run. I don't expect the stock to fall dramatically from this point. I also don't expect the stock to continue rising with such intensity, although any rise above current levels is a positive move for the dollar-cost-averaging trade. With that in mind, let's examine the strategy in its entirety, using ABC as our sample company.

AGGRESSIVE TRADE #2 : THE DOLLAR-COST-AVERAGING OPTION

When looking at the dollar-cost-averaging option, we begin with a large-cap blue-chip company in a growing industry. We want a company with a long history of earnings, some decent fundamentals and, obviously, a large following among investors. Stocks that are widely followed and actively traded provide liquidity. That's important, because this is a three-part trade. We will buy the stock and sell both a call and a put. To implement such a trade, we need a liquid stock and options.

For the dollar-cost-averaging trade, we look for companies with positive momentum. I've already talked about a couple of things you can look for to define momentum. One of the first things we can do is screen for stocks with high relative strength. Investors Business Daily provides this information on a daily basis for U.S. stocks. You can also find this information on the Internet at http://www.bigcharts.com, where you can chart different stocks and compare them with various indices. You can also look at the stocks' performance after their most recent earnings releases.

In Figure 7.4, for example, we see a one-year chart of Microsoft compared with the technology index. (The solid line in the upper chart represents the technology index). Over the previous year, Microsoft has risen by 68%, while the technology index is up approximately 17%. Also take note of the triangles representing earnings release dates, and notice the performance of the stock prior to and after the earnings are released. The earnings numbers for the previous four quarters were all better than expected, which is indicated by the upward-facing triangle. That helps us gauge the fundamentals I mentioned earlier—i.e., positive upward bias to earnings, growing faster than the underlying industry.

FIGURE 7.4

ONE-YEAR CHART ON MICROSOFT

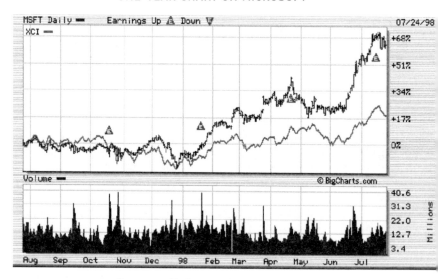

Source: www.bigcharts.com

Having narrowed the list of potential candidates, we apply a second criterion. Obviously, if the stock has long-term relative strength, it will by definition be trading well above its 200-day moving average. (We've seen how the stock was performing relative to its 200-day moving average, in Figure 7.2.)

However, in selecting the stock for the dollar-cost-averaging trade, I would like to buy into it during a consolidation period, when it takes a breather after a strong run-up. I can measure that by looking at the stock's 50-day moving average, which reflects more closely the stock's most recent movements. Preferably, I would look for a stock that's at or just slightly above its 50-day moving average. Figure 7.5 looks at ABC compared with its 50-day and 200-day moving averages.

FIGURE 7.5

ABC CORP.

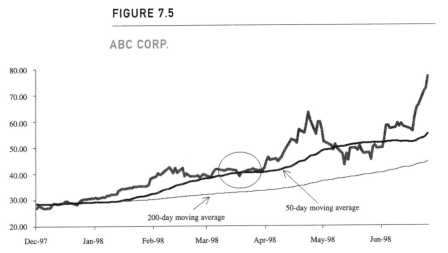

When I say I'm looking for a stock that's at or slightly above the 50-day moving average, I mean a stock that's gravitating toward its 50-day moving average, not one that has just fallen sharply. More precisely, the stock should have occupied a relatively narrow trading range for a short period, which will allow the 50-day moving average to gradually converge with the current stock price.

A stock's current price can converge with its 50-day moving average in one of three ways:

> 1. The stock price can decline sharply while the 50-day moving average remains stable;
> 2. the stock price can remain stable, while the 50-day moving average gradually rises to the current price level; or
> 3. the stock can decline in a relatively stable fashion, while the 50-day moving average slowly rises to the point of convergence.

If the 50-day moving average and the current stock price converge according to our second or third scenario, then the stock meets our second criterion. If, as in the first scenario, the stock has fallen sharply to converge with the 50-day moving average, I would not consider it a candidate for the dollar-cost-averaging option. But it may still work as a falling-for-dollars trade, as we discussed in the previous chapter.

So Rule #3 states that the underlying stock's current price must be well above the 200-day moving average, and its current price must also converge with its 50-day moving average, preferably by remaining in a relatively narrow trading range, while the 50-day moving average rises to the point of convergence. Circle marks the spot in Figure 7.5, where the dollar-cost-averaging trade could have been implemented using ABC Corp.

At this stage, we want the options to be the in the top quartile in terms of implied volatility. I'm looking for expensive options, not necessarily in terms of the historical volatility for the stock, but in terms of the average implied volatility for all equity options. Table 7.3 examines the average for all equity-option premiums as of the middle of March 1998.

TABLE 7.3

EQUITY IMPLIED VOLATILITIES

QUINTILE	LOW	HIGH
5	50.01%	and higher
4	40.01%	50.00%
3	30.01%	40.00%
2	20.01%	30.00%
1	10.00%	20.00%

Table 7.4 lists the July series of options on our hypothetical ABC Corp. along with their respective prices, on March 18th, when ABC is trading at $38.75 (inside the circle on Figure 7.5). Looking at the options on ABC, the premiums imply a volatility of 51%, which is in the top quintile of all equity options.

TABLE 7.4

ABC @ $38.75

STRIKE	JULY CALLS	JULY PUTS
30.00	10.000	1.250
35.00	6.750	2.875
40.00	4.250	5.500
45.00	2.500	8.875
50.00	1.500	12.750

To review, we have five rules that must be met before entering the dollar-cost-averaging option trade:

1. The stock must be a large-cap blue-chip company in a growing industry.

2. The stock must have solid fundamentals—a long history of earnings that are still growing, preferably above expectations (see Figure 7.4).

3. The stock must have positive momentum as defined by its strength relative to a broad stock market index, such as the S&P 500 for U.S. stocks or, for Canadian stocks, the TSE 300.

4. The stock must be trading well above its 200-day moving average, but must be converging on its 50-day moving average. The convergence must take place in a stable manner, with either the 50-day moving average gradually rising to the current price level or the stock gradually falling while the 50-day moving average rises to the point of convergence. The stock must not make a sharp decline to the 50-day moving average.

5. The option premiums must be expensive. They don't have to be high relative to the stock's historical volatility, but they must be high relative to the average of all equity options. Ideally, the option premiums must be in the 4th or 5th quintile of all implied volatilities among all equity options.

INITIATING THE DOLLAR-COST-AVERAGING OPTION TRADE

Figure 7.6 is a chart of ABC that includes our familiar trading bands. Note that on March 18, 1998, the stock is touching its 50-day moving average (see circle). The convergence took place gradually, mostly the result of ABC consolidating after a strong rally, letting the 50-day moving average rise gradually to the current stock price, an ideal situation in terms of timing a point of entry.

With all our criteria met, we enter the dollar-cost-averaging option trade using ABC Corp. With ABC trading at $38.75, we buy 100 shares and sell the July 40 call at $4.25 and the July 35 put for $2.875. The net premium received from the sale of the two options equals $7.125 per share.

When entering the order for this trade, you would ask the broker to buy a covered combination on ABC—specifically, buying the stock, selling the July 40 calls and July 35 puts for a net debit of $31.625. That's the total debit for this trade after accounting for the two option premiums.

Given that information, we can then input the numbers into the following worksheet.

FIGURE 7.6

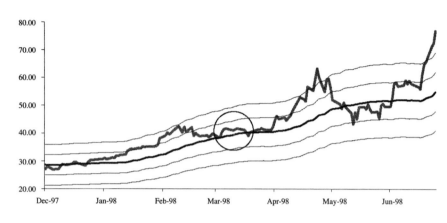

ABC CORP. WITH TRADING BANDS

ABC CASH WORKSHEET

	NET INVESTMENT CALCULATION	PRICE PER SHARE	NUMBER OF SHARES	TOTAL COST
Buy	ABC	38.750	100	3,875.00
Sell	ABC July 40 Calls	4.250	100	−425.00
Sell	ABC July 30 Puts	1.250	100	−125.00
Deposit	Cash to secure short puts	30.000	100	3,000.00
Equals	**Net Investment**			**$6,325.00**

	RETURN IF STOCK CALLED AWAY	RECEIPTS PER SHARE	NUMBER OF SHARES	NET RECEIPTS
Sell	ABC	40.00	100	4,000.00
Plus	Dividends Received	—	100	—
Plus	Cash to secure puts	30.00	100	3,000.00
Plus	Interest on cash deposit *			40.00
Less	Net Investment			−6,325.00
Equals	**Net Return**			**$675.00**
	Percent return if called away			**10.67%**

	RETURN IF STOCK UNCHANGED	VALUE PER SHARE	NUMBER OF SHARES	NET VALUE
	ABC	38.75	100	3,875.00
Plus	Dividends Received	—	100	—

continued

	RETURN IF STOCK UNCHANGED	VALUE PER SHARE	NUMBER OF SHARES	NET VALUE
Plus	Cash to secure puts	30.00	100	3,000.00
Plus	Interest on cash deposit *			40.00
Less	ABC July 40 Calls	—	100	—
Less	ABC July 30 Puts	—	100	—
Less	Net Investment			–6,325.00
Equals	**Net Return**			**$590.00**
	Percent return if unchanged			**9.33%**

	DOWNSIDE BREAKEVEN	VALUE PER SHARE	NUMBER OF SHARES	NET COST
	Cost to buy first block of shares	38.75	100	3,875.00
	Cost for second block if put exercised	30.00	100	3,000.00
Less	Dividends	—	100	0.00
Less	Interest on cash deposit *			–40.00
Less	Total Option Premiums Received			–550.00
Divide	By total number of shares		200	
Equals	**Breakeven price per share**			**$31.43**
Equals	**Percent downside protection**			**18.90%**

* Interest assumed to be 4% per annum.

In the above worksheet, we have assumed that the trade is done on a cash basis—that is, we set aside sufficient capital to buy the additional 100 shares of ABC should the short-put option be assigned.

Based on these numbers, the rate of return if ABC rises above the strike price of the short call is 10.67% over four months, or 32.01% annualized. That assumes, of course, that ABC is called away at expiration, the best-case scenario for this strategy.

If the stock remains unchanged until the options expire, the rate of return on a cash basis is 9.33%, or 27.99% annualized. Not bad for a strategy in which the underlying stock did not move.

Finally, the downside breakeven on this strategy occurs at $31.43. That's the average price for 200 shares of ABC Corp. The downside breakeven assumes that the short-put option is assigned and you are forced to buy an additional 100 shares of stock at $30 per share. In this scenario, we bought the first 100 shares at $38.75, the second 100 shares at $30 and, in the interim, received option premiums totaling $5.50 per share. If we add $3,875 + $3,000, subtract the $550 premium received ($5.50 per share or $550 per option contract), and then subtract the interest earned on the cash set aside to secure the put ($40), we end up with a dollar value of $6,285. Divide that total by 200 shares, and we have our average price of $31.43, which is our downside breakeven.

There is a certain mathematical science to determining the right options to sell. The key is to make certain that the downside breakeven price is close to the 200-day moving average, where we would expect to find solid support. The upside potential in the best-case scenario, assuming the short call is assigned, should be above the most recent highs for the stock. In this case, the maximum potential would mean you effectively sold the stock for $40 per share + $5.50 in option premium, which equals $45.50. At mid-March the most recent high for the stock was just $42.50, which occurred in the first week of the month.

USING LEVERAGE

Continuing with our ABC example, the next step is to look at the same trade using leverage. In this case, we are not setting aside any capital to support the short put. As long as you purchase the stock outright, you will have sufficient margin to cover the short put.

I recommend that you maintain at least 50% of the purchase price of the second block of shares in case the short put is assigned. You can maintain the 50% margin level as long as you pay for the first 100 shares outright.

In our ABC example, the first 100 shares will cost you $3,325 after accounting for the net premium received. The following worksheet looks at the potential and the risks for the leveraged version of this aggressive trade.

ABC MARGIN WORKSHEET

	NET INVESTMENT CALCULATION	PRICE PER SHARE	NUMBER OF SHARES	TOTAL COST
Buy	ABC	38.750	100	3,875.00
Sell	ABC July 40 Calls	4.250	100	−425.00
Sell	ABC July 30 Puts	1.250	100	−125.00
Deposit	Cash to secure short puts	—	100	—
Equals	**Net Investment**			**$3,325.00**

	RETURN IF STOCK CALLED AWAY	RECEIPTS PER SHARE	NUMBER OF SHARES	NET RECEIPTS
Sell	ABC	40.00	100	4,000.00
Plus	Dividends Received	—	100	—
Plus	Cash to secure puts	—	100	—
Plus	Interest on cash deposit *			—
Less	Net Investment			−3,325.00
Equals	**Net Return**			**$675.00**
	Percent return if called away			**20.30%**

	RETURN IF STOCK UNCHANGED	VALUE PER SHARE	NUMBER OF SHARES	NET VALUE
	ABC	38.75	100	3,875.00
Plus	Dividends Received	—	100	—
Plus	Cash to secure puts		100	—
Plus	Interest on cash deposit *			—
Less	ABC July 40 Calls	—	100	—
Less	ABC July 30 Puts	—	100	—
Less	Net Investment			–3,325.00
Equals	**Net Return**			**$550.00**
	Percent return if unchanged			**16.54%**

	DOWNSIDE BREAKEVEN	VALUE PER SHARE	NUMBER OF SHARES	NET COST
	Cost to buy first block of shares	38.75	100	3,875.00
	Cost for second block if put exercised	30.00	100	3,000.00
Less	Dividends	—	100	0.00
Less	Interest on cash deposit *			0.00
Less	Total Option Premiums Received			–550.00
Divide	By total number of shares		200	
Equals	**Breakeven price per share**			**$31.63**
Equals	**Percent downside protection**			**18.39%**

* Interest assumed to be 4% per annum.

From the above worksheet, you can see that the returns are increased by virtue of the leverage employed in the trade. Based on these numbers, the rate of return if ABC rises above the strike price of the short call is 20.3% over four months, or 60.9% annualized. That assumes, of course, that ABC is called away at expiration, our best-case scenario.

If the stock remains unchanged until the options expire, the rate of return on a leveraged basis is 16.54%, or 49.62% annualized, almost twice the rate of return you'd receive using the cash model for this trade.

Finally, the downside breakeven on this strategy occurs at $31.63. That's the average price for 200 shares of ABC. That price is just above the 200-day moving average and just slightly higher than it would be in the cash trade. Actually the only difference between the two is the interest earned on the cash trade, which you would not earn on the leverage model.

FOLLOW-UP STRATEGY

We know that the worst-case scenario for the dollar-cost-averaging trade is to have to purchase an additional block of shares at the strike price of the put. The question is, at what point does the dollar-cost-averaging strategy require us to re-evaluate it?

Assuming we have structured the dollar-cost-averaging option correctly, the second block of shares should be purchased at a price below the 200-day moving average. And the average price for both blocks of shares should be at or very close to the 200-day moving average.

Unlike the falling-for-dollars trade, this strategy gives me less cause for concern. Although the short-put option is assigned, the strategy still works. As with any dollar-cost-averaging program, we don't necessarily abandon the strategy simply because the stock has declined, especially if we feel confident that we've selected a good solid company with strong fundamentals. Given our criteria for selecting the company in the first place, the stock has a better-than-average chance of making a full recovery. In the meantime, we bought the stock at a reasonable cost—the average cost of both blocks of stock. That being said, we own two blocks of stock at this point, which means the capital required to hold the stock is not being employed aggressively. And that may require us to initiate some follow-up action.

Before doing that, however, we need to be convinced that the fundamentals that drove the stock higher in the first place are still valid. Has there been any fundamental change in the way the company does business? What is the earnings outlook for the future? Is the stock losing relative strength? Assuming the long-term fundamentals remain positive, the next step is to evaluate the option premiums.

Remember, we're looking at follow-up action because we've been assigned on the additional shares of stock. This means the call option has expired worthless. At the very least, if the puts were assigned before expiration, the call would be virtually worthless and could probably be repurchased for 1/16th or an 1/8th .

Based on these conditions, the longer-term options should be trading at a higher implied volatility than when we entered this trade. After all, for the put to be assigned, the stock must have fallen a reasonable distance. And since we were initially dealing with four-month options, the decline must have occurred quickly, suggesting heightened volatility in the stock, just as we'd expect with options in the falling-for-dollars trade. For our purposes, though, we'll assume that the options are implying the same volatility as they did when we initially established the position.

Based on these assumptions, there are two potential follow-up strategies:

1. Close out the position at a loss or, possibly, at a small profit.
2. Roll out the position by selling two longer-term at-the-money covered calls.

FOLLOW-UP STRATEGY #1: CLOSE OUT THE POSITION

There is a chance that we've made a small profit on this trade, even though we were forced to buy an additional block of stock. Remember that the strike price of the put option is usually below the 200-day moving average. It's possible that there would be strong support at that level. The stock can sometimes bounce up from that point, which might allow us to sell the shares at a price above the average cost for both blocks of stock.

With the ABC example, let's assume that the stock is trading at $27. At that price we would be assigned on the short put, forcing us to buy an additional 100 shares at $30, the strike price of the put. At that point, the average price for our 200 shares is $31.63, the downside breakeven. If we sell our 200 shares at $27, we'll close out our position at a loss, not the best scenario. But the loss is relatively small considering that the trade did not go as expected. Our balance sheet would look as follows:

CLOSE-OUT BALANCE SHEET

PARTICULARS	DEBITS	CREDITS
Buy 100 shares ABC @ 38.75	3,875.00	
Sell 1 ABC July 40 Call @ 4.25		425.00
Sell 1 AMC July 30 Call @ 1.25		125.00
Buy 100 shares ABC @ 30	3,000.00	
Sell 200 shares ABC @ 27		5,400.00
Totals	6,875.00	5,950.00

If we sell the shares at $27, our total loss is $525, or about 15.8% on our initial investment (assuming our initial purchase was in the leveraged account) over a four-month period.

This is not my favorite follow-up option for this particular aggressive trade. I don't like selling a stock when I have averaged into the purchase of 200 shares at a price well below the stock's high point and with the stock trading just below its 200-day moving average. This is not the ideal time to be selling, especially if I still like the fundamentals.

Nonetheless, we need to eliminate this option first, just as we evaluate—then, ideally, eliminate—the worst-case scenario when we have a medical problem and seek out other less-threatening solutions to our particular condition.

In fact, that's how you should approach the follow-up action with any of our trades. Eliminate the worst-case scenario first. By looking at closing out the position, you have to ask yourself if you'd buy this stock at this particular time if you didn't already own it. If you wouldn't buy it at this point, then your decision is made.

Close out your position, take your loss, protect as much of your capital as possible, and move on.

If you've incurred a loss, but this is still a stock you'd consider owning, then you should look at follow-up strategy #2.

FOLLOW-UP STRATEGY #2: ROLL OUT THE TRADE

In most cases, if I had a small loss on a position, I would opt for this follow-up action. Usually, if we've picked the company properly in the first place, the setback that caused us to buy the additional shares of stock may be temporary.

In this strategy, we assume that the original options have now expired. Further, we'll assume that ABC is trading at $29 and the following prices exist for ABC October options (see Table 7.5) Note these prices assume a 51% implied volatility.

TABLE 7.5

ABC @ $29

STRIKE	OCT CALLS	OCT PUTS
20.00	9.375	0.375
25.00	5.375	1.250
30.00	2.625	3.625
35.00	1.125	7.125
40.00	0.500	11.500

Based on these prices, I would write two October 30 covered calls. The following covered call write worksheet looks at the potential and risk from this follow-up action. Note the prices for ABC represent the average cost of the 200 shares.

By rolling out the trade, we lower our downside breakeven price to $29.01, which is where the stock is currently trading. If the stock is called away, our return is 3.43% over the three-month holding period. Not very attractive! But remember, we're following up on a losing position, and the follow-up action leaves us with a profit rather than a loss.

One final point: With this follow-up action, we're actually turning the dollar-cost-averaging trade into a falling-for-dollars trade. If the stock continues to decline, then we have to consider further follow-up action. Should that happen, then we need to review the follow-up procedures that we applied to the falling-for-dollars trade in Chapter Six.

ABC COVERED CALL WRITE WORKSHEET

NET INVESTMENT CALCULATION	PRICE PER SHARE	NUMBER OF SHARES	TOTAL COST
Buy ABC Corporation	31.630	200	6,326.00
Sell ABC October 30 Calls	2.625	200	−525.00
Equals **Net Investment**			**$5,801.00**

RETURN IF STOCK CALLED AWAY	RECEIPTS PER SHARE	NUMBER OF SHARES	NET RECEIPTS
Sell XYZ Corporation	30.00	200	6,000.00
Plus Dividends Received	—	200	—
Less Net Investment			(5,801.00)
Equals **Net Return**			**$199.00**
Percent return if called away			**3.43%**

RETURN IF STOCK UNCHANGED	VALUE PER SHARE	NUMBER OF SHARES	NET VALUE
ABC Corporation	29.00	200	5,800.00
Plus Dividends Received	—	200	—
Less ABC October 30 Calls	—	200	—
Less Net Investment			(5,801.00)
Equals **Net Return**			**$(1.00)**
Percent return if unchanged			**−0.02%**

DOWNSIDE BREAKEVEN	VALUE PER SHARE	NUMBER OF SHARES	NET COST
Net Investment			5,801.00
Less Dividends	—	200	—
Equals Total stock cost to expiration			5,801.00
Divide By number of shares held		200	
Equals **Breakeven price per share**			**$29.01**
Equals **Percent downside protection**			**8.30%**

DOLLAR-COST AVERAGING: A REAL-LIFE EXAMPLE

Having looked at a hypothetical example of the dollar-cost-averaging option, let's consider a real-life example: Merrill Lynch. We'll begin by looking at Figure 7.7. This is a chart of Merrill Lynch in the second quarter of 1998. In this particular chart, I've included all the necessary information to judge whether this stock is a good candidate for the dollar-cost-averaging option.

Note the positive earnings momentum. Over the last four quarters, the company reported better-than-expected earnings (note upward-pointing triangles). The stock has positive relative strength when measured against the S&P 500 composite index. (The S&P 500 is represented by the smoothed line.) Note especially the period at the end of April (the circle marks the spot).

FIGURE 7.7

ONE-YEAR CHART ON MERRILL LYNCH

Source: www.bigcharts.com

Now that we have ascertained that the stock fits our criteria for fundamental soundness, being a large-cap blue-chip name with a long earnings history. The next step is to determine whether it's trading well above its 200-day moving average. Figure 7.8 is the same one-year chart on Merrill Lynch, but it now includes the 200-day moving average. As we can see, the stock is indeed trading well above its 200-day moving average (the smoothed line). The 200-day moving average at the end of April was about $75 per share.

I'm also interested in the 50-day moving average and will frame that line with our trading bands in a moment. For now, I simply want to make sure this stock fits our criteria. I am most interested in the price point at which I would expect to find support. In Figure 7.8, the 200-day moving average at the end of April 1998 was crossing at approximately $75 per share. I would expect to find reasonable support around that price point.

FIGURE 7.8

ONE-YEAR CHART ON MERRILL LYNCH INCLUDING 200-DAY MOVING AVERAGE

Source: www.bigcharts.com

I have tried to find a company with strong momentum whose stock price presumably has risen on the basis of some decent fundamentals and has now begun to take off, driven for the most part by momentum investors. Again, I have screened for momentum using relative-strength analysis. Merrill Lynch performed much better than the broader market averages during the first quarter of 1998. (If you don't have access to a charting package that includes a relative-strength comparison, as in Figure 7.7, you can apply the same math as we applied to our hypothetical ABC example. That is, divide the 50-day moving average price for Merrill Lynch by the 50-day moving average of the S&P 500 composite index.)

I also think it's important to understand the company's fundamentals. You don't have to become a financial analyst, but you need to know at the very least that the company has good earnings. I'm not interested in a company that lost money but still rose in value because it beat analysts' expectations. I'm looking for companies that already have a solid earnings base. Bottom line: It's important to avoid getting caught up in the hype surrounding a particularly hot sector of the market.

For example, in the summer of 1998, Internet stocks were the hottest group in the stock market, clearly driven by momentum players and perhaps to extremes in some cases. One that comes to mind is Amazon.Com Inc., which sells books over the Internet. The chart for Amazon.Com says more about the explosive potential of the Internet than I could ever say in words (see Figure 7.9). Note how far above its 200-day moving average (the middle line) the stock has moved. Relative to the performance of the S&P 500 composite index (the line along the bottom of the chart), the comparison is rendered meaningless because of the explosive jump in the company's share price during the two-month period from June 1998 to the end of July 1998.

FIGURE 7.9

ONE-YEAR CHART ON AMAZON.COM INC.

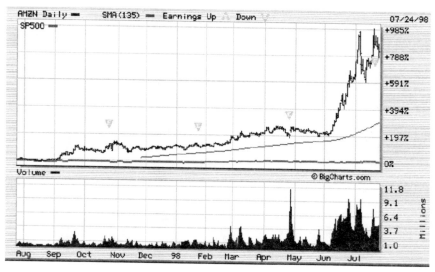

Source: *www.bigcharts.com*

By mid-July 1998, Amazon.Com Inc. had a market cap of between $5 billion and $6 billion, give or take a billion, depending on which day you check its value. This seems a bit rich for a company that's not earning any money (note the earnings triangles) but is being hyped because of its Internet presence. Note the following report from Zacks Investment Research, Inc. (available at http://www.zacks.com). The company beat analysts' consensus estimates. But that simply means that the company lost 20 cents per share instead of 40 cents per share as analysts had expected. Amazon.Com may turn out to be one of the great buying opportunities of the 1990s. But the fact remains, this company is not yet earning anything.

I'm not disputing the vast potential of the Internet. In fact, by the turn of the century, everyone may buy their books this way. But ask yourself, if you had the money, would you pay $6 billion for this company?

ANALYSTS EARNINGS ESTIMATES: AMAZON.COM

Estimates for Current Fiscal Year	–1.15 per share
Estimates for Next Fiscal Year	–0.70 per share
Actual Earnings Last Quarter	–0.20 per share
Estimates for Current Quarter	–0.40 per share
Earnings per Share Surprise Last Quarter	17% +

Source: Zacks Investment Research, Inc.

Returning to the fundamentals, I'm interested in companies that have been around for some time. That's why one of my principal rules behind all aggressive investing strategies is use only large-cap blue-chip stocks. You also have to look at the numbers, such as a company's earnings history. Stocks that have a short history but a price that reflects expectations for unlimited future earnings raise a caution flag in the Croft household.

In this context, Merrill Lynch passes hands down. It has been around a long time. It's one of the largest brokerage firms in the world and a classic takeover or merger candidate with a major financial institution. The Merrill Lynch sales force is as good a distribution channel—i.e., more retail brokers—as Smith Barney or Salomon Brothers, both of whom were taken out by Travellers Group and then merged with Citibank. So Merrill Lynch is a company that could potentially be in play.

The point is, Merrill Lynch is fundamentally sound. It's also a large-cap blue-chip company in a strong industry. Merrill Lynch also meets our conditions for momentum as defined by its relative strength, as Figure 7.7 indicates.

The stock's current price is just converging with its 50-day moving average (see Figure 7.10). And the convergence was the result of the stock falling after a sharp spike up in April while the 50-day moving average was rising. That's not quite as smooth as I like to see for this trade, but it's not bad enough to eliminate Merrill Lynch as a potential candidate.

The next step is to look at the Merrill Lynch options at the end of April 1998. Table 7.6 lists option prices based on a price of $83 for Merrill Lynch in late April.

TABLE 7.6

MERRILL LYNCH AT $83.00

STRIKE	JULY CALLS	JULY PUTS
70.00	14.375	1.375
75.00	10.500	2.500
80.00	7.250	4.250
85.00	4.875	6.750
90.00	3.000	10.000

FIGURE 7.10

ONE-YEAR CHART MERRILL LYNCH + 50-DAY MOVING
AVERAGE

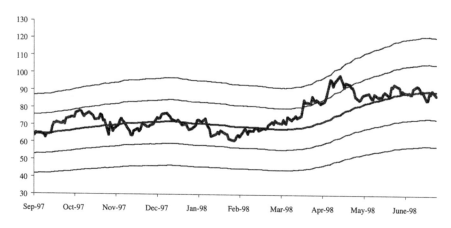

Note that the implied volatility on Merrill Lynch options is 35%. For the record, a 35% implied volatility places Merrill Lynch options at the higher end of the third quintile for all option premiums as of April 1998 (see Table 7.7). Again that conforms to our criteria that the options imply a higher volatility than the average equity option.

TABLE 7.7

EQUITY IMPLIED VOLATILITIES

QUINTILE	LOW	HIGH
5	45.01% and higher	
4	37.01%	45.00%
3	25.01%	37.00%
2	17.01%	25.00%
1	10.00%	17.00%

INITIATING THE TRADE

Having met all of our conditions, we can initiate the Merrill Lynch trade. The next step is to see whether we can implement the dollar-cost-averaging trade using the

July options—those options being three months to expiration, which is the time frame I would expect for the quickest erosion of time value. Should the put option be exercised, you will buy the second block of shares at a price below the 200-day moving average. You want the average price of the two blocks of stock—i.e., the downside breakeven price—to be just at or slightly above the 200-day moving average.

Based on the prices from Table 7.6, we would buy 100 shares of Merrill Lynch at $83 and write the July 90 calls at $3.00 and the July 75 puts at $2.50. The net per-share premium received from the sale of the two options is $5.50 per share. The following worksheet looks at the potential profits and pitfalls of the Merrill Lynch cash-based dollar-cost-averaging option. By cash basis, I mean we've kept aside sufficient capital to buy the additional 100 shares of Merrill Lynch should the short-put option be assigned.

MERRILL LYNCH CASH WORKSHEET

	NET INVESTMENT CALCULATION	PRICE PER SHARE	NUMBER OF SHARES	TOTAL COST
Buy	Merrill Lynch	83.000	100	8,300.00
Sell	Merrill Lynch July 90 Calls	3.000	100	−300.00
Sell	Merrill Lynch July 75 Puts	2.500	100	−250.00
Deposit	Cash to secure short puts	75.000	100	7,500.00
Equals	**Net Investment**			**$15,250.00**

	RETURN IF STOCK CALLED AWAY	RECEIPTS PER SHARE	NUMBER OF SHARES	NET RECEIPTS
Sell	Merrill Lynch	90.00	100	9,000.00
Plus	Dividends Received	0.24	100	24.00
Plus	Cash to secure puts	75.00	100	7,500.00
Plus	Interest on cash deposit *			100.00
Less	Net Investment			−15,250.00
Equals	**Net Return**			**$1,250.00**
	Percent return if called away			**8.20%**

	RETURN IF STOCK UNCHANGED	VALUE PER SHARE	NUMBER OF SHARES	NET VALUE
	Merrill Lynch	83.00	100	8,300.00
Plus	Dividends Received	0.24	100	24.00
Plus	Cash to secure puts	75.00	100	7,500.00
Plus	Interest on cash deposit *			100.00
Less	Merrill Lynch July 90 Calls	—	100	—
Less	Merrill Lynch July 75 Puts	—	100	—
Less	Net Investment			−15,250.00
Equals	**Net Return**			**$674.00**
	Percent return if unchanged			**4.42%**

continued

1 7 5

DOWNSIDE BREAKEVEN	VALUE PER SHARE	NUMBER OF SHARES	NET COST
Cost to buy first block of shares	83.00	100	8,300.00
Cost for second block if put exercised	75.00	100	7,500.00
Less Dividends	0.24	100	−24.00
Less Interest on cash deposit *			−100.00
Less Total Option Premiums Received			−550.00
Divide By total number of shares		200	
Equals Breakeven price per share			**$75.63**
Equals Percent downside protection			**8.88%**

* Interest assumed to be 4% per annum.

Based on these numbers, the rate of return if Merrill Lynch rises above the strike price of the short call is 8.20% over the next three months, or 32.8% annualized. That assumes, of course, that Merrill Lynch is called away at expiration. This, of course, is the best-case scenario for the strategy and assumes that Merrill Lynch is called away at expiration.

If the stock remains unchanged until the options expire, the rate of return on a cash basis is 4.42%, or 17.68% annualized. Not bad when the underlying stock did not move.

Finally, the downside breakeven on this strategy occurs at $75.63. That's the average price for 200 shares of Merrill Lynch. The downside breakeven assumes that the short-put option is assigned, and we're forced to buy an additional 100 shares of stock at $90 per share. Note that we bought the first 100 shares at $83 and the second 100 shares at $75. And we received two option premiums totaling $5.50 per share. If we then add $8,300 (original cost for 100 shares) + $7,500 (cost for second block of 100 shares) less the $550 premium received, the total dollar value is $15,250. Divide that by 200 shares, and we have our average price of $76.25. Take out the dividend received and the interest earned on the cash balance, and your downside breakeven is further reduced to $75.63 per share. Note that the downside breakeven is well above the 200-day moving average at the time the trade was initiated.

As for the upside potential in the best-case scenario, the stock will be sold at $90 per share plus the $5.50 per share in option premiums. Maximum potential pegs the upside price at $95.50 per share, which is above the all-time high for Merrill Lynch at the time the trade was initiated (i.e., April 1998).

USING LEVERAGE

Continuing with our Merrill Lynch example, the next step is to look at the trade using leverage. In this case, I recommend that you pay 100% of the cost of the first block of shares. In our Merrill Lynch example, the first 100 shares will cost you $8,300. The following worksheet looks at the potential and the risks for the leveraged version of this aggressive trade.

MERRILL LYNCH MARGIN WORKSHEET

NET INVESTMENT CALCULATION	PRICE PER SHARE	NUMBER OF SHARES	TOTAL COST
Buy Merrill Lynch	83.000	100	8,300.00
Sell Merrill Lynch July 90 Calls	3.000	100	−300.00
Sell Merrill Lynch July 75 Puts	2.500	100	−250.00
Deposit Cash to secure short puts		100	—
Equals **Net Investment**			**$7,750.00**

RETURN IF STOCK CALLED AWAY	RECEIPTS PER SHARE	NUMBER OF SHARES	NET RECEIPTS
Sell Merrill Lynch	90.00	100	9,000.00
Plus Dividends Received	0.24	100	24.00
Plus Cash to secure puts		100	—
Plus Interest on cash deposit *			—
Less Net Investment			−7,750.00
Equals **Net Return**			**$1,250.00**
Percent return if called away			**16.13%**

RETURN IF STOCK UNCHANGED	VALUE PER SHARE	NUMBER OF SHARES	NET VALUE
Merrill Lynch	83.00	100	8,300.00
Plus Dividends Received	0.24	100	24.00
Plus Cash to secure puts		100	—
Plus Interest on cash deposit *			—
Less Merrill Lynch July 90 Calls	—	100	—
Less Merrill Lynch July 75 Puts	—	100	—
Less Net Investment			−7,750.00
Equals **Net Return**			**$574.00**
Percent return if unchanged			**7.41%**

DOWNSIDE BREAKEVEN	VALUE PER SHARE	NUMBER OF SHARES	NET COST
Cost to buy first block of shares	83.00	100	8,300.00
Cost for second block if put exercised	75.00	100	7,500.00

continued

	DOWNSIDE BREAKEVEN	VALUE PER SHARE	NUMBER OF SHARES	NET COST
Less	Dividends	0.24	100	−24.00
Less	Interest on cash deposit *			0.00
Less	Total Option Premiums Received			−550.00
Divide	By total number of shares		200	
Equals	**Breakeven price per share**			**$76.13**
Equals	**Percent downside protection**			**8.28%**

* Interest assumed to be 4% per annum.

Using the leverage trade, the rate of return should Merrill Lynch rise above the strike price of the short call is 16.13% over three months, or 64.52% annualized. That assumes, of course, that Merrill Lynch is called away at expiration. If the stock remains unchanged until the options expire, the rate of return on a leveraged basis is 7.41%, or 29.64% annualized. Not bad for a strategy in which the underlying stock did not move.

Finally, the downside breakeven on this strategy occurs at $76.13. That's the average price for 200 shares of Merrill Lynch. The downside breakeven assumes that the short-put option is assigned, and you are forced to buy an additional 100 shares of stock at $75 per share. The difference between the downside breakeven for the leveraged position versus the cash position is directly related to interest earned on the excess cash reserves associated with the cash position.

The downside breakeven in the leveraged position is still below the 200-day moving average, which provides a nice balance to this particular trade. The upside potential in the best-case scenario means that you sell the stock at a price above its most recent highs that occurred in mid-April. In this case, the maximum potential would mean you effectively sold the stock for $95.50 per share. That includes the funds from the sale of the stock at the strike price of the call plus the per-share premiums received from the sale of the call and the put.

If you look again at Figure 7.10, you'll see that Merrill Lynch did indeed close above $90 per share in late July, making the maximum potential return on this trade. But also note that Merrill Lynch fell sharply in August and September, as worries over bad trades in Asia, Russia, and Latin America began to surface. This speaks to the high-risk nature of these kinds of trades and shows that you should always seek a short-term turnaround on any dollar-cost-averaging trade.

8

THE EVENT SPREAD

As a strategy, calendar or time spreads are not well understood. They're often profitable, yet rarely used. Makes for an interesting potential aggressive trade, don't you think?

A calendar spread involves the purchase of a longer-term call (or put) option and the sale of a shorter-term call (or put) option. Both options have the same strike price. For example, it's April and ABC is trading at $58 per share. A typical calendar call spread would involve the purchase of, say, the ABC October 65 calls at 4.25 (cost $425 per contract) and the sale of the ABC June 65 calls at 1.50 ($150 per contract).

Note the similarities: Both options are calls, both options have the same strike price. Note the differences: The options expire at different times. Hence the term "calendar" or "time" spread.

The calendar spread is a debit spread. You pay more for the option you buy than you get for the option you sell. In our ABC example, the difference is $275 per spread. Since the option being purchased expires after the option being sold, the short option is covered. The most you can lose from a calendar spread is the net debit. Again, in this case, the maximum potential loss is $275 per spread.

In the ABC example, both options are out-of-the-money. In other words, the strike price of the call option ($65 per share) is above the current price of the underlying stock ($58 per share). The entire option premium, then, is made up of time value.

The time value is what makes this spread so interesting. Time is a wasting asset. At expiration, an option has no time value. If an option is worth anything at expiration it will simply be the amount the option is in-the-money. For example, if ABC were trading at $70 at expiration, the June 65 call would be worth $5 per share, or $500 per contract. That's because you can exercise the call, buy 100 shares of ABC at $65 per share, and then resell the stock at $70 per share. Hence the $5 per share value, or $500 per contract. Option traders refer to this amount as the option's intrinsic value. (In the following section, we'll discuss further the concepts of time and intrinsic value.)

If ABC were trading at less than $65 per share at expiration, the June 65 calls would be out-of-the-money. They would have no intrinsic value and would therefore expire worthless. The closer the option gets to expiration, the faster the time value wastes away. Eventually it falls to zero, assuming the option is out-of-the-money at expiration. (For a quick review, you may want to revisit the time premium decay chart in Chapter Three.)

The time value in the ABC June options (which will expire in 8 weeks, using April as our starting point) will decay almost twice as fast as it would in the October options (which will expire in 23 weeks), assuming the underlying stock remains in a relatively narrow trading range. In fact, if ABC remains unchanged between now and the June expiration date, this position will likely generate a profit. Why? Because at the June expiration, the October options will still have 16 weeks to go before expiry. And, if the stock is still at $58, the October 65 call should be worth at least $3 ($300 per contract).

The best-case scenario would see ABC close at exactly $65 per share at the June expiration. At that point, the June 65 call would expire worthless, while the October 65 call would be worth approximately $6.25 ($625 per contract).

UNDERSTANDING TIME AND INTRINSIC VALUE

We know from Chapter Three how options are priced. We know that the six factors in the option pricing equation tell us how much premium to pay for an option. We can further break down that premium into its component parts: time value and intrinsic value.

Intrinsic value simply defines how much the option is in-the-money. With the ABC example at the beginning of this chapter, ABC is at $58 per share in April. Table 8.1 looks at three ABC July call options with three distinct strike prices.

TABLE 8.1

ABC CALL OPTIONS

ABC @ $58	PREMIUM	INTRINSIC VALUE STOCK PRICE LESS STRIKE PRICE	TIME VALUE PREMIUM LESS INTRINSIC
June 50 calls	8.750	8.000	0.750
June 55 calls	4.875	3.000	1.875
June 60 calls	3.750	0.000	3.750
June 65 calls	1.500	0.000	1.500

Let's first examine the cost—or premium—for the ABC June 50 calls. The total cost of that option is $8.750 per share. Since the stock is trading at $58 per share, the ABC June 50 call is in-the-money. If we exercised the ABC June 50 call, the seller of that call would have to deliver to us 100 shares of ABC at $50 per share. We could then turn around and sell that stock for $58 per share, which of course is the current market value. That's the in-the-money amount of that option, which is what we define as that option's intrinsic value.

Obviously, if we're up to speed on our understanding of options, we would never exercise the ABC June 50 call when it was trading at $8.750. Why? Because if we exercise the call, take the stock at $50 and then resell the stock at $58, our total profit is only $8.00 per share. But we could simply sell the option for $8.750 per share. The difference between the option's premium and the option's intrinsic value is its time value. This leads us to an interesting point. You would never exercise an option that still had time value in its premium. You're better off selling the option in the open market, unless of course you prefer to leave some money on the table.

From Table 8.1 we see that the total premium for the ABC June 50 and ABC June 55 calls is made up of intrinsic value and time value. Stated another way, with ABC trading at $58 per share, both the ABC June 50 calls and the ABC June 55 calls are in-the-money, the stock being above the strike price of the call.

To calculate how much of the total call option premium is accounted for by intrinsic value, we simply subtract the call's strike price from the current stock price. For example, the June 55 calls have a strike price of $55. ABC is trading at $58 per share. Subtract the strike price ($55 being the strike price) from the current stock price ($58), and the intrinsic value for the ABC June 55 call is $3.00. Time value is simply the total premium ($4.875) less the intrinsic value ($3.00), which in this case equals $1.875 per share.

Intrinsic Value: Intrinsic value is the in-the-money portion of the option's price. A call option is in-the-money if the stock price is above the strike price. A put option is in-the-money if the stock price is below the strike price.

Time Value: Time value is the part of an option's total price that exceeds the option's intrinsic value. The price of an out-of-the-money option has no intrinsic value, only time value. A call option is out-of-the-money if the stock price is below the strike price of the call. A put option is out-of-the-money if the stock price is above the strike price of the put.

(For these definitions, I'm indebted to a publication from The Options Institute called *Options: Essential Concepts and Trading Strategies*).

Finally, we need to look at the ABC June 60 calls and June 65 calls. With ABC trading at $58 per share, both of these calls are out-of-the-money, which means that the ABC June 60 and ABC June 65 calls have no intrinsic value. The entire premium is made up of time value. So we can say that intrinsic value is the amount the option is in-the-money. An option that is out-of-the-money has no intrinsic value.

Put options share the same characteristics, only the calculation is slightly different. Going back to ABC at $58 per share, look at the following three June strike prices for ABC put options.

TABLE 8.2

ABC PUT OPTIONS

ABC @ $58	PREMIUM	INTRINSIC VALUE STOCK PRICE LESS PREMIUM	TIME VALUE PREMIUM LESS INTRINSIC
June 50 puts	0.500	0.000	0.500
June 55 puts	1.750	0.000	1.750
June 60 puts	3.125	2.000	1.125
June 65 puts	7.500	7.000	0.500

Note from Table 8.2 that the total premium for the ABC June 65 and ABC June 60 puts has intrinsic value and time value. With ABC trading at $58 per share, both the ABC July 65 puts and the ABC July 60 puts are in-the-money.

That's because a put grants you the right to sell your stock at the strike price of the put. You wouldn't force someone to buy stock from you at say $55 (ABC June 55 put) if the stock was trading at $58 per share. So a put is said to be in-the-money if the strike price of the put is higher than the current price of the underlying stock.

Calculating the intrinsic value for a put, we need to subtract the current stock price from the put's strike price. For example, the ABC June 65 puts have a strike price of $65 per share. We know that ABC is trading at $58 per share. If we subtract the current stock price ($58) from the strike price ($65), we see that the intrinsic value for the ABC June 65 call is $7.00. The time value component in the ABC June 65 puts, then, equals the total premium ($7.500) less the intrinsic value ($7.000), or $0.50.

Note that the ABC June 55 put and ABC June 50 put have no intrinsic value, meaning that the entire premium is made up of time value, the wasting part of the premium.

MATHEMATICAL CERTAINTIES

The calendar spread plays to a set of mathematical certainties. We know for a fact that the time component of the option's price will decline to zero on expiration day. We also know that time value decays more quickly the closer the option is to expiration. In the options market, these are constants.

We also know from the option pricing formula that time value declines at an almost exponential rate. The time value in a two-month option declines at approximately twice the rate of the time value in a four-month option. The time value of a three-month option declines—approximately—twice as fast as the time value in a nine-month option. (Two is the square root of four; three is the square root of nine. Hence the exponential relationship.) We are assuming that all other factors remain constant. That is, the volatility implied by the two-month option is the same as the volatility implied by the four-month option, and so on.

Using our ABC example, the calendar or time spread works on the assumption that both options are fairly valued. It also works on the assumption that the underlying stock remains in a relatively narrow trading range. If the strategy unfolds as envisioned, the calendar spread will be profitable.

The calendar or time spread works even better if we can sell an option that is overvalued and buy an option that is fairly valued or better yet, undervalued. Say, for example, we can sell the June option at a higher implied volatility than the October option.

In the ABC example, we used a 40% implied volatility assumption for both the June and the October 65 call options. Suppose instead that the June options were implying a 50% volatility, while the October options were trading with an implied volatility of 40%. Using those assumptions, the June 65 calls would have been trading at $2.375. Assuming the October 65 calls were still trading at 4.25, the net debit for our hypothetical calendar spread would be $1.875 ($187.50 per spread).

Based on these numbers, we are selling an overvalued option and buying a fairly valued option. This tells us a number of things:

1. It's less costly to implement the calendar spread.
2. There's less risk, since the maximum risk is the cost of the net debit. A lower cost base, by definition, means lower risk.
3. Since we're taking advantage of price discrepancies in the market, there's a better chance this position will turn a profit.

Given the efficiency of the financial markets, is it reasonable to expect such distortions in the options market? The short answer is no, it's not reasonable, but in fact such distortions often exist.

There are at least a couple of factors that might cause such a disparity between option prices on the same underlying security. The first is volume: Usually, the volume for the October options will be much lighter than the volume on the shorter-term June options. A higher volume of transactions can sometimes distort volatility.

Second, some event might be driving up the near-month options. For example, the underlying stock may be a short-term takeover target. Such rumors heighten the activity of the short-term options, which have the most to gain if rumor becomes fact.

Events can also have a marked short-term influence on the financial markets. For example, U.S. Federal Reserve Board (FED) policy meetings can have such an effect, especially if there's uncertainty about interest rate levels.

An impending announcement could also have a dramatic short-term effect on the stock's price. For example, a drug company might be awaiting approval for a major product release from the Food and Drug Administration. Whether approved or not, the impact on the stock's price can be dramatic and usually short-lived.

A more common event is the release of a company's quarterly earnings. Earnings that stray from consensus estimates, either for better or worse, can over the short term have a dramatic effect on the value of the company's stock. Guesses about a company's earnings often cause distortions in the short-term option premiums.

Of course, the calendar spread is not foolproof. While it's a low-risk trade, it's not a risk-free trade. If the underlying stock should rise or fall substantially—which is why traders bid up the short-term options in the first place—the calendar spread will lose money. Ideally, with a calendar spread, you want the underlying stock to remain in a relatively narrow trading range, until the near-month option expires, presumably worthless.

The maximum risk is the net debit paid for this spread. However, it's not likely you would lose your entire debit if the stock didn't rise or fall too dramatically before the near-month expiration. Using our ABC example, at the June expiration, the October option will likely have some value. And the October option will always be worth more than the June option. The question is how much more.

To address the question of how much more, we need to understand that time takes a back seat to the relationship between the strike price of the option and the current price of the underlying stock. If ABC tumbled dramatically to, say, $30 per share by the June expiration, the October 65 call would be virtually worthless. At best it would be worth no more than 1/8th. In such a circumstance, you would lose almost your entire debit.

Similarly, if the stock moved up sharply (assuming we were using calls to create the calendar spread), the short-term option would rise at a faster rate than the longer-term option, and the calendar spread would at some point start to lose money. In the ABC example, assuming we sold both options using the same implied volatility, the calendar spread should be profitable if the price of the stock remained between $50 and $75 until the June expiration. Above or below that range, the position would begin to lose money. But again, the potential loss is limited to the net debit paid.

THE EVENT SPREAD: A REAL-LIFE EXAMPLE

The event spread is a calendar spread with an edge. In this case, the edge is a distortion in the volatility implied by the different option premiums. We know that distortions can be caused by a number of factors, but with this particular trade, we'll use only large-cap bellwether stocks, and we'll execute the trade only prior to quarterly earnings releases.

Essentially we're attempting to take advantage of short-term distortions in the level of option premiums. By way of example, consider options on Intel during July

1998. On July 14, after the close of trading, Intel was set to release its second-quarter earnings number. The street was expecting the company to report earnings of 68 cents per share, well down from the same period the year before, when same-quarter earnings came in at 93 cents per share.

Leading up to the earnings release, the stock rallied from the mid-$70s to $83 per share. The bulls had been comforted by the fact that Intel did not pre-announce an earnings shortfall. Intel's management has customarily reported shortfalls early, getting the bad news out before actually releasing the earnings results. But through this traditional pre-announcement period, the company was uncharacteristically quiet, leading some analysts to suggest that all was right with the giant chipmaker.

In fact, as the actual release date approached, some investors and analysts expected Intel to beat street estimates. I heard so-called whisper numbers that suggested Intel's earnings might come in at 71 cents or 72 cents per share, 5% above expectations.

On July 14, 1998, when Intel was trading intraday at $83 per share, the following prices were posted for Intel at-the-money call options (see Table 8.3):

TABLE 8.3

INTEL AT $83 PER SHARE ON JULY 14

OPTION SERIES	PRICE	IMPLIED VOLATILITY
July 85 calls	1.500	78%
August 85 calls	3.375	42%
October 85 calls	5.750	38%

Note the distortion in the volatility implied by the different option series. The July 85 calls, which were at-the-money and set to expire three days later, on July 17, were still worth $1.50 per share ($150 per contract). These options were trading with an implied volatility of 78%, reflecting the uncertainty around Intel's earnings.

In this case, you could have bought an October 85 call at $5.75 (implied volatility 38%) and sold the July 85 call at $1.50 for a net debit of $4.25 ($425 per calendar spread). I particularly like this trade because the October options were trading in line with the long-term historical volatility pattern for Intel. In other words, I would expect the October options to trade with the same implied volatility once the earnings number was out of the way.

At the July expiration, Intel closed at $83.125. The July 85 calls expired worthless, while the October 85 calls closed at $5.75. Assuming you closed out the October 85 puts at $5.75, the total profit on this trade was $1.50 per share or $150 per spread over a period of four days. Your net investment in this position was $4.25 per share ($425 net debit per spread). On a percentage basis, then, you earned 35.3% ($1.50 per share divided by the net investment of $4.25 per share).

THE EVENT SPREAD USING CALLS

With the Intel example we see the potential. But obviously, not all event spreads are so successful. That's why it's important to garner a strong edge before going into the trade.

The edge comes from the fact that you can implement this spread with either calls or puts. You can buy the longer-term calls and sell shorter-term calls or, conversely, buy longer-term puts and sell the shorter-term puts. If the short-term calls are overpriced relative to the longer-term calls, it stands to reason (because of the equivalency of positions that we discussed in Chapter Four) that the short-term puts will also be overpriced relative to the longer-term puts.

The question is, When does it make more sense to use puts rather than calls to implement the event spread? The answer boils down to where the stock is, defined by our familiar chart with the four trading bands.

I look at several factors: For example, how did the stock perform just prior to the earnings release? Was the stock rising prior to the event? This would lead me to think that the market expected the company to meet or beat street expectations. If a company expects to fall short of expectations, large-cap bellwether companies tend to pre-announce that fact some time before the actual release date.

If a company is releasing its earnings in July, for the quarter ended in June, management has a pretty good idea in early June whether or not the company will meet analysts' expectations. Pre-announcements about any shortfall in the July releases will usually occur in the first couple of weeks in June, about four to six weeks prior to the actual release date. This simply means that a company that has not pre-announced a significant shortfall—assuming that the company's standard practice is to make such a pre-announcement — will probably meet or beat earnings forecasts when it releases its actual earnings figures.

That's a bullish sign and suggests that perhaps calls would be the best approach. On the other hand, there's the tricky notion that investors buy on rumor and sell on news. In other words, they bid up the price of the shares prior to the announcement and then sell the shares once traders know what the earnings are.

As you can see, setting up this trade is not a straightforward exercise. As a rule of thumb, if a stock is falling prior to the earnings release, the market expects disappointing news. If it's rising prior to the release date, the market likely expects a pleasant surprise from the company.

Remember, the event spread is designed to generate a profit if the underlying stock remains in a relatively tight trading range over a short period. We are not trying to forecast what the company will earn or whether the company will disappoint, meet or beat expectations. Our only concern is that the market has a pretty good handle on what to expect and that its expectations are likely priced into the stock. In other words, the uncertainty is priced into the options.

Another consideration is the current price of the stock relative to the strike price of the options you're considering. This involves more art than science, since there is no definitive pattern for a stock's performance on the day earnings are released. Sometimes a stock rises prior to the release date, but management then disappoints the street. Management's outlook for the company—usually delivered at the earnings press conference—often determines the size of the hit the company takes when the stock opens for trading the next day, which is the actual release date. Sometimes that disappointment leads to a sell-off in after-hours trading. But on many occasions, stocks sell off in after-hours trading, only to rebound sharply the next day when full trading resumes. And, just to complicate matters further, on the day after a company releases a positive earnings number, its stock price might fall.

In fact, what's happening here is noise. The market is simply moving up and down during the trading day, which really tells us nothing about the fundamental direction of the underlying stock. Ideally, we want to establish an event spread that will produce a short-term profit within a reasonable trading range. We'll call it the event-spread trading range. To determine the likelihood of a stock remaining within the event-spread trading range, we can use trading bands.

Trading bands do not indicate support or resistance points, but they do play off the 50-day moving average. As I've suggested earlier, this is a pivotal short-term price point for the underlying stock. The most attractive event spread is the one that can be profitable even though the event-spread trading range breaches the trading bands above or below the stock's current price.

Now we have to decide whether to use calls or puts to implement the event spread. For stocks with positive momentum, which I would define as trading above their 50-day moving average, we would tend to use calls for the event spread. For stocks with negative momentum—trading below the 50-day moving average—we would tend to use puts.

THE XYZ EVENT SPREAD

The hypothetical company we will use for the event spread is old reliable XYZ. In this case, we'll assume it's trading at $97.50 per share. Unlike our other aggressive trades, the stock price in this case has little relevance, at least in terms of upfront costs.

With the first two aggressive trading strategies, we had to purchase the underlying stock. Therefore we had to consider the cost of buying the stock—and the stock price. And a high price might have prevented us from buying more than the minimum 100-share allotment.

Because we're not required to own shares of the underlying stock, the event spread is a pure option play designed to take advantage of a mathematical certainty. In this case, the certainty is: The closer the option is to expiration, the faster the rate at which time value decays.

That being said, there's a caveat: The shorter-term option could be exercised, in which case you'd be required to buy the underlying stock. If you were short a put, you'd have to buy the stock as part of your obligation under that contract. If a call were exercised, you'd have to deliver shares to the call buyer, which means you'd have to buy the stock and then deliver the shares, presumably at a lower price than you paid. (The holder of the option is said to exercise the option. When an option is exercised, the investor who is short the option is said to be assigned.)

Of course, an early assignment is not a likely scenario. Remember, we're selling time value. If there's time value remaining in the option it's not likely to be assigned. An option will be assigned only if its premium has no time value in it. (See our previous discussion on time and intrinsic value.) With this strategy, we are selling options with high premiums, made up almost exclusively of time value. The holder of an option that has time value in its price is almost always better off selling the contract in the option market.

Having laid this foundation, let's look at the strategy in its entirety. To do this we have to focus on the chart pattern of the underlying stock. From that, we can establish a set of rules that must be met before implementing the trade.

FIGURE 8.1

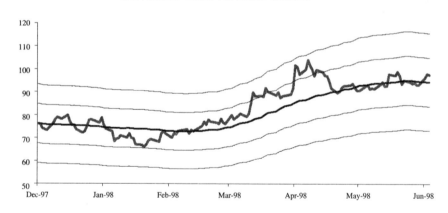

XYZ CORP. WITH TRADING BANDS

Note in Figure 8.1 how XYZ is positioned above the 50-day moving average but below trading band #3, just prior to an earnings release. Calls with the 100 strike price would be ideal for this trade, the strike price being just above the current price, which should set up an event-spread trading range that breaches trading band #1 and trading band #3. Of course, all of this assumes that the XYZ July calls are trading at a higher implied volatility than the XYZ October calls.

THE WIDTH OF THE TRADING BANDS

Before getting further into the structure of the trade, we need to spend a moment discussing the trading bands in Figure 8.1. Recall that the trading bands are based on one standard deviation around the 50-day moving average. The width of those trading bands is defined by the options' implied volatility. But which option are we using to define the width of the bands?

Since this strategy is based on selling an option with a much higher volatility than the option we're buying, we need to identify the volatility assumption we're using to create the trading bands.

Now let's look at Table 8.3: Notice that the Intel July 85 calls implied a 78% volatility, while the October 85 calls were trading with an implied volatility of 42%. Would the trading bands around Intel be based on the former or latter volatility assumption? This is an important consideration. Depending on the assumption we used, there would be a big difference in the width of the trading bands, which could affect our selection of the correct option.

We address this concern at the e-trade web site (www.canada.etrade.com) by calculating the trading bands using an average volatility assumption from all the options on the underlying stock. This means the width of the bands is based on a blended volatility assumption.

As a result, the trading bands will always be tighter than they would be if we used only the volatility assumption of the near-month options. This is what we want, because the circumstances that influence the short-term options are specific events, not long-term trends.

SETTING UP THE RULES

It's worth repeating that the event spread, like all our aggressive equity-based trades, involves large-cap blue-chip companies. In this case, the event is an earnings release date. Specifically, we're looking for companies with extremely uncertain future earnings. This uncertainty translates into higher option premiums on the shorter-term options, whose price depends heavily on the results of the quarterly earnings release.

To keep transaction costs to a minimum, we want to trade at least five option contracts. That is, we want to sell five short-term calls and buy five longer-term calls or sell five shorter-term puts and buy five long-term puts.

Ideally with the event spread we want to enter a position that can be profitable within a trading range that takes the stock one band above or below its current position. Of course, we also want to sell options that are trading at much higher implied volatilities than the options we're buying. Preferably the near-month options should be trading with an implied volatility that's at least 30% higher than the longer-term option we'll be purchasing. Finally, the company issuing the stock must be about to deliver an earnings release, and there should be a great deal of publicity about the actual numbers. Assuming we're dealing with a large-cap bellwether company, publicity is a given.

Table 8.4 looks at the XYZ options and the accompanying volatilities. We'll assume that these are the prices for XYZ options in mid-June and that the quarterly earnings are due in the second week in July.

TABLE 8.4

JUNE 15, 1998, XYZ AT $97.50

STRIKE PRICE	JULY CALLS	I.V.	OCT CALLS	I.V.
85.00	14.500	58%	17.625	45%
90.00	11.000	58%	14.500	45%
95.00	8.000	58%	11.875	45%
100.00	5.625	58%	9.625	45%
105.00	3.875	58%	7.625	45%
110.00	2.625	58%	6.000	45%

Assuming that XYZ meets our criteria for entering this trade—a large-cap blue-chip stock trading above the 50-day moving average—we should sell the July 100 calls at $5.625 and buy the October 100 calls at $9.625. This results in a net debit of $4.00 per share or $400 per spread. This is a short-term trade, the results of which will be known at the expiration of the near-month options.

Before actually implementing the event spread, we need to know the trading range in which this position is profitable. Remember, one of the first rules for the event spread is to enter a position that can be profitable at the trading range above and below the current price.

Of specific interest is the trading range between now and the July expiration. Before entering any event spread, we want to determine the event-spread trading range up to the expiration of the near-month options.

Unfortunately, the event spread is not the easiest strategy on which to assess potential profitability. In the other aggressive strategies we own the underlying stock, so the profit-and-loss potential is based on the position of the underlying stock at some point in the future. In this trade, we don't own any stock. We have to determine profitability based on two factors:

> • *where the stock is at a point in the future (the expiration date of the near-month options) and*
>
> • *the volatility assumption we'll use for the October options. After all, at the July expiration, the October options will still have three months before expiry.*

Table 8.5 looks at potential stock prices at the expiration of the July calls, about five weeks after we initiated the original event spread and three months prior to the expiration of the October calls.

Note the boldfaced numbers at the $97.50 price point. These show the profit and loss assuming the stock remains unchanged between the time we initiated the event spread and the last day of trading for XYZ July calls. For the record, the July calls actually expire on Saturday, July 18.

TABLE 8.5

PROFIT/LOSS XYZ EVENT SPREAD AT JULY EXPIRATION

STOCK PRICE	JULY 100 CALLS	OCT 100 CALLS	CURRENT SPREAD	ORIGINAL SPREAD	PROFIT LOSS PER SPREAD
85.00	—	3.125	3.125	4.000	−87.50
90.00	—	4.750	4.750	4.000	75.00
95.00	—	7.000	7.000	4.000	300.00
97.50	**—**	**8.125**	**8.125**	**4.000**	**412.50**
100.00	—	9.625	9.625	4.000	562.50
105.00	5.000	12.625	7.625	4.000	362.50
110.00	10.000	16.000	6.000	4.000	200.00
115.00	15.000	19.750	4.750	4.000	75.00
120.00	20.000	23.500	3.500	4.000	−50.00

Based on the numbers from Table 8.5, the XYZ event spread is profitable over the next four weeks if the stock remains in a trading range between approximately $86 and $119 per share. The high end of that range places the stock above trading band #3, well within our guidelines for this trade. On the downside, the XYZ event spread is profitable even if the stock closes below trading band #2.

One final point related to the trading range calculation: Note how the stock can rise more than it can fall and still remain in a profitable trading range. That simply reflects the underlying positive long-term bias of equities. (More precisely, it reflects the lognormal distribution used in the option-pricing formula. But that's a discussion best left to mathematical texts.)

This is a relatively straightforward calculation, because the July calls, at this point, have expired. The only assumption we need to make is the likely volatility implied by the XYZ October calls. For this calculation, we assume the October calls will trade with the same implied volatility as they did when we initially established the position.

That's a reasonable assumption, since the basis for the event spread is to sell overvalued options and buy undervalued or fairly valued options. In the XYZ example, we assume we sold overvalued calls (the July calls) and bought fairly valued calls (the October calls). Figure 8.2 graphs the profit and loss for the XYZ even spread at the July expiration.

FIGURE 8.2

PROFIT/LOSS PER XYZ EVENT SPREAD AT JULY EXPIRATION

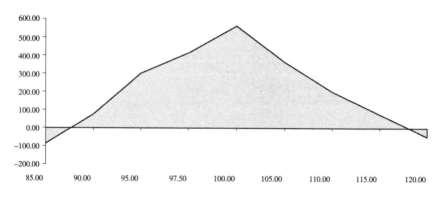

EVENT SPREAD USING PUTS

With XYZ, we assumed the stock was moving higher prior to the earnings release date, which suggested that the market thought XYZ would bring a positive surprise. The stock was also trading above its 50-day moving average, implying positive momentum. After reviewing the option premiums, we discovered that the near-month options were trading with a higher implied volatility. The implied volatility on the XYZ July options was about 30% higher than the volatility implied by the October options. We had all the pieces necessary to enter the event spread using calls.

For this example, we'll use another hypothetical company, say MNO. It's a large-cap blue-chip company, to be sure. But MNO's stock has been falling recently and is now trading slightly below its 50-day moving average. There's some concern by the market that the company may fall short of analysts' expectations. It's still the middle of June, and we expect earnings to be released in four weeks. Figure 8.3 is a one-year chart for MNO, with the familiar trading bands.

With MNO currently trading at $57 per share, the following prices exist for the XYZ July and October Puts (see Table 8.6).

FIGURE 8.3

MNO CORP. WITH TRADING BANDS

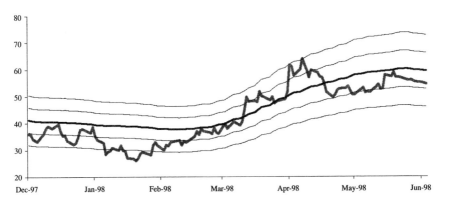

TABLE 8.6

JUNE 15, 1998, MNO AT $57.00

STRIKE PRICE	JULY PUTS	I.V.	OCT PUTS	I.V.
45.00	0.500	55%	1.625	40%
50.00	1.500	55%	3.000	40%
55.00	3.625	55%	5.250	40%
60.00	6.750	55%	8.375	40%
65.00	10.750	55%	12.000	40%

Assuming that MNO meets our criteria for entering this trade—large-cap blue-chip stock trading below the 50-day moving average—we should sell the MNO July 55 puts at $3.625 and buy the MNO October 55 puts at $5.25. This results in a net debit of $1.625 per share, or $162.50 per spread.

As with our XYZ example, we want to ascertain the trading range at which the MNO event spread would be profitable at the July expiration. Again, to calculate the event-spread trading range, we need to pick a specific point—the July expiration—and specify the volatility assumption implied by the October puts at the July expiration.

Table 8.7 looks at potential stock prices at the expiration of the MNO July puts, about five weeks after we initiated the original event spread and three months prior to the expiration of the MNO October puts.

Note the boldfaced numbers at the $57 price point. These show the profitability of this position assuming the stock remains unchanged between the time we initiated the event spread and the last day of trading for MNO July puts.

TABLE 8.7

PROFIT/LOSS XYZ EVENT SPREAD AT JULY EXPIRATION

STOCK PRICE JULY 55	OCT 55 PUTS	SPREAD AT PUTS	ORIGINAL EXPIRATION	PROFIT LOSS SPREAD	PER SPREAD
45.00	10.000	11.375	1.375	1.625	−25.00
50.00	5.000	7.875	2.875	1.625	125.00
55.00	—	5.340	5.340	1.625	371.50
57.00	**—**	**4.500**	**4.500**	**1.625**	**287.50**
60.00	—	3.500	3.500	1.625	187.50
65.00	—	2.250	2.250	1.625	62.50
70.00	—	1.500	1.500	1.625	−12.50

Note that the maximum profit for the event spread occurs if the stock closes at exactly the $55 strike price when the July options expire. Further, based on the numbers from Table 8.7, the MNO event spread is profitable over the next four weeks if the stock remains in a trading range bound by $45 and $70 per share. The high end of that range places the stock above trading band #3. The downside breakeven is well below trading band #2. Both are well within our guidelines for this trade.

FIGURE 8.4

PROFIT/LOSS PER MNO EVENT SPREAD USING PUTS AT JULY EXPIRATION

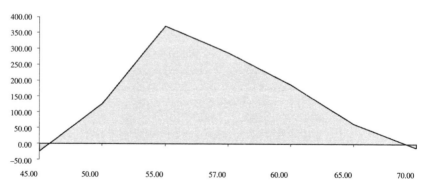

As we did with our XYZ example, we'll assume that the MNO October 55 puts will trade at the same implied volatility as they did when we initially established the position, which is a reasonable assumption, if we entered this trade when the MNO July 55 puts were overvalued relative to the MNO October 55 puts. Figure 8.4 graphs the profit and loss for the MNO event spread at the July expiration.

SUMMARY

Because the profit and loss from the event spread is based on time value eroding more quickly on the near-term options, we can implement the strategy using either calls or puts. Deciding whether to use calls or puts depends on the performance of the underlying stock prior to implementation. In general, we'd use calls for a stock with positive momentum and puts for a stock with negative momentum. We distinguish between positive and negative momentum on the basis of the stock price relative to its 50-day moving average.

A SUMMARY OF CROFT'S RULES FOR THE EVENT SPREAD

- *The stock must be issued by a large-cap blue-chip company.*
- *We enter the event spread two to four weeks prior to the earnings release date.*
- *The shorter-term options must be trading with a higher implied volatility than the longer-term options. Preferably the shorter-term options should be at least 30% more expensive than the longer-term options. For example, if the longer-term options imply a volatility of 50%, the shorter-term options should imply a volatility of at least 65% (50% × 1.30 = 65%).*
- *If the underlying stock is trading above its 50-day moving average, implement the event spread using calls. If the underlying stock is trading below its 50-day moving average, implement the event spread with puts.*
- *Use at least five contracts for every event spread. This helps to keep transaction costs in line.*
- *The event-spread trading range should allow for a profitable exit from the position, even if the stock trades one band above or one band below its current price. We calculate an event-spread trading range at the expiration of the short options. Further, we assume for the calculation that the long options will trade with the same implied volatility as they did when the event spread was established.*

FOLLOW-UP ACTION

If there's follow-up action on the event spread, it will have to take place shortly after the event. In this case, since we're looking at quarterly earnings releases, the follow-up action should occur within a couple of days of the release date.

Mind you, much depends on the actual release date. Some companies like IBM tend to announce their earnings the week after an option series expires. For example, in July 1998, the last day of trading for the July series was July 17. IBM chose to announce its second-quarter earnings on the week of July 20.

Intel and Microsoft, on the other hand, tend to announce their earnings just before an expiration date. Again, in July 1998, Intel announced its second-quarter results after the close of trading on July 14. Microsoft announced after the close of trading on July 16.

If you implemented an event spread using Intel and Microsoft, you'd have very little opportunity to follow up if the position went sour. With IBM, you'd have to base this event trade on the August options, which means you'd have more than four weeks before the August series expired.

Lest we forget, the event spread carries a limited risk element. The most you can lose is the net debit when the position was established. This allows for greater latitude when considering follow-up action.

FINDING AN ENTRY POINT

Before entering the event spread, you should have defined an event-spread trading range at the expiration of the short-term option, with the caveat, of course, that the event-spread trading range is based on our best guess about the value of the longer-term options at expiration.

You should use the profitable trading range as your guide in determining when follow-up action may be required. If the stock does not breach either end of the trading range, then it's often best to simply let the position run its course.

Even if the underlying stock does breach the event-spread trading range, follow-up action still may not be necessary. You needn't panic about this trade, because you have statistics and mathematical certainties on your side. You also have defined your limited risk at the outset. If you believe that follow-up action is necessary, perhaps as a result of the stock making a significant move up or down, then you can consider two potential follow-up strategies.

The first is straightforward: Sell your position and close it out at a loss.

The second is not so straightforward. It depends on whether the stock breaches the trading range on the upside or the downside. Either you buy back the shorter-term option at expiration or you let it expire worthless.

For example, in our hypothetical XYZ example, you would have to buy back the short July 100 calls if the stock were trading above the $100 strike price at the July expiration. This would imply that the stock rallied sharply, breaching the upside trading range by the July expiration.

On the other hand, the stock might fall sharply prior to the July expiration, breaching the downside trading range. In this case, you don't have to repurchase the short call. You simply allow it to expire worthless. The point is, you first close out the shorter-term option and then create another calendar spread. Since you would still own the XYZ October 100 calls, you might replace the short July options with, say, short August options. (I'll walk you through a couple of examples in a moment.)

CLOSE OUT THE POSITION

Recall that the ideal situation with the event spread is to have the underlying stock close at exactly the strike price of the short call at the July expiration. In such a case, the short option will expire worthless, and the long option will trade for more than you initially paid for it—the best of both worlds. Under these circumstances, close out the position. You've earned your maximum profit.

Also, since this is one of your shortest-term aggressive trading strategies, I suggest you consider closing the position if the short option expires worthless, meaning that it's out-of-the-money at expiration. It would be unusual for this trade to produce the maximum profit. However, in many instances, a profit, however small, will exist at the expiration of the short option.

If the event spread is losing money at the expiration of the short call, it's usually best to simply close out the position. At least you'll define your maximum loss, and it will be less than the net debit when you established the position.

Immediately following the event, the stock will often rise or fall quickly over the next couple of days, riding the waves of buy and sell orders placed by investors who believe the best is yet to come against investors who buy on rumor and sell on news. The rumor is the expectation factor leading up to the earnings release date; the news is the actual earnings release.

These crosscurrents immediately following the earnings release often cause a stock to move up or down. But in the end, the stock goes nowhere, creating a situation in which the short options expire worthless and the longer-term options actually trade at a higher implied volatility than they did when you established the event spread. The premium on the longer-term options reflects the short-term volatility in the stock immediately following the earnings release—sort of the best of both worlds.

ROLLING A CALL EVENT SPREAD IF THE STOCK RISES

Assuming the stock breaches the trading range on the upside, you would close out the short option and implement a calendar spread by selling the next expiration month. In our hypothetical XYZ example, we initiated the event spread by selling the July 100 calls and buying the October 100 calls. We'll assume that, by the July expiration, XYZ closed at $120 per share, and the following prices exist (see Table 8.8).

TABLE 8.8

JULY EXPIRATION: XYZ @ $120

STRIKE PRICE	JULY CALLS	AUG CALLS	OCT CALLS
95.00	25.000	25.500	27.500
100.00	20.000	20.875	23.500
105.00	15.000	16.500	19.875
110.00	10.000	12.625	16.625
115.00	5.000	9.250	13.750
120.00	0.000	6.500	11.250

The goal is to repurchase the July 100 calls at expiration. Since the options will have no time value, the cost to repurchase should correspond exactly to the difference between the current price of the underlying stock and the strike price of the short call—$20 per share ($2,000 per contract) based on the prices in Table 8.8.

The next step is to sell the August 100 calls at $25.50, thus creating another calendar spread. Only this time the spread is between the August 100 calls and the October 100 calls. The idea here is to continue selling time value against the longer-term October options. Unfortunately, since the XYZ August 100 calls are $20 in-the-money, most of the premium is made up of intrinsic value. We would be capturing only 50 cents in time value to play against the long October 100 calls.

Unfortunately, because the stock has risen so sharply, this is not usually the best follow-up strategy. There is simply not sufficient time value in the August option to offer much of a hedge against the long October 100 calls, particularly after accounting for transaction costs.

FOLLOW UP A CALL EVENT SPREAD IF THE STOCK FALLS

It's also possible that the stock may fall below the profitable trading range between the time we establish the event spread and the expiration date for the short options. In such an instance, both the short and long calls will be out-of-the-money. The short calls will expire worthless; the October calls will still have some time value remaining. For the sake of this example, we'll assume that XYZ falls to $84 per share at the expiration of the July calls. The following prices exist:

TABLE 8.9

JULY EXPIRATION: XYZ @ $84

STRIKE PRICE	AUG CALLS	OCT CALLS
95.00	1.125	3.875
100.00	0.625	2.750
105.00	0.250	1.875
110.00	0.125	1.375
115.00	0.063	0.875
120.00	0.063	0.500

We don't need to repurchase the July 100 calls at expiration; we need only sell the August 100 calls, assuming we're attempting to roll the event spread into a traditional calendar spread. It's traditional, because we can't expect the August calls to trade at a higher implied volatility than the October calls. After all, what caused the disparity in the initial trade was an upcoming earnings release. There's no such event to be played out against the August calls and thus no reason to expect them to trade at a higher implied volatility than the October options.

Obviously, the premium received from the sale of the XYZ August calls is made up entirely of time value. The problem is, there's very little value to sell. Factor in transaction costs, and the result may be meaningless, although because the stock stumbled so badly, all the XYZ options may occasionally be trading with higher implied volatilities.

In this case, it may make the most sense to simply hold the October 100 calls for a couple of weeks to see if XYZ rebounds. The downside risk from this level is minimal. The most additional money you could lose is the current value of the October 100 calls at the July expiration ($2.75 per share in this case). Often after a stock falls rapidly, it will bounce almost by reflex to the upside. And that may prove enough to allow you to sell your long October 100 calls at a breakeven price.

FOLLOW UP A PUT EVENT SPREAD IF THE STOCK RISES

What happens if a stock rallies after we establish a put event spread? In the case of MNO, what would happen if the stock trades at the $70 price point? Under such a scenario, both the short and long puts will be out-of-the-money. The short MNO July 55 puts will obviously expire worthless. The MNO October 55 puts will have some time value remaining. We'll assume that, at the July expiration, the following prices exist:

TABLE 8.10

JULY EXPIRATION: MNO @ $70

STRIKE PRICE	AUG PUTS	OCT PUTS
45.00	0.063	0.375
50.00	0.063	0.625
55.00	0.125	1.000
60.00	0.500	1.875
65.00	1.375	3.500
70.00	3.375	5.875

Since we don't need to repurchase the MNO July 55 puts at expiration, we could look at selling the August 55 puts, again, assuming we want to roll the event spread into a traditional calendar spread.

Obviously, the $0.125-per-share premium received from the sale of the MNO August 55 puts would be made up entirely of time value. But it is not sufficient to provide any real offset to the losses attributable to the initial event spread. There will usually not be enough premium to justify rolling out to a traditional calendar spread with another out-of-the-money put, especially if you factor in transaction costs.

The preferable strategy, assuming you don't want to close out the trade, is to simply hold the MNO October 55 puts, in the hope the underlying stock will snap back. Again, the downside risk from this level is minimal. The most additional money you could lose is the value of the MNO October 55 puts from Table 8.10 ($1.000 per share in this case).

ROLL A PUT EVENT SPREAD IF THE STOCK FALLS

Assuming the stock breaches the downside trading range, the best approach is to simply close out the event spread and take your loss.

If you close out the short put option and implement another calendar spread, you'll usually not capture enough time premium to justify the exercise. In our hypothetical MNO example, the initial event spread was established by selling the MNO July 55 puts and buying the MNO October 55 puts. If, at the July expiration, MNO is trading at, say, $42 per share, I would expect the following prices (see Table 8.11):

The goal is to repurchase the MNO July 55 puts at expiration. Since the options will have no time value, the cost to repurchase should correspond exactly to the difference between the current price of the underlying stock and the strike price of the short call—$13 per share ($1,300 per contract) based on the prices in Table 8.11.

TABLE 8.11

JULY EXPIRATION: MNO @ $42

STRIKE PRICE	JULY PUTS	AUG PUTS	OCT PUTS
45.00	3.000	3.875	5.250
50.00	8.000	8.125	9.000
55.00	13.000	13.000	13.375
60.00	18.000	17.750	18.125
65.00	23.000	22.625	22.750
70.00	28.000	27.375	27.500

But if you sold the MNO August 55 puts at $13.125, you would create another calendar spread, though not a very effective one. The idea is to continue selling time premium against the longer-term October options. But because the options are so far in-the-money, you would capture only $0.125 in time value to play against the long October 100 calls.

Because the stock has fallen so sharply and quickly, this is not an ideal follow-up strategy. You would be better advised to simply close out the position.

9

INDEX OPTIONS— POTENTIAL AND PITFALLS!

That aggressive investors are drawn to index options is not surprising. They're based on one basic question: Is the market going up or down? We don't have to worry about specific sectors like technology compared with, say, consumer durables or financial services. We don't even have to worry about potentially high-risk industries like tobacco, in which we'd never implement an aggressive trade because there's too much uncertainty. Nor do we have to worry about specific stocks within a specific sector. Will Dell do better than Compaq or Gateway? Is America Online a better investment than Yahoo? Who cares, when we're only interested in the broad market? Who cares, when the only issue is whether the market will rise or fall?

This is a major change in mindset. When we decide to buy a stock, we generally follow three steps to reach a decision. First, we ask what the market is likely to do. If we answer that, then we ask what sectors within the market are likely to outperform the broader market. And finally, we ask what stocks within a specific sector offer the best opportunity for advancement. In many cases, we can be right about the market and perhaps even right about a specific sector, only to find that the stock we chose failed to live up to expectations.

Index options allow us to position ourselves after answering only one question: What's the market likely to do? Fewer decisions presumably mean lower risk, although this comes with some caveats unique to index options, which we'll discuss later.

First, we need to define the market. What broadly based indices that have available options can we use for our aggressive strategies? We use the Standard and Poor 100 index (symbol OEX) and the Standard and Poor 500 Composite index (symbol SPX) both traded on the CBOE.

In addition, there are options on the three Dow averages (i.e., industrial, transportation and utilities). For our purposes, we'll pay particular attention to options on the Dow Jones Industrial Average (symbol DJX) traded on the CBOE. If you prefer options on the Dow to the OEX or SPX, simply interchange the Dow options for the SPX or OEX.

For our aggressive index strategies, however, we'll focus on the OEX and SPX. Both represent broadly based indices; both have a high correlation with the Dow (more on that in a moment); there's good option volume on both indices (meaning that we can expect narrow bid/asked spreads) and the volatility implied by OEX options is disseminated throughout the day on the CBOE Volatility Index (symbol VIX). This is important information for our strategy selection.

All three indices provide a good benchmark for the American economy, although the Dow is hardly a broad-based index, since it represents only 30 companies. But they're the 30 largest bluest-chip companies in corporate America. Within the Dow Industrial Average are such companies as General Electric, General Motors, Ford, IBM and Coca-Cola, to name a few, which represent the generals of industry. So the Dow does provide a reasonable cross-section of the American economy. In fact, you could say, as the Dow goes, so goes the American economy.

The OEX and SPX, because of the number of stocks in these indices, are defined as broadly based. Like the Dow, they also represent a cross-section of American businesses. Over shorter periods—days, weeks and perhaps months—the OEX and SPX will have a fairly high correlation with the Dow. If the Dow is up 1% on a particular day, look for the OEX and SPX to be up by 1%, give or take 10 basis points. The OEX and SPX have an even stronger correlation when measured against each other. This isn't surprising, since the 100 companies included in the OEX are also in the SPX.

It's also useful to compare the numerical performance of one index relative to another. For example, what is the ratio of Dow points relative to SPX points? Or how many SPX points equal a one-point move in the OEX? Or compare the Dow relative to the OEX.

Based on numbers in mid-August—the Dow at 8,490, the SPX at 1,080 and the OEX at 531—here are some rough guidelines:

> • *If we divide the Dow by the SPX, we get 7.86. This tells us that 7.86 Dow points represent approximately 1 SPX point. Let's call it 8 to 1, Dow points versus SPX points.*
> • *With the OEX, divide 8,490 by 531. We get 15.98, or about 16 Dow points to every 1 OEX point.*
> • *And finally, we can expect the SPX to move 2 points for every 1-point move in the OEX.*

These ratios help us to estimate the numerical change on the OEX or SPX based on how the Dow performs. This can be useful information, since most radio and TV newscasts discuss the U.S. market only in terms of the Dow Jones Industrial Average. If you're driving and you hear the Dow is up 50 points, you can calculate that the SPX is likely up 6.25 points and the OEX is up 3.125 points.

STANDARD AND POOR 100 INDEX OPTIONS

Before Dow Jones became enlightened about the possible uses of index options and about the potential licensing fees it could collect by allowing its name to be used on an index option product, investors had no way of playing their views on the stock market. They could only buy a stock that they expected to outperform, in a sector that they thought might outperform, at a time when they were bullish on the market in general.

That changed in 1983, when the CBOE listed options on Standard and Poor's 100 index (OEX). Standard and Poor's 100 index comprises 100 blue-chip stocks from diverse industry groups. Included in the index are widely held and actively traded stocks like AT&T, Coca-Cola, Du Pont, Exxon, General Electric, General Motors, IBM, Merck, Microsoft and Wal-Mart.

With a 15-year history behind the index, OEX has proven itself to be a valuable and actively traded financial instrument. In fact OEX was once the most actively traded option contract in the world, and most days it still is. In recent years, however, SPX options have traded in volumes that, on some days, come close to OEX. For aggressive investors, volume statistics on the OEX and SPX can help us draw meaningful conclusions about the likely direction of the overall stock market.

Obviously, OEX provides the next best thing to a mirror image of the movement of the broader market. Historically, the performance of OEX has a consistently high correlation to the S&P 500 index, which traditionally has been the benchmark for U.S. institutions.

THE MECHANICS OF THE OEX

We know that the value of an equity option will rise or fall based on changes in the value of the underlying stock. Similarly, index options rise and fall based on changes in the value of the underlying index, although we sometimes see some odd relationships between the call and put prices.

This is because index options are priced off the index futures market. And index futures contracts can sometimes trade at valuations quite different from the cash market. (The cash indices are the ones we see highlighted in the financial press.) Nevertheless, the index options market is extremely efficient, and perceived distortions seldom provide us with any potential advantage.

Indices are calculated and disseminated every 15 seconds during the trading day. As with equity options, each index option contract represents 100 times the current level of the index. Index option premiums are expressed in points and fractions. The price of a contract is 100 times the premium quote, which means a quote of $7.50 per unit represents $750 per contract.

OEX options are American-style as opposed to European-style options. This means that the buyer of an OEX option can exercise the option at any time prior to its expiry. The value we receive for an option at expiry is based on the closing value of the index on the last trading day. Index options, like equity options, expire on the Saturday following the third Friday of the expiration month. Close of trading on the third Friday of the expiration month is therefore the settlement value used to value in-the-money OEX options. OEX daily closing values and volume statistics appear in most business newspapers.

OPTIONS ON THE DOW

On October 6, 1997, the CBOE began trading options on the Dow Indices. In what can only be described as the greatest launch of a product in the history of the CBOE, options on the Dow Jones Industrial (symbol DJX), Transportation (symbol DTX) and Utilities (symbol DUX) averages began trading with great fanfare. On the first day, 24,700 contracts changed hands. Second-day volume quadrupled to 98,751 contracts. Trading has since tailed off, and Dow Jones index options now trade in far lower volumes than the OEX or SPX index options.

About four months before the launch, on June 5, 1997, Dow Jones and Co. made public its selection of the CBOE as the exclusive licensee to trade listed options contracts on the Dow Indices. This was a major about-face for Dow Jones.

For years the company had resisted the temptation to license its indices for such a speculative venture. Dow Jones shared the conservative view of index options as examples of the excesses of financial markets. They had no real economic value, because no tangible investment supported an index option. Equity options, on the other hand, were supported by an underlying stock certificate.

Today, index options are seen as valuable risk-management tools for portfolio managers, particularly for managers who utilize asset-allocation strategies and want to fine-tune their asset mix without making wholesale changes to their portfolio.

Investors often think of index options as being more volatile than stock options. This isn't surprising when 50- to 100-point moves on the Dow Jones Industrial Average (DJIA) are an everyday occurrence. In fact, index options are much less volatile than people think. A diversified portfolio of stocks, which is what an index is, is by nature less volatile than any single stock. The 50- to 100-point moves on the Dow, while numerically large, are really quite small in percentage terms relative to the total number of shares trading.

Options on the DJIA are based on 1/100th of the value of the underlying index, presumably so that each option on the Dow will represent the market value of the DJIA. (Remember the multiplier on an index option is 100.) For example, with the Dow at 9,000, options on the DJIA will be based on an index level of 90.00 (9,000 × 1/100th). Given the standard multiplier of 100, the underlying value for the options would be $9,000 (90.00 base index level × 100, the multiplier for an options contract = $9,000). If I wanted to buy a call on the Dow with a 9,000 strike, for example, I would actually have to buy a DJX 90 call (90 being 1/100th of the Dow 9,000).

Options on the Dow indices are European-style. (Just to confuse matters further, so are SPX options.) European-style options can be exercised only at expiration. (American-style options, of which the OEX is an example, can be exercised any time prior to expiration). Dow options are available in up to three near-term months plus up to three months on a quarterly cycle. The expiration date is the Saturday following the third Friday of the expiration month.

The settlement value is calculated based on the opening prices of the component securities in the index on the business day prior to expiration. This value is calculated by Dow Jones & Company, Inc.

In terms of the calculation, the DJIA is a price-weighted index that consists of 30 large NYSE-listed blue-chip industrial stocks. Price-weighted simply means that the prices of the 30 stocks are totaled and then divided by a divisor.

The Standard and Poor (S&P) 100 index and the S&P 500 index, on the other hand, are capitalization-weighted. That is, each component stock within the index is weighted according to its market capitalization (i.e., the share price multiplied by the number of outstanding shares).

Historically, the DJIA, S&P 100 and S&P 500 index levels have all tended to move in the same direction at the same time. However, differences in index composition and weighting methods can, on occasion, cause the index levels to move in dissimilar ways. Some traders believe these short-term distortions can be exploited. However, that's not the focus of the aggressive index strategies in this chapter.

WHY THREE INDICES?

Why use three indices, especially if all of them tend to move in unison? Why not simply pick one index? A couple of reasons:

1. Options on the OEX are American-style, whereas options on the SPX and DJIA are European-style.

2. The DJX options, which by the way, are also European-style, have strike prices at 2-point intervals, as opposed to 5-point intervals for the OEX and SPX. This doesn't present a particular advantage for most aggressive investors. However, for first-time aggressive investors, there may be some merit in being able to control more effectively the risk in their aggressive index spread strategies. With a 2-point interval, the maximum risk is 2 points ($200 per spread); with a 5-point interval, maximum risk is 5 points ($500 per spread), less any credit received when we implement our spread strategies. (This will make more sense when we examine the actual aggressive spread strategies.)

As for the other indices, OEX is particularly important because it is by far the most actively traded index option. In fact, daily volume on the OEX often equals or surpasses the total volume for all other index options and the daily volume on all equity options. For the aggressive investor, this means liquidity and ease of access. It enables the investor to move in and out quickly. This is important for the aggressive index strategies that require us to buy calls or puts.

Recently the OEX was split two for one. The CBOE wanted to differentiate the OEX index (August level 531) from the larger SPX index (August value 1,080).

RISKS UNIQUE TO INDEX OPTIONS

As we've pointed out, OEX options are American-style. This simply means they can be exercised at any time prior to expiration. Index options are unlikely to be assigned early because they usually have some time value remaining up to the last day of trading. As we know from our discussion on time and intrinsic value in Chapter Eight, options with time value will not be exercised early.

SPX and DJX index options are European-style. This means investors can't exercise the underlying options prior to maturity. This is an important feature if we're selling options. For our purposes, European settlement is important within the context of our spread strategies, because index options are settled in cash. If we exercise an index option, we receive cash; if we're assigned an index option, we pay cash, as opposed to buying or selling shares of stock. This process is more convenient, but presents a risk factor that's unique to index options.

Index options have many distinctive features that are quite different from traditional equity options. For example, the most common equity option strategy is covered call writing. As you'll recall from Chapter 6, covered call writing is part of one of our aggressive strategies, the falling-for-dollars trade. With covered call writing, the investor owns the underlying stock and sells call options against the shares. Should the calls be exercised, the covered call writer simply delivers the shares.

There is no such strategy with index options. Certainly an average investor can't deliver an underlying stock to settle an index option assignment. Until recently, an investor simply couldn't hold all the shares in the underlying index in the exact proportions in which they appeared within the index. Today, however, an investor can buy DIAMONDS (symbol DIA) or Standard and Poor Depository Receipts (symbol SPY), both traded on the American Stock Exchange, and use these securities as his or her underlying stock. They provide a perfect offset to DJX and SPX index options, although regulators do not consider a short index call to be covered simply because you hold DIA or SPY in your portfolio.

So, in theory, it's possible for you to implement a close approximation to a covered call write using an index. However, it's not usually the best approach, unless you were thinking of the falling-for-dollars trade after a major sell-off. In practical terms, however, the falling-for-dollars trade seems to work best with equity options, at least over short periods, and we want to focus in this chapter on trades that are better suited to index options.

Because an investor can't deliver a specific security if an index call is exercised, the exchanges had to come up with an alternative that would facilitate index option trading. So they made a rule that index options have to be settled in cash. If we exercise an index call option, we receive the difference in the closing value of the index that day, less the strike price of the option, multiplied by 100 (note that the multiplier for index options is the same as it is for equity options).

For example, if we exercised an OEX June 500 call option, and the value of the OEX at the end of the trading day was 531, we'd receive the difference between the strike price of the call (500) and the current closing value (531) of the index, times the underlying multiple (100). Specifically, we'd receive 531 less the 500 strike price = 31 × 100 = $3,100 cash per contract (less applicable commissions). The $3,100 would be credited to our trading account the next business day. The key point is the index level and particular date that are used in facilitating an exercise notice. If we receive an assignment notice first thing Wednesday morning, the price that will be used to calculate the cash owing will be based on the closing value of the index on Tuesday night.

For index spread traders, that's a risk, especially with the spreads we discuss in this chapter. For our purposes, a spread involves the purchase and sale of call options—or put options—with different strike prices. The objective is to establish a position with limited return potential and limited risk.

Let's assume that it is May, and the OEX is at 500. An example of a bear call spread would be the sale of, say, OEX June 480 calls at $25 together with the simultaneous purchase of OEX June 500 calls at $15. This bear call spread strategy would create a net credit in our account of $10 per share or $1,000 per spread. In this case, the short June 480 call is worth more than the long June 500 call.

If the S&P 100 index closes below 480 when the options expire in June, both calls will expire worthless, and the investor will pocket the $1,000 per spread net credit received. If the index experiences a sharp rally, the position will lose money, but the losses are limited. Any loss on the short June 480 call will be offset by a profit on the June 500 call. The maximum loss on this spread is the difference in the strike prices less the net credit received when the position was established. The difference in strike prices (500 – 480) is 20 points or $2,000 per spread. The net credit received when the position was established was $1,000. So in the worst case, our maximum loss is limited to the difference in strike prices, $2,000, less the net credit received, $1,000, for a net risk of $1,000 per spread (see Table 9.1 and Figure 9.1).

Note the shape of Figure 9.1. A bearish call spread begins to lose money as the index rises, from left to right on the graph. (The index values can be found along the X axis at the bottom of the chart.)

This is the kind of graph I would expect to see with a bear call spread. However, the graph could be severely distorted if the short call were assigned early. That's not a big risk, I admit, but with an American-style option, the risk does exist.

TABLE 9.1

PROFIT/LOSS OEX BEAR CALL SPREAD*

INDEX VALUE	SHORT OEX JUNE 480 CALLS	LONG OEX JUNE 500 CALLS	NET CREDIT RECEIVED	PROFIT LOSS
450.00	0.00	0.00	1,000.00	1,000.00
460.00	0.00	0.00	1,000.00	1,000.00
470.00	0.00	0.00	1,000.00	1,000.00
480.00	0.00	0.00	1,000.00	1,000.00
490.00	−1,000.00	0.00	1,000.00	0.00
500.00	−2,000.00	0.00	1,000.00	−1,000.00
510.00	−3,000.00	1,000.00	1,000.00	−1,000.00
520.00	−4,000.00	2,000.00	1,000.00	−1,000.00
530.00	−5,000.00	3,000.00	1,000.00	−1,000.00
540.00	−6,000.00	4,000.00	1,000.00	−1,000.00
550.00	−7,000.00	5,000.00	1,000.00	−1,000.00

* Values are assumed to be at expiration.

FIGURE 9.1

PROFIT AND LOSS OEX BEAR CALL SPREAD

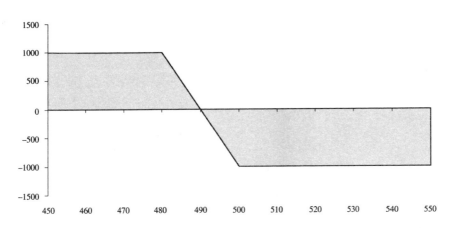

Consider an example: Suppose the S&P 100 index rallied and closed at 530, well above the 500 strike price of the long call option. No problem. Your risk is limited to $1,000 per spread as defined by Table 9.1. Right? Well maybe, maybe not.

What happens if the buyer of the OEX June 480 call decides to exercise it, presumably because there was no time value remaining in the call? In that unlikely event, you would be required to deliver, in cash, the difference between the index value at the close of trading (530) and the strike price of the short call (480) multiplied by 100. Total cash settlement per contract, then, would be $5,000.

Again, no problem, at least at first glance. After all, the OEX June 500 call would be worth at least $30 ($3,000 per contract), reducing the overall loss on the position to $2,000 per spread, less the $1,000 net credit received, when the position was established. The problem, of course, is there is no guarantee that the OEX June 500 calls would be worth $3,000, because there's no guarantee that the S&P 100 index will open the next trading day at 530.

Your risk is limited only if you can exercise the long OEX June 500 call and receive the same index value as you used to calculate the loss on the short OEX June 480 call. This works with equity options because you can exercise the long call and take possession of the stock, ultimately delivering the shares to satisfy the assignment notice.

But index options are settled in cash, so that approach won't work. For one thing, you won't know about the early assignment—on your short OEX June 480 call—until the next business day, when your options account will be debited $5,000. You can't simply exercise the OEX June 500 call, because you'll receive only the difference between the strike price of the call and the closing value of the index that night. And there's no reason to expect the index to close at the same value tonight as it did the night before.

Since exercising the long OEX June 500 call is not a reasonable alternative, you're left with the frustrating task of attempting to sell that call option after the market has opened. And that could take some time. On some days, the opening rotation in the OEX pit can take more than 30 minutes to complete; in that time, the market can move significantly.

The idea behind a spread strategy is to limit the trader's risk. However, if the short side of a spread trade is assigned early, as in this case, the investor is left with a position far removed from the initial intent. In the example above, the original strategy was bearish but, by virtue of the early assignment, the trader is left with a bullish position. (Recall this idea was also discussed in Chapter 3.)

We've now come full circle in this discussion, and we're back to the issue of how the options are structured. A European-style option can be exercised only on the last trading day. As such, we never need to face the potential problems from having the short side of a spread strategy assigned early. European-style settlement, especially on index options, eliminates the timing problems associated with an early assignment. When using spreads, we can at least define with certainty the maximum risk.

INDEX TOOLS FOR THE AGGRESSIVE INVESTOR

So far, we've laid the foundation for using the OEX and SPX indices and considered the differences between American-style OEX index options and the European-style SPX index options. Let's look at some tools we can use when setting up specific index strategies.

The first tool is the put-call ratio that we introduced in Chapter Five, with the promise of showing you how to use it in this chapter. The put-call ratio is a contrarian-sentiment indicator, the modern-day version of the old short-interest ratio. (The short-interest ratio compared the number of shares that were sold short—i.e., sold with the intent of buying them back at a lower price—with the number of shares outstanding on the New York Stock Exchange [NYSE].)

A high short-interest ratio presumably indicated pent-up buying power. Investors who sold stock short would eventually have to buy it back to close out their position. If stocks began to surge, investors who were short would have to buy back the stock as prices rose. Theoretically, if the market began to rise, the shorts would panic and buy in, adding more fuel to the upward move, thus defining the contrarian nature of the indicator. As the number of short sellers increased, the likelihood that the market would advance also increased, suggesting that the majority of short sellers were on the wrong side of the market at the wrong time. That being said, one could never draw any significant conclusions when the short-interest numbers were low. Historically, a low short-interest number was never a good indicator that it was time to sell the market.

The short-interest ratio became so popular that technical analysts began to break down the numbers, creating a short-interest number for individual investors and another for NYSE specialists. (A specialist is the professional trader who works on the floor of the NYSE.) You want to be on the opposite side of the fence to the individual investor, but on the same side of the fence as the specialist. If specialists are shorting stock in a big way, then you should be taking a bearish view on the market.

In the end, the short-interest ratio was a victim of its own success, which tells us that any technical indicator will work until it doesn't. If too many investors follow a particular indicator, the market at some point stops reacting as expected. In fact, the short-interest number hasn't worked very well since the advent of exchange-traded options.

Nevertheless, it leads us to the theory underpinning the put-call ratio. Remember that a high short-interest ratio meant that investors would have to buy-in their short positions to cut their losses, usually in a panic. Of course, the idea that one will panic is based on the notion that one is not hedged. With the advent of options, short equity positions could be hedged with long calls. In fact, most modern-day shorts are hedged with an offsetting option position. This means there's no urgency to close out when the market begins to rise. With no pent-up buying power, the short-interest ratio becomes meaningless.

The put-call ratio works much the same way as the short-interest number. Essentially, we're measuring the number of OEX puts versus OEX calls traded on a given day. Behind the put-call ratio are a number of assumptions. We assume, for example, that most investors trading OEX options are individual investors. That's a reasonable assumption, because institutions tend to use SPX options, since the S&P 500 composite index is a better benchmark for portfolios held by U.S. institutions.

That's why you tend to see such high open-interest numbers relative to daily volume trends on the SPX options versus the OEX options. Institutions tend to establish option positions as hedges against movements in their portfolio. As such, an institution will often hold an SPX position until it expires. Note from Table 9.2 that the open-interest numbers on the SPX options are almost four times as large as the open-interest numbers for the OEX. Note also the distortion in trading volume. This happened to be a day when the market was declining. Note that, on the OEX, more calls than puts were purchased, in direct contrast to the volume numbers for the SPX options.

TABLE 9.2

OEX (S&P 100 INDEX OPTIONS)

Total Call Volume	96,273	Open Interest Calls	309,219
Total Put Volume	91,576	Open Interest Puts	257,069
Total Volume	187,813	Total Open Interest	566,288

SPX (S&P 500 INDEX OPTIONS)

Total Call Volume	57,851	Open Interest Calls	951,234
Total Put Volume	107,429	Open Interest Puts	1,370,277
Total Volume	165,280	Total Open Interest	2,321,511

To calculate the OEX put-call ratio, we divide the OEX daily put volume by the OEX daily call volume. From Table 9.2, we would divide 91,576 (number of puts traded on this day) by 96,273 (number of calls traded on that day). The put-call ratio, then, is 0.95.

Table 9.3 and Figure 9.2 show the daily S&P 100 put-call ratios from the sixth of July 1998 to the middle of August 1998, together with the trailing three-day moving average. (I'll explain the rationale behind the moving average in a moment.)

A put-call ratio above 1.00 indicates that more puts than calls traded on a given day. A ratio below 1.00 indicates more calls than puts have traded. The idea is to look for extremes in the measure. Some technicians look for signals when the ratio is above 1.25 (indicating 125 puts for every 100 calls traded) or below 0.75 (75 puts for every 100 calls). The former would be considered a bullish sign, the latter a bearish sign.

TABLE 9.3

DATE	DAILY PUT-CALL RATIO	THREE-DAY MOVING AVERAGE
06-Jul-98	1.10	1.06
07-Jul-98	1.11	1.16
08-Jul-98	0.99	1.07
09-Jul-98	1.02	1.04
10-Jul-98	1.35	1.12
13-Jul-98	1.46	1.28
14-Jul-98	0.86	1.22
15-Jul-98	1.08	1.13
16-Jul-98	1.02	0.99
17-Jul-98	0.90	1.00
20-Jul-98	1.11	1.01
21-Jul-98	1.13	1.05
22-Jul-98	1.09	1.11
23-Jul-98	0.95	1.06
24-Jul-98	1.10	1.05
27-Jul-98	0.95	1.00
28-Jul-98	0.98	1.01
29-Jul-98	1.03	0.99
30-Jul-98	0.94	0.98
31-Jul-98	0.92	0.96
03-Aug-98	0.93	0.93
04-Aug-98	0.88	0.91
05-Aug-98	1.10	0.97
06-Aug-98	0.95	0.98
07-Aug-98	1.08	1.04
10-Aug-98	1.05	1.03
11-Aug-98	0.95	1.03
12-Aug-98	1.22	1.07
13-Aug-98	0.97	1.05

Technicians who use the put-call ratio as a contrarian indicator believe that when too many individual investors are bearish and buying puts, the market is about to bottom. Similarly, when too many individual investors are bullish and buying calls, the market is about to make a short- to medium-term top. Ideally, we buy the market—as in calls on the OEX—if the put-call ratio gets too high, or sell the market—as in buying puts on the OEX—if the put-call ratio gets too low.

The problem with the put-call ratio is that it has become a victim of its own success. It is so widely followed that its usefulness as a stand-alone indicator is suspect. You tend to see as many false signals as true ones.

This is why I prefer to use the put-call ratio only as a confirmation—a first signal—rather than a trigger, which tells us when to consider a trade.

Because we're using the put-call ratio only as a back-up, we can fine-tune the numbers by creating a three-day moving average. Using the three-day moving average as a confirmation indicator, the next step is to define when the put-call ratio is at an extreme reading. In other words, when do the numbers become a trigger? For our purposes, we'll consider a signal only if the put-call three-day moving average is above 1.25 or below 0.85. And even then, we'll use this signal only to confirm our trigger. Figure 9.2 graphically displays the numbers from Table 9.3.

FIGURE 9.2

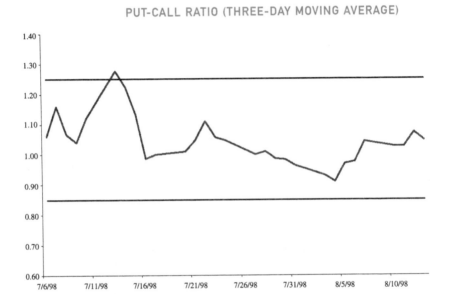

PUT-CALL RATIO (THREE-DAY MOVING AVERAGE)

The CBOE publishes two put-call ratios. The first is the put-call ratio on the OEX; the second is the equity-only put-call ratio. The principals are the same and, since this is just one of the tools we'll use in setting up our index strategies, we'll stick with the OEX put-call ratio. The daily numbers can be found at the CBOE website (www.cboe.com) under market data. In fact, fill out a form on the site and the CBOE will e-mail you this information on a daily basis.

THE CBOE VOLATILITY INDEX

Up 100 points one day, down 100 points the next. Seemingly going nowhere. Such triple-digit moves on the Dow Jones Industrial Average have in recent years become expected. This has led to many discussions in the financial press about the volatility of the market.

What seems to be missing from the discussion is a sense of whether the current volatility is within normal bounds. The market will move up and down. It always has and always will. The question is, what constitutes an extreme move? We know, for example, that 100 Dow points is about 12.5 S&P 500 points and 6.25 OEX points. But still, what's extreme?

The easiest way to approach market volatility is to look at historical returns. Calculate the percentage changes in the market on a daily basis, and then compute a volatility number. This is referred to as historical volatility. But again, it's useful only if it tells us something useful, and I'm not certain it does. For example, if I tell you that the 20-day historical volatility on the OEX is 17%, what have you learned? For practical purposes, practically nothing. If I then say that the normal volatility for the market is 17%, we have at least established a basis of comparison. At least we know that, over the last 20 days, volatility was normal. But then, what do we mean by normal? In this example, the answer is: 17% volatility. Now we're back to square one: What does the 17% mean?

Statistically, volatility is a measure of dispersion around a mean. And since 17% is an annual volatility, it indicates that one year from now the OEX has a 66% chance of being 17% up or down from where it is today.

To translate this annual volatility number into a trading range, simply multiply the percent volatility by the current value of the underlying index. For example, with the OEX at 531, a 17% trading range equals 90 points. So there's a 66% chance that the OEX will be between 441 and 621 one year from now. That's the one standard deviation number we have been using since the beginning.

Now, if you want to calculate a daily trading range, simply divide the annual trading range (i.e., 90 points) by 16. The actual formula requires us to multiply the annual volatility number by the square root of time. Time in this case is one trading day divided by 252 trading days in a year. The square root of 1 divided by 252 is 16. With this rule of thumb, the normal daily trading range for the OEX is about 5.6 points.

Remember there are 16 Dow points in one OEX point. So the OEX trading range translates roughly into 90 Dow points (5.6 OEX points × 16 Dow points = 89.6). Suddenly the 100-point daily swings in the Dow don't seem so extraordinary.

So far we've talked only about historical volatility, a measure of previous fluctuations in the market. Implied volatility, as discussed in Chapter 5, is the more common measure used by options traders. Implied volatility represents the opinion of option traders about the market's future volatility. It is calculated using actual market prices for specific options.

The Chicago Board Options Exchange calculates during the day the implied volatility on OEX options. The results are graphically displayed in the Volatility Index (symbol VIX). Note the one-year performance of the VIX in Figure 9.3 from September 1997 to August 1998. Note the spikes just after the 550 + point decline in

October 1997 on the S&P 500. Volatility spikes in December 1997, January 1998, and August 1998 (Figure 9.3) followed corrections in the S&P 500, which are graphed in Figure 9.4 (the arrows mark the spots).

FIGURE 9.3

CBOE VOLATILITY INDEX—ONE-YEAR CHART

Source: www.bigcharts.com

Considering efficient market theory and all, you might expect implied volatility to be the same as historical volatility, over the long term. In fact, they're much different.

In the case of the OEX, implied volatility is almost always higher than historic volatility. According to the VIX index, the average implied volatility on the OEX is 20%. Historical volatility is 17%, which suggests that options on the OEX are almost always overpriced. Good for option sellers, not so good for option buyers. There's no definite reason why index options are always overpriced, although ease of use is one possible explanation.

Of course, if the options are always overpriced, what's the harm in paying too much? You'll sell them before they expire (presumably they will still be over-valued), and recover the cost, right? This may be true for short-term trades, but I'm not certain that traders should expect as much success over the longer term.

The alternative, if you don't want to buy an overpriced index option, is to buy a number of equity options on stocks that should move in line with the market. For most investors, however, that's not a reasonable alternative. If they have an opinion about the market, most investors will gravitate to the convenience of index options, which means increased demand on the buy side.

FIGURE 9.4

S&P 500 COMPOSITE INDEX—ONE-YEAR CHART

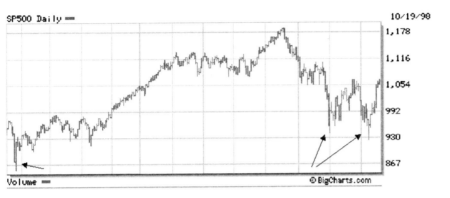

Source: *www.bigcharts.com*

It's also more difficult to sell naked index options. In fact, some brokerage firms will not allow an individual to trade a naked index option. That means less supply on the sell side. More demand + less supply = higher prices.

To come full circle in this discussion, we need to ask whether the VIX index can help traders make better trading decisions. The answer is not clear, although it's generally believed that the VIX is a contrarian indicator.

When the VIX index is trending higher, it means that investors are bidding up index-option premiums, presumably because they believe that the market is about to make a significant move. Often, however, the market does just the opposite of what individual investors anticipate. That is, when option premiums are rising, or when premiums have spiked higher, the market will often settle into a narrow trading range.

Conversely, when option premiums are trending lower, investors are lowering the price they are willing to pay in the belief that the market will remain in a relatively narrow range. That's often the point where the market will move dramatically. The problem, of course, is that even if we accept the notion that the VIX index can help us ascertain only when an explosive move is likely to occur, it won't tell us anything about direction.

Because of that, I prefer to use the VIX index as a tool to help define the width of the familiar trading bands about the OEX 50-day moving average. Then, when there's some concern about strategy selection, I use the VIX index as the deciding factor.

For example, there are four basic strategies we'll discuss using index options: two bullish and two bearish. The idea is to determine whether it's best to buy or sell options when taking a specific position. We'll look at one bullish position in which we sell puts and another bullish position in which we buy calls. We'll do the same with the bearish trades: in one, we sell calls; in the other, we buy puts.

When we sell options on the index, we need to be careful not to overextend ourselves. Remember, we don't want to sell uncovered options at any time. We always want to be able to define our worst-case scenario. And since we can't buy a security that we can use to deliver against an assignment notice from the options market, we always need to protect our downside by defining a worst-case scenario before going into the position.

With this in mind, we'll sell index options only using spreads. We discussed one type of spread in Chapter Eight, the so-called event spread. In this chapter, we'll look at bull put spreads and bear call spreads. Both of these trades create a credit in your trading account, which is what we're looking for in this particular transaction.

Before going any further, we need to define spreads and, in particular, make certain we understand the spreads we'll be using with our index option trading.

WHAT ARE SPREADS?

Spread is a term used to define any position in which you've bought and sold options of the same type (either calls or puts) on the same underlying security.

To be considered a spread, the following conditions must be met:

1. There must be a buy and a sell order.

2. Both the buy and the sell order must use the same type of options, i.e., long and short calls or long and short puts.

3. The buy and sell order must be on the same underlying security, i.e., long calls on the SPX, short calls on the SPX; long puts on the SPX, short puts on the SPX.

4. The long option (the option that was purchased) must expire at the same time as or after the short option (the option that was sold). In other words, we can sell an October SPX 1100 call and buy an SPX October 1120 call. The long call expires at the same time as the short call. If we sold the SPX October 1100 call and bought the SPX November 1120 call, that too would be considered a spread, because the long call expires at a later date than the call we are short. The same applies to trading put spreads.

Let's assume the following prices exist for call options on the Standard and Poor's 500 composite index (symbol SPX) on May 11, 1998 (Table 9.4). Given these options, we could initiate the following spreads:

1. Buy the July 50 calls and sell the July 60 calls. This is known as a debit spread, because the cost of the option you bought is higher than the premium received from the option you sold.
2. Buy the August 60 calls and sell the August 50 calls. This is a credit spread, because the premium received from the sale of the August 50 call is greater than the cost of the August 60 call.
3. Buy the October 60 call and sell the August 60 call. That's our familiar calendar or time spread, discussed in Chapter Eight. This spread also creates a debit, because the October options cost more than the August options.

TABLE 9.4

XYZ @ $55 IN MAY

STRIKE PRICE	JULY CALLS	AUG CALLS	OCT CALLS
45.00	10.500	10.875	11.625
50.00	6.625	7.500	8.625
55.00	3.750	4.625	6.000
60.00	1.875	2.625	4.000
65.00	0.875	1.500	2.625

What about this position? Assume you purchased the July 50 call and sold the August 50 call. Look closely and you can see that this is not a spread. It does not meet the fourth condition, in that the short August call expires after the long July call.

THE ADVANTAGES AND DISADVANTAGES OF A SPREAD

So far, we have examined the spread from the perspective of how it's constructed. Spreads can be bullish, bearish or neutral. They can cost you money or create a credit in your account. It all depends on how the spread is constructed. It's also important to note that any spread that can be created using calls can be replicated using puts.

Whether we're using calls or puts, a spread is bullish if the strike price of the short option is higher than the strike price of the long option; a spread is bearish if the strike price of the short option is lower than the strike price of the long option.

The aggressive trades used with our index strategies are all credit spreads. That is, we use only a bullish put spread—created with a credit—or a bearish call spread, also created with a credit.

Spreads are an attractive strategy because they're consistent with the option's ability to limit risk. However, while the risk in a spread is always limited, so too is the potential reward. The maximum profit on any spread occurs at the strike price of the short option.

Finally you need to be aware of transaction costs. Some brokerage firms will not accept a spread order, forcing us to place two separate orders. In such a case, we pay a commission to enter the buy order and another to execute the sell order. The same costs apply when we close out the position (assuming the spread is closed out prior to expiration). These costs, if not factored into the position, can eliminate any of the potential advantages of the spread.

Two points to consider:

1. If your broker doesn't accept spread trades, then get another broker.

2. If you're trading spreads, trade a minimum of 10 contracts.

BULL PUT SPREADS

Option traders have a number of ways to take advantage of a view on an underlying security. For instance, if we were bullish on the outlook for OEX, we could buy a call option or buy a call option and sell an option with a higher strike price (a bull call spread).

We know that any position a trader can take with call options can be replicated with put options. This may seem surprising when you consider that puts are generally used when the trader expects the underlying stock to decline.

However, as we've seen when comparing naked put writing to covered call writing, puts can be used to take a bullish position, just as call options can. The bull spread is simply another example of this.

A bull spread can be established with put options by purchasing a put at the lower strike price and simultaneously selling a put at the higher strike price. For example, with SPX trading at 1,060 we could implement a bull put spread by selling say, the SPX August 1,100 puts (we'll assume they're trading at 50) and buying the OEX August 1,040 puts, which we'll assume are trading at 20. The net credit for this position is $35 per unit, or $3,000 per spread.

This position is bullish, because we want the SPX to close above the strike price of the short put by the August expiration. If SPX is trading above 1,100, both series of SPX options will expire worthless, and we make the maximum profit of $30 per unit or $3,000 per spread.

I like this type of spread, because I receive a credit when the position is established. The credit is my maximum potential profit, which will occur if both options expire worthless, and I don't have to return the credit. I find it easier to ride out a position if I'm holding the cash. I hate giving back the credit. I also earn interest on the credit balance, as long as the position remains open.

The maximum loss on our SPX spread occurs if the index falls to 1,040 at expiration. At that point, the SPX 1,100 put, which we're short, would be worth $60

($6,000 per spread), while the SPX August 1,040 put, which we're long, would expire worthless. We'd have to return the $30 per unit ($3,000 per spread) net credit, plus another $30 per unit ($3,000 per spread) to cover the shortfall in this position. The maximum potential loss, then, is $60 ($6,000 per spread), less the $30 per share ($3,000 per spread) net credit received.

BEAR SPREADS USING CALLS

The bear call spread is also established with a net credit. In this case, however, we want the underlying index to decline. The bear call spread, like its sister strategy, the bull put spread, is often referred to as a vertical spread. In this case the underlying security must decline or, at the very least, remain neutral for the trader to profit.

A bear spread is established when a trader buys a call option at the higher strike price while simultaneously selling a call option at a lower strike price. In most cases, the options have the same expiration date.

With the SPX at 1,060, let's look at the same strike prices we used with our bull put spread, only this time we'll buy the SPX August 1,100 calls at, say, 10 and sell the SPX August 1,040 calls at 40. This is a bear spread, in that we want the index to close below 1,040. Below that level at expiration, both calls expire worthless.

This is also a credit spread, because the short SPX August 1,040 call is worth more than the SPX August 1,100 call. The net credit received is $30 per unit, or $3,000 per spread. The maximum profit would occur at the strike price of the short option.

The maximum risk is also limited to the difference between the strike prices of the options, less the original credit. In most cases, particularly when premiums are expensive, that's better than paying up to buy index puts.

AGGRESSIVE TRADES ON THE INDEX

All the aggressive trading strategies we'll discuss will focus on the U.S. indices, specifically the OEX and SPX indices. We'll base each aggressive trade on three indicators:

- *The trading bands about the index will be our trigger.*
- *The put-call ratio will be our back-up confirmation.*
- *The VIX index will help us assess whether we should be buying or selling options.*

We'll enter an aggressive trade only if the index is at or below trading band #2 (sector one) or at or above trading band #3 (sector four). If the index reaches either of these two bands, we'll consider an aggressive trade, but only if we get a confirming signal from the put-call ratio.

We've defined the points where we would look at the put-call ratio to provide back-up or confirmation before entering an aggressive trade. These occur when the put-call ratio reaches extremes as defined by our aggressive trading patterns—i.e., above 1.25 or below 0.85. We won't use the put-call ratio as a stand-alone indicator because we'd expect it to issue false signals about half the time.

Figure 9.5 looks at the performance of the S&P 500 index, plus the 50-day moving average and the four trading bands that move about that 50-day average. The width of the trading bands is based on the volatility implied by the options on the SPX. This raises an issue that needs some explanation.

The volatility implied by the SPX options is usually the same volatility implied by the OEX options. Certainly the two sets of options tend to trade in unison. That's important, because the numbers on the VIX index represent only the volatility implied by OEX options. And we'll use the VIX index for the last step in making our aggressive trade decision.

The point is, SPX options should closely approximate the implied volatility of the OEX options, if not in exact percentage terms, at least in direction. In other words, SPX options might imply a 32% volatility when the OEX options are implying a 35% volatility. But both are expensive relative to their historical norms. Bottom line: We can implement trades on the SPX using the same criteria as we'd use with the OEX.

LAYING THE FOUNDATION FOR AN AGGRESSIVE INDEX TRADE

In this section we'll walk through some examples. In some cases, we'll initiate a trade; in others, we'll pass if one of the signals doesn't measure up. These examples will help you lay a foundation before making any index trades.

First, we'll look at a bullish position on the S&P 500 composite index (SPX options). Figure 9.5 is a chart of the S&P 500 composite index from April 1997 to mid-August 1998. I want to draw your attention to August 12, 1998, when, for the first time since the correction on October 27, 1997, the index fell below trading band #2—the first trigger in our aggressive index trades.

Table 9.5 looks at the closing values on the S&P 500 composite index, as well as the value for trading band #2, the closing value for the VIX index and, finally, the three-day moving average of the put-call ratio—all the indicators we'll use for each of our aggressive index trades.

In this particular example, the index closed below trading band #2. That's the point where we would consider a bullish trade. The question then is, should we buy calls if premiums are relatively inexpensive, or should we sell puts with a bull put spread?

To answer the buy-or-sell question, we need to look at the VIX index. We know that index-option premiums are almost always high relative to the historical volatility on the index. But what constitutes an extreme? We'll use an implied volatility of 25% as the demarcation line. If the VIX were above 25% when we're considering a

FIGURE 9.5

S&P 500 COMPOSITE INDEX

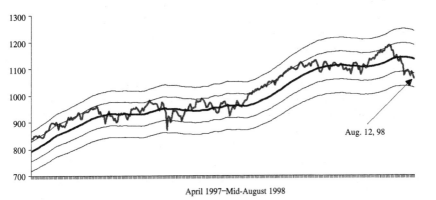

April 1997–Mid-August 1998

TABLE 9.5

AGGRESSIVE TRADE TRIGGERS AND CONFIRMATIONS

DATE	S&P 500 CLOSE	TRADING BAND #2	VIX INDEX	PUT-CALL RATIO
03-Aug-98	1,113.13	1,088.23	26.3%	0.91
04-Aug-98	1,073.13	1,088.12	33.1%	0.97
05-Aug-98	1,085.94	1,087.98	30.3%	0.98
06-Aug-98	1,090.63	1,087.35	28.3%	1.04
07-Aug-98	1,092.50	1,086.85	27.1%	1.03
10-Aug-98	1,086.72	1,086.47	28.4%	1.03
11-Aug-98	1,071.25	1,085.58	30.9%	1.07

position, then we'd sell options, and the spread would be the strategy of choice. If it were below 25%, then we'd normally buy options—calls if we're bullish, or puts if we're bearish. In this example, the VIX index closed at 30.9%, which indicates a bull put spread.

Finally, we want to look at the put-call ratio for confirmation that we've found a point at which to enter an aggressive bull put spread. In this case, the three-day moving average for the put-call ratio is 1.07, meaning that 107 puts were traded for every 100 calls over the previous three days. That's not high enough to provide us with a confirmation. Remember, the put-call ratio must be above 1.25 to confirm a bullish signal on the underlying index.

That doesn't eliminate this potential trade. We'll just put the index on a watch list and look for opportunities to enter the trade if the index remains in sector one and the put-call ratio rises above 1.25.

THE BEARISH INDEX TRADE

Figure 9.6 looks at the S&P 100 composite index (symbol OEX) over the same period used in Figure 9.5. But this time I want to draw your attention to December 5, 1997. Note that the OEX is in sector four, the point at which we'd look to enter a bearish aggressive trade.

FIGURE 9.6

S&P 100 INDEX (SYMBOL OEX)

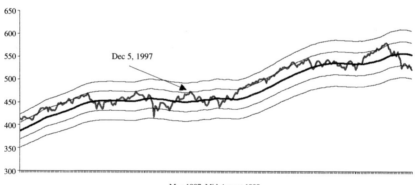

May 1997–Mid-August 1998

Table 9.6 looks at the closing values on the S&P 100 composite index (symbol OEX), as well as the value for trading band #3, the closing value for the VIX index and, finally, the three-day moving average of the put-call ratio—all the indicators we'll use for each of our aggressive index trades.

In this particular example, the OEX index closed in sector four. That's the point where we would consider a bearish trade. The question then is, should we buy puts if premiums are relatively inexpensive, or should we sell calls using a bear call spread?

To answer the buy-or-sell question, we again turn to the VIX index. In this case, the VIX index indicates that the OEX options are trading with an implied volatitlity of 22.1%. That's below our 25% demarcation line, suggesting that we should buy puts in this example.

TABLE 9.6

AGGRESSIVE TRADE TRIGGERS AND CONFIRMATIONS

DATE	S&P 100 CLOSE	TRADING BAND #3	VIX INDEX	PUT-CALL RATIO
01-Dec-97	468.14	465.62	24.8%	0.77
02-Dec-97	466.13	465.62	25.1%	1.09
03-Dec-97	468.20	465.68	22.8%	1.25
04-Dec-97	467.52	465.82	24.1%	0.73
05-Dec-97	473.53	466.31	22.6%	0.73
08-Dec-97	472.49	466.90	22.1%	0.86

Finally, we look at the put-call ratio for confirmation that we've found a point at which to enter an aggressive bearish trade in which we'll buy puts. In this case, the three-day moving average for the put-call ratio is 0.73 on December 5, meaning that 73 puts were traded for every 100 calls over the previous three days. That's below the 0.85 line, giving us a confirmation to proceed. (Remember, the put-call ratio must be below 0.85 to confirm a bearish signal on the underlying index.)

Having ascertained that, we can enter a bearish aggressive-index trade, based on the VIX. We should consider buying puts rather than a bear call spread, but which are the best puts to buy?

To help us, Table 9.7 looks at three series of OEX put options with various strike prices.

TABLE 9.7

OEX AT 473.53 ON DECEMBER 5, 1997
IMPLIED VOLATILITY 22.6%

STRIKE	DECEMBER	JANUARY	FEBRUARY
440.00	0.875	4.375	8.750
445.00	1.125	5.275	10.000
450.00	1.675	6.500	11.500
455.00	2.500	7.875	13.125
460.00	3.500	9.500	15.000
465.00	5.000	11.375	17.000
470.00	7.000	13.500	19.375
475.00	9.375	16.125	21.875
480.00	12.250	18.750	24.500
485.00	15.500	21.675	27.250
490.00	19.250	24.875	30.375

Picking the right option is as much an art as a science. It involves balancing the time to expiration with the cost of the option. When buying options, I prefer to pay up for time, looking for options that do not expire in two weeks, as the December options do. Based on the data from Table 9.7, there are only 10 trading days left in the December options.

However, the February options may cost too much in terms of added time value. If we have a bearish signal because the index is trading in sector four, that signal is confirmed by a low put-call ratio, and the VIX index suggests that we buy rather than sell our options, then I would expect the move—if a move occurs—to take place quickly.

I would try to be in and out of this position within two weeks—ideally, after doubling my initial investment.

Again, this is more art than science. But when selecting the right option to buy, the first step is to determine how much time you want to buy. Once you have established a period for your aggressive trade, the best option is usually the OEX option with the highest open interest in the expiration month of your choice. Usually you'll find that this option is just slightly in-the-money or slightly out-of-the-money—in this case, either the January OEX 475 put or the OEX January 470 put.

With two choices, you should opt for the put that's just slightly out-of-the-money. It's a little less expensive, and it will give you a slightly bigger bang for your investment dollar.

When you've set up a bearish index trade and, as in this case, decided to buy puts, you need to have an exit price in mind. Any time you're long an option, you should aim to double your initial investment. This doesn't always happen, but if you have all the signals in place, it may happen sooner than you think.

CONCLUSION

We could use a number of examples for index-option trading. But with all of them, we'll focus on three basic criteria:

1. Where is the underlying index relative to sector one and sector four? If it's in sector one, consider a bullish trade and move to step 2. If it's in sector four, consider a bearish trade and move to step 2.

2. Having determined that the underlying index has fallen below trading band #2 or risen above trading band #3, we now have to determine costs, looking at the VIX index for an indication of the implied volatility priced into the OEX options. If the implied volatility is above 25%, consider using a spread—a bull put spread if you're bullish, a bear call spread if you're bearish.

3. Finally, we need to look at the put-call ratio three-day moving average for confirmation. If the index falls below trading band #2,

we want a put-call ratio above 1.25, indicating that at least 125 puts had traded over the previous three days for every 100 calls. On the other hand, if the underlying index has broken above trading band #3, then we want a put-call ratio below 0.85, indicating that fewer than 85 puts traded for every 100 calls over the previous three days.

APPENDIX: DIAMONDS ARE FOREVER

Diamonds are forever, a girl's best friend and, as of January 20, 1998, a security that will trade on the American Stock Exchange (ticker symbol DIA). DIAMONDS are a single investment security encompassing a proportionate interest in all stocks within the Dow Jones Industrial Average (DJIA). With more than 100 years of history behind it, the DJIA is an index of 30 blue-chip U.S. stocks.

The new shares are licensed by Dow Jones and Company and will trade like shares of stock on the floor of the AMEX, in much the same way as Toronto Index Participation Units (ticker symbol TIPs) trade on the Toronto Stock Exchange.

DIAMONDS are administered under an Investment Trust that holds all 30 stocks in approximately the same proportion as they're represented in the DJIA. Essentially, DIAMONDS work like an index fund that tracks the performance of the DJIA—no better, no worse.

DIAMONDS are quoted at 1/100th the value of the DJIA. If the Dow's at 8,000, DIAMONDS trade at US$80.00 per share. Investors will also be entitled to monthly cash payments representing the dividends paid by the underlying stocks in the DJIA.

The pricing of DIAMONDS will allow investors to take positions that mirror options on the Dow Averages. Options on the DJIA trade on the Chicago Board Options Exchange (ticker symbol DJX), with strike prices set at 1/100th the value of the average. As such, investors can employ many of the same option strategies as equity investors, albeit with some caveats.

The most obvious example would be covered call writing. Investors could purchase DIAMONDS and write, say, the DJX June 90 calls against the shares. Any losses that accrue on the short call options, should the value of the index rise above 90, would theoretically be offset by gains on the DIAMONDS. As with any equity covered call writing strategy, investors sacrifice upside potential above the strike price of the call in exchange for immediate income and limited downside protection.

However, owning DIAMONDS and writing DJX call options is not really a covered call write. To be covered, the options must be exercisable into the underlying security. Intel call options, for example, are exercisable into shares of Intel. Assuming you hold Intel, the shares cover the obligation inherent in the short call options.

Index options are cash-settled. At expiration, in-the-money index call options have an intrinsic value equal to the difference between the current value of the index and the strike price of the call.

For example, if at the June expiration the value of the DJIA were 9,400, that would translate into a value of 94 for the DJX index underlying the Dow options (i.e., 9,400 divided by 100 = 94). At expiration, the DJX June 90 calls would be worth the difference in cash between the index level (94) and the strike price of the call (90) or US$400 per contract. (Note the underlying multiple for index options is 100.) DIAMONDS can't be used to cover an assignment submitted by the holder of the DJX June 90 calls.

Still, all things being equal, one would expect DIAMONDS to be worth US$94 at the June expiration, with the value of the DIAMONDS mirroring the performance of the underlying index. Although the option assignment is settled in cash, the return at expiration on the overall position—i.e., long DIAMONDS, short DJIA June 90 calls—would be similar to a traditional covered call write.

In the longer term, DIAMONDS provide a cost-effective way for investors to track the performance of the bluest of blue-chip stocks in the U.S. "Expenses and fees for DIAMONDS [presently 0.18%] are expected to be among the lowest for investments of this type," said Joseph B. Stefanelli, Executive Vice President of Derivative Securities at the Amex. In addition, says Stefanelli, "holders of these securities also may anticipate lower capital gains taxes, because turnover in the portfolio of stocks in the DJIA has been historically low and because shares of the Trust are redeemed for the actual stocks in the DJIA."

Mirroring the blue-chip segment of the market has other advantages. It means that you'll likely beat the returns on 80% of all U.S. equity mutual funds in any given year. You also have greater flexibility. As an exchange-traded trust, DIAMONDS allow investors to move in and out of the market during the trading day, versus end-of-day settlement for most mutual funds. Shares of the Trust will trade in minimum increments of 1/64th, or 1.56 cents (U.S.), suggesting tighter bid-ask spreads than you'd find on most U.S. stocks. Generally stocks in the U.S. trade in 1/16th or 6.25-cent increments.

Holding DIAMONDS in your portfolio, you'll be 100% invested in the blue-chip end of the U.S. market at all times, again something that's not guaranteed with equity mutual funds, since active fund managers tend to hold a percentage of their portfolio in cash.

As a long-term investment, DIAMONDS are a cost-effective alternative to index funds at the high end of the U.S. stock market. In terms of risk management, intra-day access means that DIAMONDS can be used to complement trading in DJX options.

10
CASH MANAGEMENT

One of the advantages of buying an option is that our risk is limited and predetermined. The most we can lose is the premium we've paid. Buy one XYZ January 50 call for $5 per share ($500 per contract), and the most we can lose per contract is $500.

Did you also know that one of the principal risks of trading options is that we can lose our entire investment, which is the premium we've paid to buy the option? Buy one XYZ January 50 call at $5 ($500 per contract) and, if XYZ is below $50 by the January expiration, we can lose our entire $500 investment.

So the cost of an option is both an advantage and a risk. Confused? Don't worry. Regulators have never been particularly clear about the best approach to citing the possibilities and the pitfalls of trading options.

Whether we view the premium paid as an advantage or a risk depends on our approach to cash management within the context of our overall aggressive trading strategies.

For example, assume we have $10,000 to invest. XYZ is at $50 per share, and the XYZ January 50 call costs $5 per share. If we like XYZ, there are three potential strategies:

    1. We could buy 200 shares of the stock.
    2. We could buy two calls for a total investment of $1,000 and invest the balance ($9,000) in risk-free treasury bills.
    3. Or, we could buy 20 calls, for a total investment of $10,000.

Most investors understand the risk of buying 200 shares of the stock. We can lose our entire investment, although XYZ would have to decline to zero. That's a possibility, but assuming XYZ is a large-cap blue-chip company, it's unlikely.

The second strategy—long two calls + treasury bills—is the least risky. If the stock declines to zero, we lose $1,000, less any interest earned from the treasury bill. The $9,000 invested in treasury bills is basically risk-free. (Note how the limited risk involved in investing in options works to our advantage.)

Finally, if we spend the $10,000 to buy 20 calls—the most aggressive strategy—we incur the greatest risk. If the stock remains unchanged until the January expiration, the XYZ January 50 calls will expire worthless. As with our second strategy, our loss is limited to the premium paid for the calls. But unlike the second strategy, this one puts our entire investment at risk.

So we have two points of view:

- *a limited-risk advantage of buying options, and*
- *the potential to lose all our money if we buy options.*

These two perspectives are directly related to how we manage our cash flow.

Here's another insight into the importance of cash management. At lunch a while ago with a money-manager friend, we spoke about the role of options in portfolio management. We talked about aggressive trading strategies, how options can be used to define the risk levels within a balanced portfolio, and, in general terms, the pros and cons of options trading.

He made an interesting observation: In the first year he ever traded options, he made over $100,000 in profits, almost quadrupling his initial investment. Stellar returns in anyone's book.

Interestingly, he believed that the returns from his first year of trading options were probably the worst thing that could have happened to him. He explained: Huge profits have a tendency to mask reality. You can imagine how an investor might feel after making over 400% in a year. From such lofty heights comes a false sense of security, which doesn't serve investors well when their fortunes change. Better, he observed, to learn how to deal with failure sooner rather than later.

Wise words, if you believe, as I do, that we tend to learn more from our failures than we do from our successes. With failures, we tend to analyze what we did wrong, in the hopes of not making the same mistake twice. This stands in stark contrast to the bull-in-a-china-shop mentality that accompanies repeated successes.

I believe all aggressive investors can learn from my friend's observation. No one wants to endure losses today to reap successes tomorrow. But if you can learn from your mistakes, your lessons will serve you well over the long term.

If you quadruple your capital and learn nothing, or lose all your capital and never trade again, the results over the long term are the same: You won't trade successfully in the future. This means, for the options trader, that cash management is probably the most important issue for long-term success.

Clearly, one of the most difficult things for an investor is to admit that he or she is wrong. Not only is it psychologically damaging, it also lightens the pocketbook. Yet, admitting your mistakes early will save you thousands over the long haul, as long as you can learn from them.

A mistake is not a failure, if you treat it as a lesson paid for in hard dollars. It's an investment that's well worth the effort if you learn something that will make you a better trader in the future. Think of it as your price of admission to the school of aggressive trading tactics.

CASH MANAGEMENT PRACTICES

As mentioned in Chapter One, I manage a number of small high-risk options accounts, which I call my performance portfolios. In these high-risk ventures, cash management is my greatest concern. The idea is to manage the cash flow in such a way that I can be wrong 50% of the time and still make profits, a feat that, unlike most things with aggressive investing, is more science than art.

The performance portfolios are designed to cover a one-year period. The client invests at the beginning of each year and must remain invested for a full year. On December 31, I cash out each performance portfolio. During the year, clients can't withdraw funds from the portfolio, nor can they add funds. The end-of-year results are based on the amount they start with.

There are no management fees attached to my performance portfolios. Clients pay transaction costs to the brokerage firm. Costs are relatively low, since we trade in bulk, buying and selling hundreds of contracts at a time. I don't earn anything from the transaction fees.

My performance fees are based on the performance of the portfolios during the year. We establish a minimum return threshold at the beginning of each year, set at the rate payable on one-year GICs + 600 basis points (6%). In 1998, for example, the minimum return threshold was set at 10%. We allowed that one-year GICs were paying 4% (which was generous for 1998) and added to that 600 basis points (6%) to reach the 10% figure.

I receive a fee equivalent to 25% of any return earned above the minimum return threshold. If the performance portfolios lost 10% during 1998, I wouldn't earn anything. If the performance portfolios returned 10% during 1998, I would still not earn anything. I would earn performance fees only if the portfolios generated a return exceeding 10%. If the performance portfolios earn 20% in 1998, I earn 2.5% in performance fees, leaving the client with a net return of 17.5% for the year.

The problem with this type of portfolio—assuming one places no restrictions on the manager—is that it favors high-risk strategies. The portfolio manager has nothing to lose. It's your money at risk. And since the manager can't make anything unless the portfolio's returns exceed minimum standards, a portfolio manager without restrictions has nothing to lose from pursuing the highest-risk strategy and everything to gain.

This is important to understand, because it goes to the heart of cash-management practice. Of the three approaches we could use with XYZ, the aggressive portfolio manager may well choose to buy 20 XYZ January calls with the $10,000. If she's right, the gain from the options could add 50% to the portfolio in a short period. The manager earns a healthy bonus, and the clients are happy.

If XYZ falls and the options expire worthless, the portfolio manager earns nothing. But the portfolio manager doesn't lose anything either. Only the client loses—in this case, the entire $10,000 investment. But presumably, the client was aware when he made the investment that the money in this high-risk portfolio was at risk.

I've never liked this particular approach to money management, no matter how aggressive the investor wanted to be. I believe that, with some disciplined cash-management practices, the client can play the aggressive-investing game with limited risk. I believe it's one thing to say to clients that we're attempting to earn better-than-average returns. It's quite another to assure clients that not all of their capital is at risk.

I approach cash management in a relatively straightforward way. I begin each year with specific objectives in mind. My first objective is to define for a client a worst-case scenario. On January 1, my clients know exactly what could happen in their worst-case scenario, no matter how many mistakes I might make during the year.

My first trade is a covered call write. That is, I buy a large-cap blue-chip company and sell a one-year at-the-money call against the shares. In 1998, for example, I used Dell Computer. In a typical portfolio, which is about $25,000, I bought 500 shares of Dell Computer at $43 per share. I then sold five Dell January (1999) 45 calls against the stock, for which the portfolio received $9 per share. These Dell 45 calls expired in January 1999, one year from the date the position was established. I used no margin to buy Dell stock, so the shares were fully paid for at the beginning of the year.

The sale of the five Dell 45 calls netted the portfolio $9.00 per share or $4,500 in premium income. The premium is then put at risk in the options market. The idea is to profit from the premium received through some judicious trading during the year. Assuming every trade I make throughout the year ends up in a loss, the most the client forfeits is the premium received. This allows us to take advantage of the limited-risk element within the option contract. The stock position is never touched. At the end of the year, the premium may be lost, but the investor still owns the stock.

No matter how badly I trade the portfolios during the year, the client ends up with 500 Dell shares, fully paid for, even in a worst-case scenario. At the end of the year, the shares could be trading at some price below the initial $43-per-share purchase price. Dell could fall from $43 per share to, say, $35 per share. In that circumstance, the account would lose money. But at no time will investors lose all of their capital, assuming the underlying company doesn't go bankrupt.

I don't count on being right more than 50% of the time. Nor should you. It's nice if one is right more often than not, but don't run your portfolio with such an expectation. Fortunately, if you focus on cash management, you don't need to be right more than 50% of the time.

The following example explains why: During 1998, the shares of Dell Computer rallied from $43 per share to a high of $124 per share. By the end of the summer, the shares were still trading at $115 per share. In hindsight, the performance portfolios would have been much better off if I'd never sold the January 45 calls. I was wrong about the outlook for Dell during 1998. The decision to sell the calls reduced the potential returns in the performance portfolio. But that's okay, because the decision to sell the calls was a cash-management decision.

It's likely that Dell will be trading above $45 per share come January 1999. The calls will be exercised, my clients will deliver their stock and receive $45 per share. So even if I lose the entire option premium—which is all that's at risk in the account—each portfolio during 1998 will earn at least $2 per share in profit during the year, even under the worst-case scenario.

ESTABLISHING A TIME FRAME

As I mentioned, my first objective when managing my performance portfolios is to define a worst-case scenario. My second objective is to establish a specific time frame. For my performance portfolios, I use a calendar year.

My performance-based fee is determined by how well the performance portfolios do during a specific calendar year. The performance portfolios start up every January 1. Money must be deposited into the account before trading begins. The performance portfolios settle on December 31 each year. I'm paid only one fee, once a year, after all the accounts are settled, after December 31.

I believe that a one-year time frame is an excellent starting point for all aggressive investors. A calendar year forces you to keep cash-management front and center in your approach. For example, I would never risk all the premium received from the sale of the Dell calls in the first quarter. What money could I invest in the second, third and fourth quarters? If I lose all the premium, I'm out of the game until next year.

I believe aggressive investors should apply some of the same principles: set objectives in terms of a worst-case scenario over a predetermined period. Having established that as a foundation, the aggressive investor must then set short- and medium-term performance goals.

AGGRESSIVE STRATEGIES

Having established a period—a calendar year—and having defined a worst-case scenario for that period, you can begin your aggressive trades. If you apply the principles we've discussed so far, you'd use the premium from the sale of a covered call to set what I refer to as the Maximum Capital at Risk (MCAR) during any calendar year.

For example, let's assume that you have $25,000 to commit to aggressive trading strategies. We'll also assume that we can purchase 500 shares of XYZ at $50 per share and sell five XYZ one-year 50 calls for a total premium of $9.00 per share.

Our MCAR is $4,500 during the calendar year. For our purposes, we'll assume that XYZ remains unchanged for the year and is called away at $50 per share in January 1999.

The next step is to divide the calendar year into four quarters. You can use two approaches when dealing with the MCAR:

> 1. The Level Risk approach: Risk no more than one-quarter of the MCAR during any specific quarter.
>
> 2. The Elevated Risk approach: Risk an ever-larger percentage of the MCAR during each successive quarter. The idea is to risk one-quarter of the MCAR in the first quarter, a third of the remaining MCAR in the second quarter, half the MCAR in the third quarter and 100% of the remaining MCAR in the fourth quarter. This approach is more aggressive than the first approach, but may appeal to young aggressive investors with healthy cash flows. We'll examine both approaches using the Dell example in the following sections.

THE LEVEL RISK APPROACH

We'll examine the Level Risk approach assuming an MCAR of $4,500. With this approach, we'll risk approximately $1,125 or 25% of the MCAR in each of the four quarters—never more, never less.

Risking only $1,125 may make it difficult to implement some of our aggressive strategies that don't guarantee limited risk such as the falling-for-dollars trade or the dollar-cost-averaging trade. I would suggest that you consider either an index strategy or the event spread. In both strategies, the risks can be defined before entering the trade, at least at the beginning of the year.

We'll assume that your first trade produces a $512.50 profit, which is a 50% return on your initial investment. Table 10.1 looks at your balance sheet at the end of the first quarter. Total portfolio value equals $30,070.

TABLE 10.1

PORTFOLIO VALUE AT END OF MARCH

XYZ shares	25,000.00
MCAR	4,500.00
Profit (loss) first quarter	512.50
Total Portfolio Value	$30,012.50

In the second quarter, we again risk 25% of the initial MCAR, or $1,125. We'll assume that the second aggressive trade produces a 100% loss on the capital at risk in the second quarter, or $1,125. At the end of the second quarter, the portfolio looks like this:

TABLE 10.2

PORTFOLIO VALUE AT END OF JUNE

XYZ shares	25,000.00
MCAR	5,012.50
Profit (loss) second quarter	–1,125.00
Total Portfolio Value	$28,887.50

In the third quarter of your calendar year, the Level Risk approach requires us to risk no more than $1,125. We'll assume that, in the third quarter, you are again unsuccessful and produce a $600 loss, which equals 53% of the capital at risk in the third quarter. Table 10.3 looks at the portfolio at the end of September.

TABLE 10.3

VALUE AT END OF SEPTEMBER

XYZ shares	25,000.00
MCAR	3,887.50
Profit (loss) third quarter	–600.00
Total Portfolio Value	$28,287.50

In the fourth quarter you risk the last $1,125. This time you're successful, producing a $1,000 profit or an 88% return based on the capital at risk in the fourth quarter. The results are shown in Table 10.4.

TABLE 10.4

VALUE AT END OF DECEMBER

XYZ shares	25,000.00
MCAR	3,287.50
Profit (loss) fourth quarter	1,000.00
Total Portfolio Value	$29,287.50

Over the year you had two losing aggressive trades (–100% and –53%) and two winning aggressive trades (+50% and +88%). Although in percentage terms the total loss of the two losing trades exceeded the total gain from the two successful trades, your portfolio still grew by 17.15%, from an initial investment of $25,000 to $29,287.50.

To be fair, we're assuming that XYZ remains stable during the year, and the shares are called away at the end of the year. However buying XYZ stock and selling the covered call was a cash-management strategy. The goal of the Level Risk approach is to assure that you retain some of the option premium at the end of the year, unless, of course, you were to lose on all four aggressive trades over the period.

THE ELEVATED RISK APPROACH

We begin, as we did with the Level Risk approach, using an MCAR of $4,500. But this time, we'll increase the risk levels during each quarter. We'll begin by risking 25% of the MCAR ($1,125) in the first quarter. Again, that's too small an amount to apply against some of our aggressive strategies. It's more suitable as a starting point for an index strategy or an event spread.

Keeping with this theme, let's assume that your first trade produces a $512.50 profit. Table 10.5 defines the results at the end of the initial trade.

TABLE 10.5

PORTFOLIO VALUE AT END OF MARCH

XYZ shares	25,000.00
MCAR	4,500.00
Profit (loss) first quarter	512.50
Total Portfolio Value	$30,012.50

The difference this time around is that we can increase the amount of capital at risk in the second quarter. We now have an MCAR of $5,012.50 ($4,500 original MCAR + $512.50 profit from first quarter = $5,012.50). In the second quarter, using the Elevated Risk approach, we can risk one-third of $5,012.50, or approximately $1,650.

Let's assume that you enter your second aggressive trade, only this time you produce a 100% loss on the capital at risk in the second quarter, which equals $1,650. Table 10.6 looks at your portfolio at the end of the second quarter.

TABLE 10.6

PORTFOLIO VALUE AT END OF JUNE

XYZ shares	25,000.00
MCAR	5,012.50
Profit (loss) second quarter	−1,650.00
Total Portfolio Value	$28,362.50

In the third quarter of your calendar year, you can risk 50% of your total available risk capital. At the end of the second quarter your MCAR is $3,362.50 ($5,012.50 less $1,650 loss in second quarter = $3,362.50) or approximately $1,680.

In the third quarter, we'll assume that you are again unsuccessful and produce a 53% loss on the capital at risk, or $890. Table 10.7 looks at the portfolio at the end of September.

TABLE 10.7

VALUE AT END OF SEPTEMBER

XYZ shares	25,000.00
MCAR	3,362.50
Profit (loss) third quarter	–890.00
Total Portfolio Value	$27,472.50

Your MCAR as you enter the fourth quarter, then, is $2,472.50 ($3,362.50 – $890 = $2,472.50). But since this is the last quarter in the year, you can risk all of your total available risk capital. Remember this is an aggressive trading book for BOLD investors, and this is the boldest cash-management approach.

In the fourth quarter, we assume that you earn an 88% profit on capital at risk, or $1,977.60 ($2,472.50 capital at risk × 0.88% return = $1,977.60). Table 10.8 looks at the value of your portfolio at the end of the year.

TABLE 10.8

VALUE AT END OF DECEMBER

XYZ shares	25,000.00
MCAR	2,472.50
Profit (loss) fourth quarter	1,977.60
Total Portfolio Value	$29,450.10

Over the year you had two losing aggressive trades (–100% and –53%) and two winning aggressive trades (+50% and +88%). However, with this approach, we raised the bar in each successive quarter, and the net return in the portfolio was slightly better. At year end, using the Elevated Risk approach, the portfolio grew by 17.8%, from an initial investment of $25,000 to $29,450.10.

CASH MANAGEMENT SUMMARY

I'm not suggesting that one cash-management strategy is better than the other. Both have merits. Clearly, the Elevated Risk approach is more risky than the Level Risk approach. The latter is designed to protect profits throughout the year. The former is designed to become more aggressive throughout the year. Both cash-management strategies are designed to allow you to survive to trade another day.

Choosing the approach that makes the most sense depends on your current financial position, your level of comfort with losses, and how quickly you learn from your experiences with the aggressive trades discussed in this book.

BENCHMARKING AGGRESSIVE STRATEGIES

The 1997 Berkshire Hathaway annual report makes interesting reading, especially the commentary of Chairman Warren Buffett. According to Buffett, his 36% return in 1997 "was no great triumph."

At first blush, one can dismiss such talk as Buffett eccentricity. But looking beneath the surface, there's merit in his commentary. In 1997, the Standard and Poor's 500 composite index returned 33.3%, before converting to the Canadian-dollar equivalent. Buffett was merely assessing his fund's return within the context of a reasonable passive benchmark.

This raises an interesting question about benchmarking in general. Specifically, how do aggressive traders benchmark their results? It's easier said than done. In fact, I'm not aware of any specific passive index that we can use to measure the performance of our aggressive-trading tactics.

It's a problem I've wrestled with in my own practice. I collect a performance fee if the percentage return in the performance portfolio exceeds the minimum-return threshold. But if I earn 25% in a year, is that good or bad? Without some benchmark against which to make a comparison, I'm in the same boat as Mr. Buffett. It may well be that 25% per year is no great triumph.

On the other hand, if you can earn 20% a year, year in and year out, you'll eventually find yourself quoted as a guru in financial textbooks. Very few money managers consistently attain that kind of return. That's probably as good a quick-and-dirty measure as you'll find for evaluating an aggressive trading strategy. At 20% per year, a $10,000 investment grows six-fold in 10 years.

Another more sophisticated tool used as a benchmark for commodity managers is the Sharpe Ratio. Essentially, this is a mathematical tool that evaluates period returns relative to risk. The Sharpe Ratio takes the return for a period less the risk-free rate and divides the result by the standard deviation.

The Sharpe Ratio is well respected, but works only if the return for a period is greater than the risk-free rate. If your return is 2% and the risk-free rate for the period is 3%, you end up with a negative number in the numerator. When you divide standard deviation into a negative number, the result is meaningless.

Along the benchmark trail, I came across an article penned by Patrick Young, editor of Applied Derivatives (www.adtrading.com). In it, Mr. Young offers some interesting, albeit subjective, ways to benchmark aggressive trading tactics.

He begins with the most obvious benchmark, the risk-free rate of return. What are treasury bills yielding in the host country? If you're trading U.S. options, for example, what is the base rate of U.S. treasury bills? Similarly in Canada, if you're trading Canadian options, what's the rate paid on Canadian treasury bills?

On the surface, measuring an aggressive portfolio against treasury bills is akin to comparing the performance of a Corvette to a pick-up truck. But measuring against the risk-free rate at least provides a wake-up call. If you can't beat the yield on treasury bills, then get out of the aggressive-trading business.

Another approach is to compare your performance against the return on the stock market in the host country. This, too, has some merit, considering that each of the aggressive strategies discussed in this book relates in some fashion to the stock market. But again, we're talking about aggressive trading tactics, and the name of the game is performance. If you're investing aggressively in the U.S., you need to earn at least 12% compounded annually to beat the long-term returns of the S&P 500 composite index. If you can't do that, why take the risk?

Perhaps a better system is one that looks at the trading range of the assets in which you're invested. According to Young, look at the changes from the high to the low (or vice versa) in a given year, then ask how much of that move you were able to capture.

If you captured more than the move from the high to the low, then pat yourself on the back. Remember, we're talking aggressive trading strategies. You may be in and out of a position 10 times in a year. Five good trades against five small losses may result in a total return greater than the high-to-low numbers on the underlying asset.

On the other hand, don't dismiss your performance out of hand, if you failed to capture the entire move. Look at your return and determine what percentage of the total high-to-low move you captured.

For example, say the asset you were trading went from 50 to 70 in a year. That's a 20-point move. Say you captured 12 points in the year, or 60% of that move. Suppose next year, the asset you're trading moves from 50 to 70, only this time you capture 14 points or 70% of that move. You've now captured more of the move than you did in the previous year, which implies that your trading techniques have improved. And isn't the role of a good benchmark to make an aggressive trader a better trader?

Young also talks about using "the highest implied (or if you prefer, historical) volatility in your market and comparing this to your notional percentage gain." If you're trading Intel options, then Intel is your market. If you're trading OEX options, then the S&P 100 index is your market.

Using Intel as an example, assume the options are implying a 40% volatility. Using that implied volatility, aggressive traders should strive to earn at least 40% on Intel options over the course of the year. At least, writes Young, this approach "takes into account some measure of just how fraught a particular market was at its extremes of excitement."

Finally, you could look at your performance in terms of what you earned on a daily basis. However, writes Young, this method is "best employed as a retrospective measure." You don't want to become fixated on the idea that you must earn some fixed-dollar amount on any given day. Traders who do that often lose their focus. They hang on to a winning position too long, simply because it didn't quite pass their daily dollar quota.

The last point serves to illustrate the downside of benchmarking, particularly for aggressive traders. You don't want to get caught up with the idea that you must beat some rigid benchmark and, in the process, forfeit the go-with-the-flow habits that make an aggressive trader successful.

FINALLY SOMETHING TO PRACTISE ON: THE OPTIONS TOOLBOX

Want to learn more about options in the comfort of your home with no risk of capital? If so, consider *The Options Toolbox*, a software package geared towards individual investors. Distributed by the Options Institute, the educational arm of the Chicago Board Options Exchange (CBOE), this Windows-based software describes the fundamentals of exchange-traded options, from basic definitions to pricing theory to how to place an order. Presumably, by learning how options are priced and traded, investors can enhance their performance by drawing from a variety of available strategies.

The newest Windows version—version 2.1—provides an options position modeling feature, as well as discussions and position modelling for LEAPs. The idea is to simulate the performance of your planned positions under a variety of conditions. Test before you invest!

The position modeling allows investors to construct and simulate option positions to see how changes in various factors can affect an option's value. That should help investors learn which strategies are consistent and most effective, given a bullish, bearish or neutral opinion about the underlying stock or index.

Included with the software package are:

1. a glossary;
2. an explanation of the characteristics and risks of standardized options;
3. a guide to taxes (although these are US taxes);
4. a recommended reading list, and
5. an options directory, with updates available for a small fee.

The cost is U.S. $29.95 for a supported version (updates are U.S. $6). If you don't need the support feature, you can download a free version from the CBOE website (www.cboe.com).

Aggressive investors who want more information can go to the CBOE website or call 1-800-OPTIONS.

AND FINALLY . . .

Take note of the comments in the section above. I believe strongly in the notion of testing before investing. Take these aggressive trading strategies out for a test drive. See how you do in a risk-free environment, before venturing into the real world of aggressive trading.

I want to finish with a caveat. Aggressive trading carries great risk. That's why we call it aggressive trading. I believe aggressive trading can yield stellar returns. But it's best served as one course in a full-course investment meal, with the main course being a balanced portfolio that you hold for the long term.

Having said that, look me up on the e-trade Canada website at www.canada.etrade.com. On this site, we'll look at aggressive trading strategies throughout the year. And, with the low commissions available from e-trade Canada, we'll help you build aggressive trades more cost-effectively.

INDEX